THE PRACTICE OF SOUL-CENTERED HEALING

Vol. I: Protocols and Procedures

An Instructional Manual

Thomas Zinser, Ed.D.

Copyright 2013 by Thomas Zinser, Ed.D.

All rights reserved. No part of this publication may be reproduced, stored in a retrieval system, or transmitted, in any form or by any means, electronic, mechanical, photocopying, recording, or otherwise, without the prior written permission of the publisher.

Paperback, ISBN 978-0-9834294-2-5

Published by
Union Street Press
2701 Union SE
Grand Rapids MI 49507

For Aaron and Rachel

Contents

Foreword 7
Acknowledgements 11
Introduction 13

Part 1: The Opening Protocols 23
    Chapter 1   The Protective Part of the Mind 25
    Chapter 2   Contacting the Higher Self 31
    Chapter 3   Identification Protocol 35
    Chapter 4   The Higher Self Review 47

Part 2: The Clinical Protocols 59
    Chapter 5   The Ego-State Protocol 61
    Chapter 6   Past-Life Protocol 87
    Chapter 7   The Spirit Protocol 95
    Chapter 8   When Spirits Refuse 127
    Chapter 9   The Shutdown 135
    Chapter 10 Dealing with Souls in Darkness 149
    Chapter 11 The ET/Dimensional Protocol 175
    Chapter 12 Protocol for External Ego-States 197
    Chapter 13 Protocol for Created Entities 215
    Chapter 14 Protocols for Clearing Devices and Energies 227
    Chapter 15 Mixing and Matching Protocols 237
    Chapter 16 Soul-Centered Healing: Closing Comments 253

Appendix A: Trance Induction 261

Foreword

When I read the introduction to Tom Zinser's first book *Soul-Centered Healing*, I saw that Tom's journey of discovery resembled my own very closely. We were both practicing psychologists using clinical hypnosis and we were both coming across cases and information that conventional psychological theories could not explain and therefore tended to dismiss.

I find this situation ironic. While one may be mocked as being "unscientific" for holding views such as those stated in this volume, a true scientist should accept the evidence before their eyes regardless of whether it clashes with their pre-existing beliefs or no matter how uncomfortable it makes them feel. A psychologist will tell you that this clash of judgments creates a state of cognitive dissonance, whereby two conflicting views of the world result in anxiety for the individual trying to make sense of the order of things. In order to reduce that anxiety, many people will reject the new information and stick with the old. Being open-minded is not easy.

The undeniable truth is that many of the clinical problems we frequently see in therapy are not amenable to conventional therapy or medication. Some phobias, for instance, can be treated quite easily with conventional techniques, and yet these same techniques are completely ineffective when treating a different patient suffering from the same type of phobia. Why should this be the case? Many clinicians will simply shrug their shoulders, express their sympathy to the patient, and move on. However, given there must be a reason for everything, it would appear that we simply do not understand the underlying structure that accounts for these different clinical results.

The courage it takes to write about these cases and the clinical challenges they represent cannot be underestimated. I know from first-hand experience how hard it is to present alternative views to one's colleagues. Trying to convey to psychologists the therapeutic benefits of hypnosis is hard enough, but getting them to explore the subject matter of the soul and 'soul-related' therapy is even more challenging.

Tom's two books in this field represent a major leap of progress and an important contribution for clinicians. They are an invaluable gift for both the novice and the advanced practitioner, and I am immensely grateful to Tom for his work for several reasons.

The first is his courage in publishing his findings in the face of certain skepticism and even hostility from his peers. Tom knew these risks but they did not deter him.

The second is that Tom's books finally provide an expanded and coherent framework for understanding what we are really up against in deep clinical work. They shed new light in what had been a dark and little understood area of the psyche.

Finally, I am grateful to Tom for documenting his innovative methods with extensive case histories. Working with transcriptions of years of sessions is time-consuming and demanding work, and Tom has persevered admirably in the task. He gives case histories for each technique presented, illustrating the variations of where things can go with a patient. This takes a lot of dedication and commitment to teaching.

After I read Tom's first book which explained what was going on in the deep psyche, I realised this new information could explain a lot of the blocks I had encountered with patients in the past, blocks that my normally effective techniques could not seem to shift. I was itching to get started and have another crack at those blocks, but I bemoaned the lack of a 'how to' manual included in the book. It was a case of being so near and yet so far. In my frustration I wrote to Tom to enquire further and we struck up a correspondence. Tom explained that his upcoming second book would cover the 'how to' side and would be the manual for his actual techniques. Hearing this I was fairly chomping at the bit to get my hands on it, and I finally did.

With this second book, Tom has provided a detailed and systematic explanation of the way he works in deep hypnotherapy, making his methods clear, easy to understand, and thus accessible to a larger clinical audience. After reading his books I finally understood how things fit together and what kind of approaches would be needed in which circumstances. Before that, in contrast, I was flying blind. Tom also saves practitioners from wasting a lot of valuable time and resources chasing red herrings, going up blind alleys, or prematurely giving up on a patient.

After applying the techniques described in this second volume for several months now, I can confirm that the way I work has been changed forever. It is likely that you too may have the same experience. You have in your hands a book that could revolutionize the way you work with clients and your success rate with difficult cases. Enjoy the learning and where it will take you, and know that you are now equipped to help people in ways you perhaps did not even dream of when you were starting out.

Have a great read and thank you, Tom, for your contribution.

—Felix Economakis
Chartered psychologist, clinical hypnotist
Director of *The Heath Therapies in London*;
author of *Take Charge of Your Life With NLP* and
Harden Up: Building Resilience In A Changing World.

Acknowledgements

I am grateful to all those clients who shared with me their healing journey and soul stories. Without them there would be no Soul-Centered Healing.

I am grateful to Gerod whose information and guidance played an essential part in identifying the many phenomena I encountered with my clients and learning what approach to take in resolving them. Without Gerod there also would be no protocols or Soul-Centered Healing.

I am grateful to Katharine, who channeled Gerod, for her commitment to helping others who might benefit from Gerod's information and guidance. I am grateful for our long collaboration to help others beyond just my own clients. Through her ability to act as a clear channel, Katharine played a central role too in the development of Soul-Centered Healing.

I want to give special thanks to Dr. Alan Sanderson, of London, for his editing of the original manuscript. Thanks also to Felix Economakis, Michael Kivinen, and Mary Kay O'Neil who proofread the manuscript and made a number of corrections. This book reads much better because of their help.

Finally, I want to thank my wife, Jane, who has given her support to me and to this work for thirty years despite its demands and the sacrifices it required.

Introduction

To Hypnotherapists

This book is written for hypnotherapists who want to learn more about Soul-Centered Healing (SCH) and who may want to incorporate some of its methods and techniques into their own practice. This book assumes that you are 1) already practicing hypnotherapy or are involved in training, and 2) that you are familiar with the basic hypnotic techniques, including *ideomotor signaling*. If you are not familiar with this technique, there are many books and articles that can teach you how to use it. Ideomotor signaling is one of the basic tools in SCH and it's a prerequisite for practicing this method.

The powerful thing about ideomotor signaling is that it quickly bypasses the conscious mind and establishes direct communication at unconscious levels. Verbal behavior is such a conscious activity that many people have difficulty maintaining the trance state and also responding verbally to the hypnotherapist. It's as though the client is pulled back to some level of consciousness in order to articulate and report to the therapist. As a result, the client often begins to doubt and have second thoughts about whether what they are reporting is truly information from the unconscious or whether it's the conscious mind just coming up with thoughts or images. This pull back to consciousness also can activate the defenses that normally operate when a person is functioning consciously. This in turn defeats the very purpose of trance work, which is to avoid these blocks and defenses.

Unless all of your clients are excellent trance subjects, you will need ideomotor signaling to bypass the conscious mind and its defenses.

An excellent trance subject is one where this dissociation happens quickly and the ego gives up control of the voice to those parts existing at unconscious levels. We don't understand why some people so easily dissociate and others do not. There's no question that it is easier and more engaging to work with a client who is able to easily dissociate in trance. It allows the higher self, ego-states, and outside entities to communicate verbally without the conscious mind becoming involved or interfering. However, I find only a small percentage of my clients have this ability. Most of my work with clients is done through ideomotor signaling.

Beside some expertise in hypnosis, this book also assumes that you have read my first book, *Soul-Centered Healing*. If you have not, then that is the place to start. This book is an extension of that one. I'll refer to *Soul-Centered Healing* throughout this book and build upon it. Unlike the first book, though, the focus here is on application. It's a *how-to* manual. If you are practicing hypnotherapy, then you should be able to test out for yourself the techniques and methods presented here. It's like learning to swim: you only really know in doing it.

This approach to healing grew out of my own clinical practice, which was based on ego-state therapy. The healing and integration of ego-states is still a primary focus in SCH. These parts of the self, understood as conscious beings, are often the source of a client's pain, conflict, or confusion. This is especially true at the emotional, psychological, and psychic levels. However, ego-states often affect the physical body as well. Most ego-states are created during a physical experience, and therefore, their experiences most often have a body component. Identifying these dissociated parts of the self and bringing them into integration with the conscious self and the soul is usually going to be a part of a client's healing process.

A second major focus in the practice of SCH is the intrusion or interference by spirits or other beings that are separate from the client's own self/soul. The emphasis here is on separate. There are many different entities and energies that can interfere with a person at different levels of consciousness. This kind of intrusion and violation of a person at unconscious levels can also, like ego-states, be a source of a client's problems. This issue does not come up with every client, but it's not rare. So, identifying and clearing a client of these spirit/entity involvements is often a part of the healing process.

A third major focus in the process of Soul-Centered Healing is a client's past lives. Unresolved conflicts or trauma from past lifetimes can be triggered in a client's present life and cause a wide range of symptoms or difficulties. These can extend from the physical to the mental to the spiritual. In general, we can say this is true for all of us. We are all affected in ways by our soul's past-life experiences. For certain clients, though, these past life conflicts are particularly strong and able to break through into the present life.

In Soul-Centered Healing, a client's healing process will more than likely involve other lifetimes. Sometimes it's a major issue, other times not. I have worked with a few clients where present life ego-states were the exclusive focus and past lives never came up. (This may depend on the client's conscious belief and attitude toward reincarnation.) It has happened the other way, as well. A client's inner work dealt almost exclusively with past lives, and present-life ego-states never came forward. Most of the time, though, you can expect both.

Finally, the fourth area that is frequently a focus in Soul-Centered Healing is the most difficult to talk about. I call it *energetics*. SCH recognizes that there are subtle energies and energy fields that cannot be directly perceived by our physical senses. Soul-Centered Healing also recognizes that each person is not only a physical body, but is comprised of what Eastern traditions call *subtle energy bodies* as well. From within this framework, each of these energy bodies is regulated by an energy center called a chakra. From the root chakra at the base of the pelvis to the crown chakra at the top of the head, each chakra is thought to regulate an energy body. These energy levels are much more extensive and complex than I'm stating here, but the acknowledgement of the seven major chakras is a good place to start.

In Soul-Centered Healing it is not unusual to find blockage or damage in one or more of a client's chakras. In that case, restoring a chakra's balance and energy flow becomes a goal in the healing process. The blockage may involve ego-states, spirits, physical illness, emotional wounding, or psychic energies and devices. The higher self may indicate that a client's chakra is in need of immediate attention, or it may become a secondary goal to come back to later. Ideally, we want to see each client's chakras and energy bodies functioning at a healthy level.

There are other problems that can be considered energetic. There might be holes in a person's aura; there might be energy deposits described as "toxic" or emotional "sludge" that need to be expelled. I cannot predict or define all the forms that energy might take. I can only say that in working with a client I'm on the lookout for energies and etheric devices that may be a source of blocking or interference in a client's healing process. I'll talk more about these energies and devices later in the book. I will also give examples and the protocols for dealing with them.

In general, ego-states, intruding spirits/entities, past life influence, and energetics are the phenomena that most frequently present in a client's healing process. One or more of these phenomena are often the source of, or a contributing factor in, the client's problem area. This book presents the methods and protocols used in Soul-Centered Healing to work with and resolve these different phenomena. While we cannot predict what will present in a person's healing process, I would say most of the time it will fit one or more of these categories. This book is about how to identify the presenting phenomena and select the protocol that will help resolve it.

Each protocol is a series of specific steps for dealing with a particular phenomenon. The protocols can also be quite specific as to what to ask and when to ask it. One protocol, for example, is used to work with sub-personalities, while a different protocol is used for dealing with attached spirits.

The Protocols

Part One presents three different protocols. The first one is used to establish communication with a client's protective part of the mind. This protocol is normally used just once with each client. The second protocol is used to establish communication with a client's higher self and this protocol will be used throughout the client's healing process. The third protocol is the Identification Protocol. It is also used throughout the healing process to identify anyone or anything that is presenting in the healing work.

Part Two presents the clinical protocols. Each protocol is a series of steps designed to deal with a particular phenomenon using ideomotor signaling. Once someone or something that needs to be addressed has been identified, the therapist can use the protocol designed for that particular phenomenon. The protocols should not be viewed as rigid formulas to be applied in a 'cookie cutter' fashion. The protocols act as step-by-step guides to engaging and resolving the different kinds of entities, devices, and energies that can present in the course of the healing process. At the same time, there are specific words, questions, and statements that I use throughout the healing process. I developed this language and phrasing over time, and I have found it to be the most reliable and efficient way of communicating with the inner world. You can judge for yourself about this. What is most important are the aims of each protocol, not necessarily the steps it takes to get there.

Paradigm Shift

The idea or belief in a higher self is not new. Many religions and spiritual traditions recognize a higher self. It goes by many different names, though, and is colored by the culture it comes from. The problem in our Western culture, however, dominated as it is by empirical science, is that we have no conceptual framework for talking about phenomena like the higher self. Empirical science does not recognize, let alone explore and study, nonphysical phenomena like the higher self, spirits, psychic phenomena, past lives, etc.

Empirical science reaches a boundary at this point. It cannot address metaphysical realities, even hypothetically, without contradicting its most fundamental assumption, i.e. that matter is the ground of reality. To even posit the possibility of nonphysical realities, empirical science would have to abandon its own basic foundation. It would be like cutting itself off at the knees. To accept the existence of metaphysical realities would require a shift in paradigms, one in which *consciousness*, not *matter*, is the ground of reality. It's a paradigm in which consciousness is recognized as a force in itself, independent of matter.

What is true for empirical science is also true of our modern psychology. It stands at this same boundary, caught in the same paradox. It cannot recognize the psychic and spirit dimensions of the self without abandoning its assumption that matter—the body—is the final definition of who a person is.

This book is not going to address the dichotomy between the empirical and metaphysical paradigms. That's far beyond the scope of this book. As for Soul-Centered Healing, it's already decided on the point. It clearly belongs in the second camp. SCH recognizes the psychic and spirit dimensions of the self. It recognizes also that there are nonphysical phenomena, conditions, entities, and energies that can affect a person for good or ill.

I believe the day will come when people commonly accept the existence of these other dimensions of consciousness and reality. I believe science, driven by the human desire to know, will reach these boundaries, and find a way to cross them. I also believe that the public acknowledgement of these realities will be a core element in the shift from an empirical to a metaphysical paradigm.

Meanwhile, as healers and therapists in the day-to-day world, we are always straddling these paradigms, and we have to recognize that a client who enters into this process of healing most likely will have to straddle them too. Many of my clients feel they cannot talk about their problems or their healing process when it involves these kinds of phenomena. Because of this, some feel isolated and alone. There are other clients who are already quite comfortable with the metaphysical realities. These are clients who have established some kind of workable compromise in their day-to-day world. They know with whom they can or cannot talk about these things.

For those clients who are just opening up to these realms, this adjustment to a new paradigm can affect them at many levels. Psychologically and cognitively, lifelong assumptions and strongly held beliefs about reality are being challenged and threatened with collapse. This can be confusing and, at times, frightening for a client, as they try to recalibrate and integrate this new perspective. Opening to these realms can also affect one's social relationships. As it is now in our Western culture, there is still great stigma attached to these phenomena. There are people—family, friends, and co-workers—who clients feel they cannot talk to for fear of being rejected, thought of as strange, or even crazy. For this reason, when a client is just awakening to these levels, the effects of the change on him or her need to be monitored. If the client does run into trouble in adapting to this shift, then the issue can be addressed in therapy.

It also is not uncommon for someone to seek treatment who is going through what is called a *spiritual emergency*. This is when metaphysical or spiritual realities are breaking into one's awareness and there is no way for the person's ego-consciousness to comprehend what is happening. I would guess that most people go through a spiritual emergency at some point in their life, perhaps more than once. I would also guess that many, if not most, are painful awakenings. This is only natural. For some people, however, these crises are so extreme that they need active support and treatment to help them through the process of reintegrating at a different level of consciousness. In Soul-Centered Healing, the higher self can be worked with to help a person sort through what is happening, determine if there is outside interference involved, and to find those parts of the self, from past lives or present, that are reacting to changes occurring at the conscious level.

Who is a Candidate for Treatment?

There are few hard and fast rules that apply in determining who is an appropriate candidate for Soul-Centered Healing. It depends on the person, the phenomena, or issues involved, and the client's own judgment about the effects or not of the healing process. In general, I do not work with children younger than eighteen years old. I don't believe children and most adolescents have the ego strength or identity development yet that is needed to start working intensely at psychic and spiritual levels. This is especially true if the child has suffered abuse or extreme trauma. The healing process is likely to bring up this pain and trauma and could threaten to overwhelm the child again. An exception to this is when a very specific issue like a spirit attachment or a past-life memory appears to be causing a significant problem. In these cases, I will work with a child if I believe the particular issue can be treated with such a focused and limited intervention.

In regard to adults, a person is not a good candidate for treatment if he or she is entrenched in a victim position. This doesn't mean a person has not been *victimized* in their life, but that is different than being a victim. This kind of determination usually cannot be made before a person begins treatment. I've worked with many people who came into treatment with a strong victim mentality and early in the course of treatment began to change their perspective and move out of this position. From a Soul-Centered Healing point of view, this in itself is a healing step. However, if a person cannot make this shift, at least cognitively, then that itself will become the focus of the therapy. Often, such a client will end the therapy before it ever reaches this point.

I will not treat someone who is actively psychotic and does not have the necessary social support to help them deal with abreactions and defenses that may be triggered in the treatment sessions. In modern psychology, the term *psychosis* refers to a person who suffers a cognitive break from reality. That reality is assumed to be the physical, three-dimensional reality, which we know through our senses. Modern psychology does not address the issue that there may be other dimensions of reality and the psychotic person may be entangled in one or more of these realities.

I believe Soul-Centered Healing may offer an effective treatment for some people diagnosed as psychotic. When a person has the necessary support, I will assess whether the treatment might be helpful. If it looks promising, I will follow up with an initial hypnosis session to assess the response of the inner world, especially regarding the higher self's ability to communicate. From a Soul-Centered Healing point of view, there are many phenomena, both within and from outside the client, that may be breaking into or strongly affecting his or her consciousness. These experiences can be profoundly frightening, confusing, or alien to the conscious person. If treated as a figment of the person's imagination or strictly the result of a biochemical imbalance, treatment becomes one of suppression and denial.

Whether to work with a person exhibiting psychotic symptoms is, in the end, a judgment call by the therapist. As usual, there are many factors to take into account. The point here is that some psychoses, if not most, involve other levels of reality and consciousness that are a source of the person's psychotic symptoms.

Conscious Level Therapy

In Soul-Centered Healing, the emphasis is on the inner work. There are times, however, with every client that calls for conscious level therapy, or what some call talk therapy. A client, for example, whose inner work is opening up memories or flashbacks of abuse, may need help in consciously dealing with what is coming forward. A client may be experiencing conflict or crisis in their everyday world and need to focus on that during the therapy session or over several sessions. This is really standard therapy practice, so I don't feel a need to go into it. I am assuming that, as practiced therapists, you know when a client needs to process or deal with something at a conscious level. I just want to make the point that in Soul-Centered Healing the emphasis is on inner work, but the process moves back and forth between conscious-level therapy and inner work.

About the Book

There are several things that I want to alert the reader to ahead of time about the book. Since it is addressed to hypnotherapists, I've taken the liberty of writing the book in three voices. The predominant voice is third person—the clinician and scientist. I will be presenting and explaining different phenomena and the methods used in dealing with them. I'll be writing about the specific protocols and procedures used in Soul-Centered Healing from a more objective point of view.

In the second voice, I will address you directly as a practicing therapist and colleague. I do not presume to know you personally, but I do assume that, as hypnotherapists, we share some common experience, language, and knowledge.

Finally, I've used first person narrative to speak from personal experience about what I have observed and learned or what I believe about these different realities.

I hope this change from one voice to another is not a distraction, but adds different levels of depth and perspective to a difficult work.

I have also taken the liberty of including a great many clinical examples to illustrate the different protocols for dealing with different phenomena. The examples are in the form of printed transcripts of the dialogue between the therapist and the client's inner world. This can be tedious and demanding reading unless you have a specific interest and want to get into the details of how it works.

This is where the book is like a how-to manual. Dialogue that takes thirty seconds to speak may take several minutes or more to read and comprehend. It slows down the natural speed and rhythm of the spoken dialogue, like listening to music being played at the wrong speed. There is also a good deal of repetition as the same phenomena are addressed from different points of view. For therapists, I hope the examples offer an understanding of the principles on which the protocols are based. They can then be used with flexibility. The examples also give specific wording that can be used verbatim and act as models in formulating effective protocols for your own specific clients and situations.

Use of Terms

There are several terms I use in the book in a particular way. I want to alert the reader to them in order to avoid confusion:

1) For the purposes of this book, the terms healer, therapist, and facilitator are used interchangeably.
2) The terms Light, God, Allah, Divine, Source, All That Is, Creator are also used in this book interchangeably. I don't believe words can capture the reality of the Divine. From my point of view, these terms all refer to a higher power and consciousness that created souls and is beyond our human comprehension.
3) In the example dialogues, I use the terms "yes finger" and "first finger" interchangeably. They both indicate that the client's index finger is lifting. Which term I use depends on the question I am asking or the context of the client's inner situation. I also use both terms to introduce some variation into my dialogue. The same is true for the terms "no finger" and "second finger." They also are used depending on the context and to add variation to my questions and dialogue.
4) Abbreviations used in the example dialogues are:
   - TH—Therapist
   - HS—Higher self
   - ES—Ego-state
   - SP—Spirit
   - DS—Dark soul
   - PL—Past life ego-state, no gender identified
   - PM—Past-life male ego-state
   - PF—Past-life female ego-state
   - EES—External Ego-state
   - ET—Extraterrestrial

Trance Induction

In Appendix A, I have included a transcript of what I consider my standard induction for clients and the establishment of ideomotor signals. Every hypnotherapist has his or her favorite methods for inducing trance. There's nothing special about the one I use. I include it for those who are curious or who might find some of its elements useful. My own induction incorporates different elements from other practitioners that I have found useful, as well as techniques I have developed myself. Whatever induction method is used, however, the aim is for the conscious self to step aside and allow communication with parts of the unconscious.

Part 1
The Opening Protocols

1

The Protective Part of the Mind

The first step in Soul-Centered Healing, once a client has entered trance, is to communicate with the client's *protective part of the mind*. This is a part of the mind that is conscious and aware and is always focused in the present reality. The protective part is, at base, a survival function. While it is not completely independent from the conscious self, it appears to function with a high level of autonomy. Its perception is focused in the present because that's where the body is. This is its primary purpose—to ensure the survival and safety of the body.

The protective part, though, as part of human consciousness, came to take on the function of emotional and psychological protection as well. Pain is pain—whether originating from inside or outside—and any pain taken too far begins to threaten the body. So the protective part, in its narrow consciousness, will react to emotional and psychological pain and threat, as well as physical. This includes the pain or threat of pain that a client feels at any time in the healing process. After I learned from Gerod about the protective part, it occurred to me that the protective part must have been a significant source of the blocking that I encountered with past clients. Since healing so often involves past pain and trauma, whether from a client's present life or a previous lifetime, I thought that the protective part of many clients probably perceived me as a bull in a china shop.

Given this understanding, and speaking in general, the protocol for dealing with the protective part has several steps. The first is to establish communication with the protective part from the beginning. Once the protective part is engaged, the next step is to make sure it understands what the healing process is about and why past pain is being opened up in the present. Often, the client's protective part is already aware of this if the therapist has discussed the process with the client before the trance work begins. If the protective part does not understand, then the therapist can give a brief explanation about the process of sharing, release, and integration. The other method, and the one that I use most frequently, is to have the client's higher self communicate this understanding to the protective part. This is usually quite effective once the protective part is willing to receive the communication. The final step, then, is to elicit the protective part's agreement to cooperate by not blocking the process when painful material is coming forward.

The protective part is almost always in agreement with the healing process because, in the end, it recognizes it as strengthening of the self and a potential relief from pain. This is in accord with the protective part's own constant aim as well.

So, once the client is in trance, and the signals have been specified, the protective part is asked to come forward. You can assume it is listening. Its focus is in the present and in this moment that means its focus is on you and what you are saying and doing. What you cannot assume is that the *protective part* will respond to that name. This has to be made clear in the beginning. For this reason, when asking for the protective part, I'll include a description of its general function. I use this kind of phrasing.

> TH To the protective part of the mind, that part that is always aware here in the present, that part that has always served to protect (<u>Client's Name</u>) from threat, hurt and pain. To the protective part of the mind, are you willing today to communicate with me?

Usually, the protective part is willing to communicate and will respond with a yes signal. If there is no response after several attempts, there is a good chance its communication is being blocked by someone or something else. If this happens, then the block(s) will need to be resolved before being able to establish communication with the protective part. The identification and resolution of such a block requires a different protocol. This situation will be addressed in a later chapter.

There are times, though, when it is the protective part itself that is refusing to respond. If so, then it's likely that it still perceives the healing process as a threat and will need to be reassured or given more information. Making sure the protective part understands about the healing process is often sufficient to gain its cooperation. In the end, the protective part will always do that which is—in its perception—in the best interest of the self. In this case, relief from pain and improved health is perceived by the protective part to be in the self's best interest. So ultimately, it will respond with a yes to the healing process once it understands its purpose. The protocol for dealing with the protective part, then, looks like this:

- Establish direct communication with the protective part.
- Confirm that it understands the purpose of the healing process.
- Elicit its agreement to cooperate in the healing.
- If refused, address any reservations directly or through higher self, and again ask for its agreement.

The following is a typical example of engaging the protective part and obtaining its cooperation.

Engaging the Protective Part: Example 1

Once the trance induction is complete, the first question is addressed to the protective part.

> TH I'm asking now that the protective part of the mind, that part that is always aware here in the present, and has always served to protect Nancy from threat, hurt or pain… To the protective part, as long as it is safe, are you willing now to communicate with me? If so, the yes finger can lift, if not, the no finger.
> PP Yes finger lifts.
> TH To the protective part of the mind: do you have an understanding now about the healing process that Nancy and I have been talking about here at a conscious level?
> PP Yes finger lifts.
> TH Are you in agreement, then, with the healing process and our work with those parts inside for healing and release?
> PP Yes finger lifts.
> TH To the protective part: are you receiving Light now for yourself there?
> PP Yes finger lifts. (If it says no, then have the higher self bring it Light which may lead to quick cooperation.)

TH To the protective part: with your agreement, I'm going to ask that you step back now and allow the higher self to come forward. Is that agreeable?
PP Yes finger lifts.
TH Before you do that, would you like higher self to send you more of that Light/Love energy?
PP Yes finger lifts.

The above example is short and simple and it usually is this short and simple as long as the protective part is not being blocked. In communicating with the protective part, you also want to make sure it is receiving Light. I have worked with more than one person where his or her protective part was not aware or receiving Light—and maybe hadn't been for a long time. So, as a last step, even when the protective part is receiving Light, I will ask if it is willing for the higher self to send it Light, or send it more Light.

If the protective part refuses the Light in this initial contact, I would consider that a problem. Either there is something painful that it is shielding or reacting to, or someone or something is interfering. In this case, after confirming it is the protective part that is communicating, assisting it in receiving Light or resolving any blocks in the way would become the priority.

Engaging the Protective Part: Example 2

TH I'm asking now that the protective part of the mind —that part that is always aware here in the present, and has always served to protect Nancy from threat, hurt or pain—to the protective part, as long as it is safe, are you willing now to communicate with me? If so, the yes finger can lift. If not, the no finger can lift.

No response.

TH To the protective part: we are here to help. We want to help all parts of the self to be free of pain, hurt and fear. To the protective part: as long as it is safe and nothing is forced, are you willing to communicate with me about this?

No response.

TH To the protective part: I'm still not aware of a signal. I'm not sure whether someone or something is blocking you from communicating. To the protective part: are you able to communicate with me if

you choose to?
PP Yes finger lifts.
TH Is there some scare or concern for you about this healing process?
PP Yes finger lifts.
TH Are you aware of parts inside that carry pain or distress?
PP Yes finger lifts.
TH If those parts could be free of all fear and pain, would you want that for the self?
PP Yes finger lifts.
TH Would you be willing to have more information sent to you about the healing process?
PP Yes finger lifts.
TH Higher self, I'm asking now that you send to protective part that information about the Light and the healing process, how each part inside can be free and released of all pain and fear. And to the protective part: first finger lifting when you've received that information, second finger if you do not.
PP First finger lifts.
TH Did your receive that information?
PP Yes finger lifts.
TH Does that make sense to you?
PP Yes finger lifts.
TH Are you receiving Light for yourself now?
PP Yes finger lifts.
TH Are you willing then for us to work with those inside for healing and release?
PP Yes finger lifts.

Once the protective part says yes to the healing process, then usually you will not have to communicate with it again in subsequent sessions. There are exceptions to this. There are times in the healing process that the protective part will be triggered because something intensely painful has been touched on, or there are inner parts reacting to what is coming up and the protective part needs to slow the process down. In these cases, though, when it is the protective part blocking, it will still be cooperative and willing to communicate about why it is blocking. The therapist can then offer appropriate reassurances that its concerns can be addressed and resolved to make the process safe.

If the protective part is being blocked, however, then identifying and resolving the block becomes the focus of the session. At this point, there is a different protocol and strategies to use to identify such a block and to deal with it. You will no longer be addressing the protective part, and will have to come back to it when the block has been resolved. I will discuss this protocol and its strategies in a later chapter.

Let's assume for the moment, though, that everything goes smoothly. The protective part comes forward, is able to communicate, has contact with the higher self, and agrees not to block the healing process.

2

Contacting the Higher Self

The second step in Soul-Centered Healing is to establish direct communication with the client's higher self. Most of the time, this will be a quick and simple procedure. Unless something or someone is blocking it, the higher self is always willing to communicate and is always in support of healing. The more difficult part will be 1) confirming that it is the higher self that is communicating, and 2) establishing a working relationship with it. This will take a little longer. I think of the first two or three sessions with a client as a calibration period. It's a time to make sure the ideomotor signals are well established. It's also a time to communicate and work with the higher self and judge whether it is functioning freely and well.

Like with the protective part, establishing communication with the higher self is a one-time step. It's like a formal introduction and only needs to happen once. Unlike with the protective part, however, the healer will communicate and work closely with the higher self throughout the client's healing process. The higher self possesses a wide range of abilities by which to assist in the healing process.

As healers, we need to know what a higher self can and cannot do in order to know the right questions to ask. If you're working with a client whose higher self is able to communicate verbally—without contamination or interference by the conscious self—then this is much less a concern. Having to communicate to a client's higher self with only *yes/no/don't know* responses requires some precision of language. It will be important that the healer and higher self have clear communication and understanding throughout the process about 1) what is being dealt with at any given moment, 2) what it is we want the higher self to do, and 3) whether we know that it is capable of what we ask. What is accomplished in these first sessions with a client will also act as confirmation or not that it is the higher self with whom you are communicating.

Because of cultural and language differences, when I first ask for the client's higher self to come forward, I'll use several adjectives to describe the part of the self I'm asking for. Like with the protective part, the higher self may not recognize itself immediately by the term I am using. This doesn't happen very often, but there are cases where a client's higher self appears to have been dormant or suppressed. In these cases, it's as though the therapist needs to help the higher self awaken and *rev its engines,* so to speak. Once this happens, the higher self usually comes up to speed pretty quickly.

One of the most important things to understand about the higher self is that it is not a "chooser." It won't tell a person what to do. It won't say whether to take a new job, make a move, or get married. These are choices the self must make. The higher self won't violate that free choice. It is not even in its nature to do so.

At the same time, we can ask the higher self whether one thing or another is aligned with the Light, or of the Light. If a person (or the therapist, by proxy) asks the question, the higher self is free to answer. As usual in our interactions with the Light, it will not intrude and it will always say *yes* when invited. Same way with the higher self; it won't say what to do but it will Light the path or act as a beacon if the person asks.

By asking yes/no, black/white questions we have to be careful not to ask higher self questions that require a choice that belongs to the conscious self. If in doubt about a particular question, I can ask higher self whether it's a question that it is free to respond to. Then, if there is a yes, I'll proceed; if not, I'll ask the question in another way or move to a new line of questioning.

The questions that make up the protocols are ones I have found that the higher self is usually free to answer, and that lead most directly to the desired results in the healing process. Besides asking for Light, many questions are asking higher self for knowledge or information. As long as it doesn't violate the person's choice, the higher self is usually free to give information, about present life and past lives. The line can be fuzzy between questions that are okay to ask and those that cross the line. Making it even more difficult, based on its higher level perspective, the higher self at times can answer questions that would appear to violate one's choice but which are allowed from that soul level. We can't know this ahead of time. My best guidance here, beyond the questions in the protocols, is to keep in mind that the higher self may not be free to answer in the way the question has been posed.

These are not the only questions that can be asked of the higher self. I imagine all kinds of exploration can be done with one's higher self, consciously or in trance, alone or in groups. These explorations, though, are not necessarily part of the healing process, and so that avenue is not discussed here. Some clients, in their own spiritual search, may wish to explore and there is nothing wrong with that. The examples below, however, are focused on the healing process.

Establishing Contact with the Higher Self: Example 1

TH   To the protective part: I'm asking then that you step back and allow the higher self to come forward here with me. Is that agreeable?
PP   Yes finger lifts.
TH   I'm asking now for the higher self, that deeper part of the self/soul, that part that is aware of so much more and knows so much more than the conscious self... To the higher self, are you willing today to communicate with me?
HS   Yes finger lifts.
TH   To the higher self: do you know about the healing process we are starting today?
HS   Yes finger lifts.
TH   And are you in agreement that we continue?
TH   Yes finger lifts.

Asking the higher self to communicate and asking for its agreement to the healing process seems only a formality. As long as it is not blocked, the healer can always expect a yes response to these two questions. The higher self is always willing to assist the self in whatever ways it can for the person's highest good. This is so consistent that if you don't receive a *yes* signal to both these questions, then you can be almost certain that the higher self is being blocked or interfered with. If the no finger lifts, then you can be sure that you are not communicating with the higher self.

If the higher self is blocked in this initial attempt at contact, then identifying and resolving that block becomes the immediate aim of the session. Some blocks are simple and easily addressed, like an ego-state that is afraid of the Light. Other blocks are complex and might require more than one session to resolve. Different protocols and strategies are used to deal with these blocks. The priority at this point is still to establish direct communication with the higher self. So, once a block to the higher self (or a series of blocks) is resolved, the healer asks again for the higher self to communicate. If the higher self is still blocked, then the protocol for finding and resolving the block is repeated until the higher self is free to communicate.

Establishing direct communication with a client's higher self at this early point in the healing process is important for two reasons. First, the higher self, with its many abilities, will play a central role, not only in the person's healing process but also in every session. In fact, without the higher self's assistance, I'm not sure how far one's healing would progress before it became blocked. Therefore, it is imperative that communication between the client's higher self and the therapist be open and clear. This goes not only for the initial session, but for all subsequent sessions as well. The therapist contacts the higher self at the start of each session to make sure it is free to communicate, to ask it for information and guidance, and to initiate action.

The second reason for establishing direct communication with the client's higher self is because it's a kind of barometer of how strong and open the connection is between the self and soul. If the higher self is able to communicate right from the start, it's a good sign. If it is blocked from communicating in this initial session, it can be indicative of deeper level conflicts or blocking in this conduit between the self and soul. It's possible, for example, that a client's higher self has been shrouded, suppressed, or blocked for some time, maybe even since childhood. This would be a case where the therapist may need to help activate the higher self. As Gerod once described it, " you may have to remind it of what it is."

For the moment, we'll assume that there is no blocking and the higher self has responded with a *yes*, that it is in agreement with the healing process. When you reach this point where the protective part is cooperating, and the higher self is communicating directly, then you are ready to explore the client's presenting symptoms or complaints.

3

Identification Protocol

The First Two Questions

The next step in the Opening Protocol is to ask the higher self to review the particular problem area or areas that have been identified by the client. The purpose of the higher self's review is to determine whether something is happening at an energetic, psychic, or spiritual level, either to cause a client's problem or as a significant contributing factor. If the higher self says *yes*, that it has identified someone or something, then the challenge is to identify what it has found using only ideomotor signals. (If you are working with a client whose higher self is able to communicate verbally, then this is not so much an issue. You would still follow the protocol, but verbal communication makes the whole process much easier.)

Over hundreds of clinical sessions, aided by Gerod's information and guidance, I began to recognize patterns in the kinds of phenomena that presented with clients, the questions and suggestions that each kind responded to or not, and how each phenomenon needed to be dealt with in the healing process. Over time, I developed a protocol—a standard sequence of yes/no questions—that enabled me to quickly determine the particular kind of phenomenon that the higher self had identified in its review.

I found, generally speaking, that the phenomena I encountered fit into eight categories. So, when presented with an unknown phenomenon, the protocol assumes that it belongs to one of the eight. These categories are:

1) Ego-states (Present-life or past-life)
2) Spirits

3) Extraterrestrials
4) Dimensional beings
5) Created Entities
6) External ego-states
7) Device/objects
8) Autonomous energies

In order to identify which category a presenting phenomenon belongs to, the Identification Protocol begins with two questions. One question is whether the phenomenon presenting is *someone* or *something*. The other question is whether the presenting phenomenon is part of the client's self/soul energy or is separate. By *someone* I mean a conscious being that is an ego-state, a separate soul (spirit, extraterrestrial, dimensional), a created entity (a thought-being), or some part from another soul (an external ego-state). By *something*, I mean a physical or etheric device or an autonomously operating energy that is acting as a block or is negatively affecting the self in other ways. These devices and energies can be created either of the client's own self/soul energy or be separate from the soul and inserted from the outside.

These distinctions are important because a *someone* is treated differently than a *something*, and what is part of the client's self/soul energy will be treated differently than someone or something that is separate. In general, if someone or something is part of the self/soul, then the aim of treatment is usually integration. There are exceptions to this, especially in dealing with devices or energies. (This will be covered in a later chapter.) If it is separate, then the aim is dissipation and/or removal.

Based on these categories, then, the first two questions in the protocol will lead to one of four possibilities. When you encounter a new phenomenon, it is either:

- Someone – part of the soul
- Something – part of the soul
- Someone – separate from the soul
- Something – separate from the soul

We can view this as a decision tree where the two questions result in four primary branches leading to the eight phenomena. (See Figure 1.)

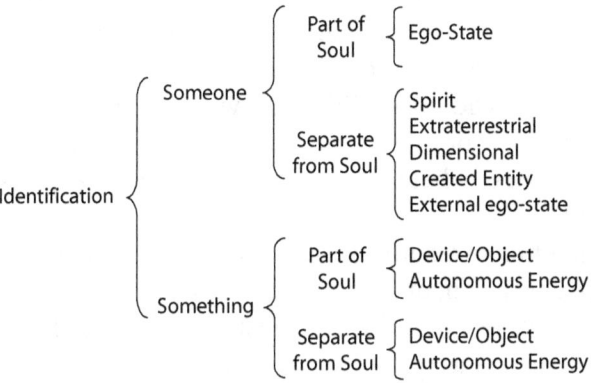

Figure 1

In practice, however, there is a complication. Using ideomotor signaling, only one question can be asked at a time and, depending on the situation, the two questions can be asked in reverse order. In effect, this means there are really two versions of the protocol depending on which of the two questions the therapist asks first. If the first question is whether a presenting phenomenon is part of the self/soul or not, the result is a different decision tree. They both lead to the same eight phenomena, but through a different sequence. The second version of the protocol would look like this:

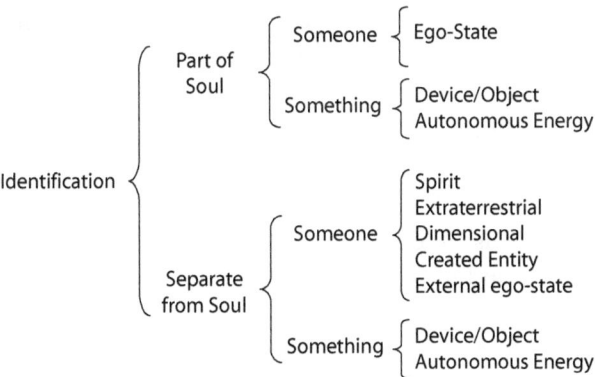

Figure 2

Which question to ask first will usually depend on what has been happening in the session up to that point. It depends, too, I think, on the therapist's experience and intuition. You do develop a feel for the various situations and possibilities and which question is most likely to elicit a response. For myself, I would say that most of the time I start with the question of whether the presenting phenomenon is *someone* or *something*.

Which question to ask first is usually not a critical issue. It sometimes can result in confusion, or take several steps longer than necessary, or trigger a negative reaction. For the most part, though, if one question doesn't work, then you try the second one. In my mind, the importance of the first question is a therapeutic one. I don't want to ask someone from the start a question they cannot answer, that frightens them, confuses them, or leads them to shut down. I want to ask a question that engages them and establishes an immediate connection. I want a positive interaction if possible, not a negative one. This first question also sets the stage for the questions that follow, some of which may be frightening or threatening to the ego-state or entity I'm communicating with.

Here are two simple examples illustrating the difference.

Identification Protocol: Example 1

TH   Higher self, were you able to find the source of that block?
HS   Yes finger lifts.
TH   If it is someone, the first finger can lift. If something, like a device or energy of some kind, then the second finger. If it's not clear, the hand can lift.
HS   First finger lifts.
TH   Higher self, is that one part of the self/soul?
HS   Yes finger lifts.
TH   I'm going to ask, then, that you help that one to come forward here with me... and to this one: are you willing today to communicate with me?
__   Yes finger lifts.
TH   Do you know yourself to be part of this self and soul I'm working with?
__   No finger lifts.

Identification Protocol: Example 2

    TH   Higher self, were you able to find the source of that block?
    HS   Yes finger lifts.
    TH   Higher self, is it part of the self/soul?
    HS   Yes finger lifts.
    TH   If it is someone, the first finger can lift. If something—like a device or energy of some kind—then the second finger lifting. If it's not clear, the hand can lift.
    HS   First finger lifts.
    TH   I'm going to ask, then, that you help that one to come forward here with me… and to this one: are you willing today to communicate with me?

Twenty-Six Possibilities

Usually, it doesn't matter which question is asked first, as long as both get answered. Either way, it leads to one of these four branches, and then to one of the eight phenomena. The protocol, however, goes further to identify more specifically *who* or *what* is presenting. That's because within each category of phenomena, there are different types. There are different types of ego-states, different types of spirits and dimensional beings. There are different types of etheric devices ranging from simple to sophisticated.

Within the category of ego-states, for example, there are past-life ego-states, present-life ego-states, mirror personalities, or ego-states that have left the soul. Each type needs to be treated in a slightly different way or requires a particular kind of resolution. It becomes important, then, to be able to identify what type of ego-state you are working with in order to know how to treat and resolve it. Ideally, every ego-state could move through its sharing and release without any difficulty. The therapist wouldn't need to know anything more about the ego-state than what it shares, and then move to the next one.

I want to emphasize that the different types of phenomena within each category are based on my clinical experience. This isn't to say there aren't other types. Over time, I recognized patterns among the different phenomena that presented independently in my work with many clients. Some of these presented so consistently and frequently that they were added to the protocol as a *type* of a particular phenomena to rule in or out.

When I sat down to analyze the protocols that I had been using in the healing process, I came up with twenty-six possible categories. Don't let the number intimidate you. Some of the differences between types are so small that the same protocol still works for each or requires only a minor tweak. In practice, there are about fourteen protocols for dealing with all twenty-six types of phenomena.

In Part 2, I will discuss the different phenomena and present the clinical protocols for dealing with each category and type of phenomena. Right now, staying with the Identification Protocol, I want to just list the twenty-six possible phenomena, along with their identifying characteristics. Also, each line represents the sequence that the protocol follows in identifying the particular phenomenon. It's a list that won't make complete sense right now, but it will as you move through the book. Also, it's a list you can refer back to when necessary.

Not every phenomenon you encounter will need to be identified to this level. The following list, however, applies to those cases where you do, in order to resolve it. It is a list of the phenomena along with the treatment each requires.

Someone

Part of Soul

- Someone – part of soul – an ego–state – created in present life – is present within the soul – needs to move through sharing, release, and integration.
- Someone – part of soul – an ego-state – presently outside the soul – needs to be retrieved – needs to move through sharing, release, and integration.
- Someone – part of soul – an ego–state – created in a past life – is present within the soul – needs to move through sharing, release, and integration.
- Someone – part of soul – an ego-state – created in a past life – presently outside the soul – needs to be retrieved – needs to move through sharing, release, and integration.

Separate from Soul

- Someone – separate from client's self/soul – a discarnate soul (spirit) – present within the client's energy – needs to connect with Light – voluntarily leaves or is forcibly removed.
- Someone – separate from client's self/soul – a discarnate soul (spirit) – operating from outside the client's energy – needs to connect with Light – sever ties.
- Someone – separate from client's self/soul – an incarnate soul, from off-planet or another dimension – present within the client's energy – needs to connect with Light – voluntarily leave client or be forcibly removed and ties severed.
- Someone – separate from client's self/soul – an incarnate soul, from off-planet or another dimension – operating from outside the client's self/soul energy – needs to connect with Light – sever ties with the client's soul.
- Someone – separate from client's self/soul – a created entity (a thought being) – present within the client's energy – needs to be dissipated or removed from the soul.
- Someone – separate from client's self/soul – a created entity (a thought being) – operating from outside the client's energy – needs to be dissipated and/or sever ties from the client's soul.
- Someone – separate from client's self/soul – external ego-state – present within the client's energy – needs to connect to the Light – voluntarily return to own soul or be forcibly removed and ties severed.
- Someone – separate from client's self/soul – external ego-state – operating from outside the client's energy – needs to connect to the Light – sever ties from the client's soul.

Something

Part of Soul

- Something – part of soul – an object/device of some kind – present within the soul – needs to be infused with Light and reintegrated.
- Something – part of soul – an object/device of some kind – present within the soul – needs to be dissipated and expelled.
- Something – part of soul – an object/device of some kind – pres-

ently outside the soul – needs to be retrieved and reintegrated with self/soul.
- Something – part of soul – an object/device of some kind – presently outside the soul – needs to be dissipated and/or sever its ties to soul.
- Something – part of soul – an autonomous energy – present within the soul – needs to be reintegrated with soul.
- Something – part of soul – an autonomous energy – present within the soul – needs to be dissipated and expelled.
- Something – part of soul – an autonomous energy – presently outside the soul – needs to be retrieved and reintegrated.
- Something – part of soul – an autonomous energy – presently outside the soul – needs to be dissipated and ties severed.

Separate from Soul
- Something – separate from client's self/soul – object/device – has entered the soul – needs to be expelled, or dissipated and expelled.
- Something – separate from client's self/soul – object/device – outside the soul – needs to be dissipated and/or all ties severed.
- Something – separate from client's self/soul – an autonomous energy – has entered the soul – needs to be expelled, or dissipated and expelled.
- Something – separate from client's self/soul – an autonomous energy – operating from outside the soul – needs to be dissipated if possible, or at least all ties severed.

If we extend the decision tree to include these other possibilities, it looks like the diagram in Figure 3. For all practical purposes, this is a diagram of the complete Identification Protocol.

Identification Protocol

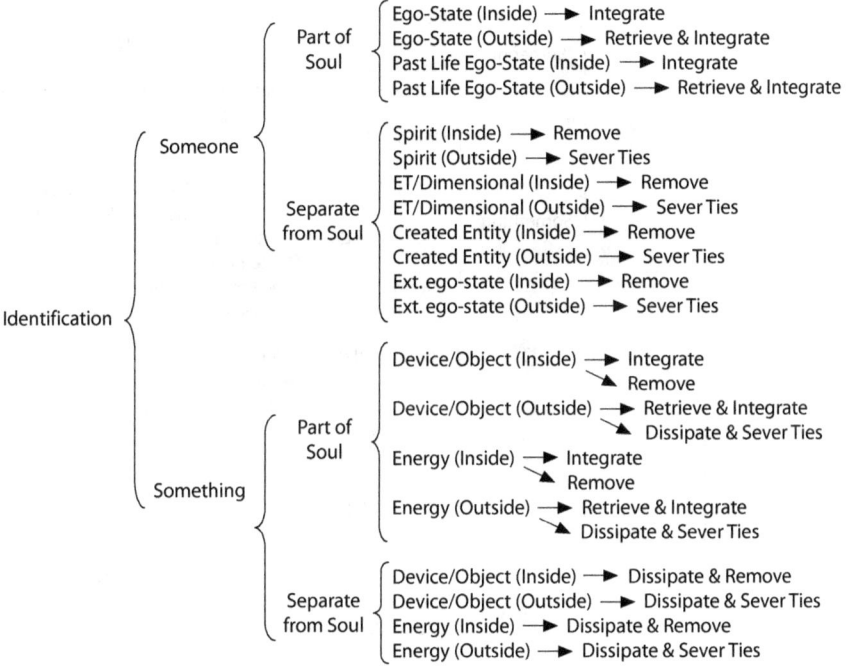

Figure 3

You might only encounter two or three of these phenomena with a particular client. The problem is, we never know which two or three we will encounter. Just as we saw earlier, there is a second version of the protocol. The diagram in Figure 3 starts with the distinction between someone and something. If the protocol begins with the distinction between what is part of the client's self/soul and what is separate, then the following diagram would apply. (See Figure 4.)

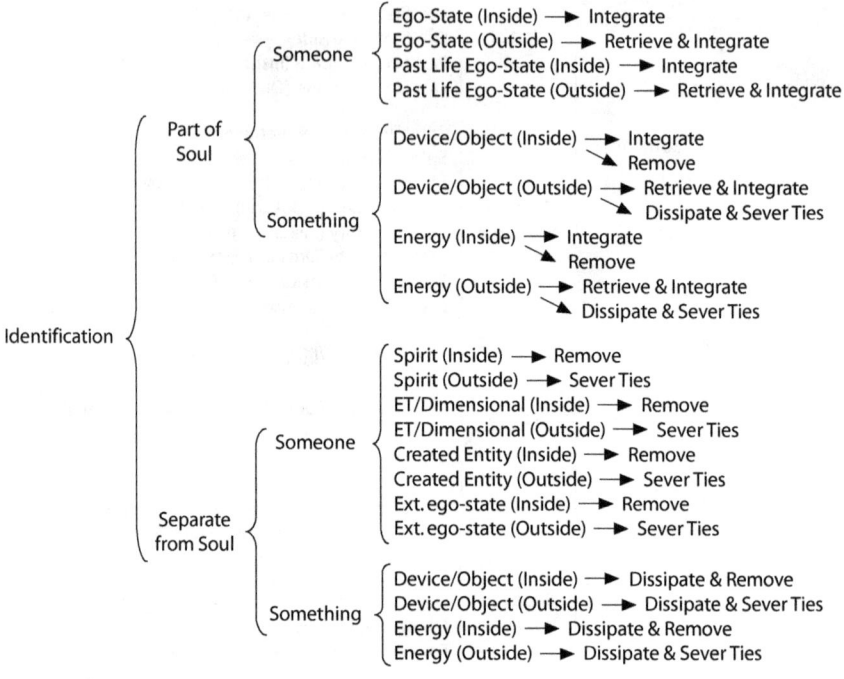

Figure 4

Again, each version identifies the same possible phenomena and prescribes the same treatment, only they arrive there by a different sequence of steps.

The decision tree is easy enough to learn. It is basically a series of if/then questions that eliminate possibilities as it moves to identify a specific phenomenon. It will take practice, though, to gain facility in using the Identification Protocol as a basic tool and be able move efficiently through the decision tree of possibilities. Before long, you will find yourself adept at thinking in this *yes/no* structure.

You will see the Identification Protocol woven throughout the rest of this book as different examples are given of the clinical protocols. The rule of thumb in the practice of Soul-Centered Healing is to always know who or what you are dealing with at any given moment. The Identification Protocol will help you answer that question so you can decide which treatment protocol to use. This process of identification also creates a clear trail, so the therapist can backtrack when necessary. It's somewhat like the police who have to maintain the chain of evidence as they carry out an investigation.

When the higher self has finished a review, the Identification Protocol is used to identify specifically who or what it has found. This is the necessary first step. The therapist must know who or what he or she is dealing with at any moment in order to know how best to treat it or deal with it. This situation is constantly occurring throughout the healing process where the therapist may encounter a block or interference and must identify its source in order to resolve it. For this reason, I view the Identification Protocol as a utility tool that is used in conjunction with all the clinical protocols and should always be ready at hand. The Identification Protocol tells you *what* you're dealing with; the clinical protocols tell you *how* to deal with it.

The use of the Identification Protocol, however, extends far beyond this initial contact with the higher self. During a session, the protocol is used anytime someone or something new has been identified or is presenting on its own. In addition, the protocol is used not only with the higher self, but also with anyone with whom the therapist is communicating, such as an ego-state or a spirit.

4

The Higher Self Review

Going back now to the Opening Protocol, we left off with the higher self communicating a yes, that it is in agreement with the healing process. The next step then is to ask the higher self to do an internal review regarding the identified problem areas or symptoms. The following examples illustrate how the exchange might go.

Higher Self Review: Example 1

TH To the higher self: John and I have talked at a conscious level about his panic attacks this past week. Higher self, have you been aware of these panic attacks?

HS Yes finger lifts.

TH Higher self, I'm going to ask that you look inside and see if someone or something is involved in triggering these panic feelings. Is that agreeable?

HS Yes finger lifts.

TH Please look inside, then, and see if there is anyone or anything at an unconscious level involved in the panic feelings. First finger lifting when that review is complete; second finger if the review is stopped. (Pause)

HS First finger lifts.

TH Higher self, were you able to review that area all right?

HS Yes finger lifts.

TH Did you find someone or something involved in these panic attacks?

HS Yes finger lifts.

TH If it's someone, the first finger can lift; if something, the second finger lifting; if neither of those fit, the hand can lift.

Higher Self Review: Example 2

TH To the higher self: Paula and I have talked at this conscious level about the fear she has in going to bed at night. Higher self, are you aware of that fear?

HS Yes finger lifts.

TH Higher self, I'm asking that you review inside and see if someone or something is involved in that fear. First finger when the review is complete. Second finger if it's stopped.

HS Second finger lifts

TH Higher self, was that review blocked or stopped?

HS Yes finger lifts.

TH Higher self, I am asking that you find the source of that block. First finger when you have found it. Second finger lifting if you do not.

HS First finger lifts.

TH Higher self, if it is someone, the first finger can lift; second finger if something or some energy; the hand lifting if none of those fit.

HS First finger lifts.

TH Higher self, are you in agreement that we have that one come forward here to communicate?

HS Yes finger lifts.

TH To this one: do you know yourself to be part of this soul I'm working with?

__ No finger lifts.

TH If you believe you are separate from this soul, the first finger can lift. If you're just not sure, the second finger can lift.

__ Second finger lifts

TH To this one: are you willing to receive a communication about whether you are or are not part of this soul?

__ Yes finger lifts.

TH On three, then, it will come to you. Beginning, one, two, three... and higher self or a guide, send to this one that information about themselves, whether they are or are not part of this self/soul energy. And to this one: yes finger when you've received that, second finger if you do not.

Higher Self Review: Example 3

TH To the higher self: Ben and I have talked about this rage that he felt yesterday, and at other times. Higher self, I'm asking that you look inside and see if there is someone or something involved in triggering that rage? First finger when that review is complete, second finger, if it is stopped.

HS First finger lifts.

TH Higher self, were you able to complete that review all right?

HS Yes finger lifts.

TH Higher self, did you find someone or something involved in triggering that rage?

HS Yes finger lifts.

TH If it is someone, the first finger can lift. If some thing or some energy, the second finger. If none of these fit, the hand can lift?

HS First finger lifts.

TH Higher self, I'm asking that you help that one come forward here with me. And to this one: do you know yourself to be a part of this self and soul I'm working with? If so, the first finger can lift, if you believe you are separate from this soul, second finger lifting. If you're not sure, the hand can lift.

__ Hand lifts.

TH To this one: are you receiving Light/Love energy for yourself there? If so, first finger lifting. If not, second finger. If you don't know, the hand can lift.

__ Second finger lifts.

TH To this one: are you willing to have some Light/Love energy sent to you now?

__ No finger lifts.

TH Is there some scare for you about this?

__ Yes finger lifts.

TH To this one: are you willing to have a tiny piece of Light sent—you can stop it immediately if you need to—or if you like it, you can keep it for yourself. The Light will not force itself on you. Would you be willing to try just that tiny piece of Light and make your own choice about it?

__ Yes finger lifts.

TH I'm going to ask higher self then to send you that small piece of

Light. Let yourself touch that and make your own decision. First finger when you see that Light, second finger if you do not.
__ First finger lifts.
TH To this one: did you receive that Light?
__ Yes finger lifts.
TH If you needed to stop it, first finger. If you decided to keep it for yourself, second finger lifting.
__ Second finger lifts
TH To this one: does it seem now that you are part of this self – that's the first finger; if you believe you are separate, the second finger lifting; if you're still not sure, the hand can lift.
__ First finger lifts.
TH To this one: it seems you are part of this soul, is that right?
__ Yes finger lifts.
TH Are you one first created in this present life of Ben's?
__ No finger lifts.
TH Do you believe you are from a past or different lifetime?
__ Yes finger lifts.

Higher Self Review: Example 4

TH Higher self, were you able to complete that review all right?
HS Yes finger lifts.
TH Did you find someone or something involved in that voice that Jerry keeps hearing?
HS Yes finger lifts.
TH Higher self, first finger if it is someone; second finger if something or some energy; the hand lifting if none of those fit.
HS First finger lifts.
TH Higher self, are you in agreement that we have that one come forward to communicate?
HS Yes finger lifts.
TH To this one: do you know yourself to be part of this soul I'm working with?
__ No finger lifts.
TH If you believe you are separate from this soul, the first finger can lift. If you're just not sure, the second finger can lift.
__ Second finger lifts

TH To this one: are you willing to receive a communication about whether you *are* or *are not* part of this soul?
__ Yes finger lifts.

At this point, the therapist would start with the protocol for past-life ego-states.

This was the general protocol for engaging the higher self and initiating its role as an inner guide in the healing process. Once I have established direct communication with a client's higher self and it has carried out a review, it marks the next step in the process. From this point on the higher self will be your ally and play a central role in the client's healing process. As you'll see, the higher self also plays a central role in each of the clinical protocols.

I usually make direct contact with the higher self at the start of each session. Once the client is in trance, I'll ask the higher self whether it is able to communicate with me again. It's a way of making sure that communication with the person's higher self is still open and clear and that it is free to assist in what we are about to do in the healing session.

If I don't receive a *yes* to this question, then I know that someone or something is blocking or interfering. Once communication is established with the higher self in the Opening Protocol, it will always be willing to communicate. If you get a *no* to this request—in this first session or in later sessions—then you know it's not the higher self communicating. If that happens, then you switch to the Identification Protocol in order to identify the source of the blocking or interference. Later, I'll discuss how to apply the Identification Protocol to those situations where you encounter a block.

For right now, staying with our best-case scenario, once the higher self signals that it is able to communicate I will usually seek its guidance on where the best place is to start the session, or I will ask whether it is in agreement that we start with a particular issue. Usually, I will name the two or three most significant issues my client has on the table at that moment. It might be a painful area we left off with in the previous session. It may be about a terrifying dream that the client just reported having the night before. Or it might be several panic attacks that he or she experienced in the past week.

In listing these possibilities for the higher self, I always include the choice that none of the options I'm suggesting would be the best thing to address. This gives the higher self the opportunity to signal that it perceives someone or something else as more important to address first. If the hand lifts, signaling that none of the choices fit, then I'll begin working with higher self to identify who or what it perceives as the best place to start. Here are five example scenarios.

Higher Self Review: Example 5

TH   Higher self, Larry and I have talked about the disturbing dream he had this week. Also in the last session we left off with a group of six ego-states. Higher self, are you still aware of the group of six we were working with last time? If so, first finger. If not, second finger lifting.
HS   First finger lifts.
TH   Higher self, if that group is the best place for us to start the session today, the yes finger can lift. If it would be better to start with the dream, the second finger can lift; if we should start with someone or something else, then the hand can lift.
HS   Second finger lifts.
TH   I see the second finger. Higher self, is the dream the best place for us to work with first?
HS   Yes finger lifts.
TH   I'm going to ask then that you review that dream and see if there is someone or something involved in the dream that needs to be addressed. First finger lifting when the review is complete; second finger if it is stopped or blocked.
HS   First finger lifts.
TH   Higher self, were you able to do that review all right?
HS   Yes finger lifts.
TH   Higher self, did you find someone or something involved in the dream that needs to be addressed?
HS   Yes finger lifts.
TH   If it is someone, first finger lifting, if something, the second finger can lift.
HS   First finger lifts.
TH   Higher self, is that one part of Larry's self/soul?
HS   No finger lifts.
TH   If that one is itself a soul, first finger lifting, if it is a created entity or a part from another soul, then the second finger can lift. If none of those fit, the hand can lift.

HS First finger lifts.

At this point, the therapist would use the protocol for addressing a spirit(s).

Higher Self Review: Example 6

TH Higher self, if it would be good to address the dream or panic attacks that Nancy and I talked about, first finger lifting. If someone or something else needs to be addressed first, the second finger can lift.
HS Second finger lifts.
TH Higher self, if it's someone we should address, first finger lifting; if something or some energy, then the second finger lifting. If none of those fit, the hand can lift.
HS First finger lifts.
TH Higher self, is this one part of the self/soul?
HS Yes finger lifts.
TH Higher self, are you in agreement that we bring that one forward to communicate?
HS Yes finger lifts.
TH Higher self, I'm going to ask, then, that you help that one come forward here with me. (Pause) And to this one: do you know yourself to be part of this self and soul I'm working with?

At this point the therapist would use the Ego-Sate Protocol.

Higher Self Review: Example 7

TH Higher self, are you willing again today to communicate with me?
HS Yes finger lifts.
TH Higher self, are you aware of the group of three we worked with in our last session?
HS Yes finger lifts.
TH If that's the best place for us to continue right now, first finger lifting. If we should address the dream Nancy and I talked about or the panic attacks, then the second finger lifting. If none of those fit, then the hand can lift.
HS Second finger lifts.
TH If we should address the dream, then first finger. If the panic at-

tacks, then the second finger. If neither of those, then the hand can lift. (I still want to give the higher self a way out of the two options presented.)
- HS First finger lifts.
- TH Higher self, if there's someone involved in the dream that we should communicate with, the first finger lifting. If it's something or an energy we should address, then the second finger lifting. If none of those fit, the hand can lift.
- HS Second finger lifts.
- TH If it's something like a device, an object, or a cord, first finger lifting. If it's more like an energy, the second finger can lift.
- HS Second finger lifts.
- TH Higher self, is that energy part of the self/soul energy?
- HS Yes finger lifts.
- TH Is there more than one?
- HS Yes finger lifts.

At this point the healer would switch to the Energy Protocol.

Higher Self Review: Example 8

- TH Higher self, I see the first finger lifting. Were you able to do that review all right?
- HS Yes finger lifts.
- TH Higher self, did you find someone or something involved with Jim's frequent headaches?
- HS Yes finger lifts.
- TH Higher self, if it's someone, first finger lifting; if something or some energy, the second finger lifting.
- HS First finger lifts.
- TH Higher self, is that one part of the self/soul? If so, first finger lifting. If it is separate, the second finger can lift
- HS Second finger lifts.
- TH Higher self, is that one itself a soul? If so, first finger. If it's a created entity or a part from another soul, the second finger can lift. If you're not sure, higher self, the hand can lift.
- HS First finger lifts.
- TH Higher self, has that spirit entered the soul?
- HS Yes finger lifts.

The Higher Self Review

TH Higher self, if this is one I should communicate with directly, the first finger can lift. If we should just remove it now, second finger lifting. If something else, the hand can lift.
HS First finger lifts.
TH I'm asking, then, higher self that you help that one come forward here with me. … And to this one: do you know yourself to be a soul? If so, first finger lifting. If not, second finger. If you're not sure, the hand can lift.
SP First finger lifts.

At this point the healer would use the Spirit Protocol.

Higher Self Review: Example 9

TH Higher self, did you find anyone or anything at the unconscious level that's involved in these panic attacks?
HS Yes finger lifts.
TH If it's someone, first finger; if some thing, the second finger; if neither of those fit, the hand can lift.
HS First finger lifts.
TH Higher self, is this one part of Jodie's own self/soul energy? If yes, then the first finger lifting, if they are separate from the soul, the second finger can lift. If you're not sure, the hand can lift.
HS First finger lifts.
TH I'm asking, then, higher self, that you help that one to come forward here with me. And to this one: are you willing now to communicate with me?
___ Yes finger lifts.

I don't want to give the impression here that control over the direction of the client's healing process is just handed over to the higher self. Weight is also given to the client's concerns, whether focused on a specific issue like panic attacks or on an experience the client had during the week. When something quite traumatic or significant has happened, the client's felt need to deal with it can take priority and the higher self most often will be in agreement that it's an appropriate issue to address first.

It makes a difference, though, how you ask the question. If asked like this: "Higher self, are you in agreement that we address this panic attack that Cindy and I have talked about today?" A *yes* signal from the higher self supports working on the panic attacks, but that *yes* signal should not be interpreted to mean that the higher self is in agreement that it's the *best* place to begin the session. If the client chooses consciously to focus the session on a particular issue, the higher self will usually not oppose that. I give the higher self two or three options along with lifting the hand for "none of these" in order to avoid this situation. I do not want to put the higher self, or anyone else inside, into a forced choice where neither choice is correct for the question we've asked. By using the hand signal, it's as though we are giving the one we're communicating with an opportunity to say, "Hey, you're asking the wrong question."

For now, staying with our best-case scenario, the higher self signals that it has completed its review.

Choosing a Protocol

This is the point, as healers, where we cannot predict what the higher self has found and who or what is going to present. This goes for the first review the higher self does and it goes for every subsequent session. We don't know what we are going to encounter next. There are many possibilities, and in practice, the healer needs to be ready for any of them.

In my own experience, I have found that what presents will generally fall into one of eight categories. The reader will recognize these from the Identification Protocol. Each one calls for a different approach and different protocol in order to identify and resolve it. The eight categories of what might present at any time are:

1) An ego-state(s).
2) A past life ego-state.
3) A spirit (discarnate soul).
4) A created entity (Not a soul, more a *thought being*.).
5) An external ego-state from another soul (EES).
6) An extraterrestrial or extra-dimensional being or entity. (Some are souls, some not. Some would be considered incarnate, others discarnate.)
7) An etheric device or object created of the client' own self/soul energy or created from separate energy and inserted from the outside. These device/objects carry out certain functions or serve different purposes at an unconscious level. These device/

objects can be present within the self/soul, or acting on the soul from outside.
8) Some form of energy—created either of the client's self/soul energy or separate energy—that is affecting the self in negative or painful ways. These energies can be operating within the self, or acting on the soul from outside.

These are broad categories, and within each category there can be a wide variation of phenomena. I'm also quite sure these categories do not cover all phenomena, but they are the ones I've seen most frequently with my clients.

In Soul-Centered Healing, there is a different protocol for dealing with each category of phenomena. The protocol for dealing with an ego-state, for example, is very different than the protocol for dealing with an attached spirit. Once we know which category the presenting phenomenon belongs in, then a decision can be made as to which protocol to use to address it. You may have to adapt the protocol to the specific phenomenon you're dealing with, but it still follows the basic steps from identification to resolution.

In Part 2, I'll discuss each of the protocols and how to use them.

Exercise 1

The best first step in learning Soul-Centered Healing is to practice establishing communication with a person's protective part and higher self. With willing friends, family, or selected clients, use the Opening Protocol to establish communication with his or her protective part and higher self. I would suggest doing this with at least seven or eight subjects and more if possible. The goal would be to develop a feel for working with these parts of the self. I consider the first few sessions with a client to be a calibration period for establishing reliable ideomotor signals.

Keep in mind that a protective part and/or higher self can be blocked. If, after trying several safe questions you cannot establish communication with either part, then close the session with positive suggestions and discontinue the trial. Try again with the next person.

Normally, if this blocking happens in practice, the therapist would move to the next step of identifying the source of the block. This can involve very complex situations and we have not addressed these yet. So for now, the emphasis is on a direct and safe communication with the protective part and higher self.

I consider this exercise to be safe in the sense that these are both positive parts of the self that are inherently supportive of the person's healing and are not being asked to do anything beyond communicating directly.

Once you have communicated with a person's protective part and/or higher self, thank those parts and bring the session to an end.

Part 2
The Clinical Protocols

5

The Ego-State Protocol

Unlike with the protective part and higher self, there is not just one ego-state per client. There are many. They come from the client's present life and from past lives. Usually they are in human form, but not always. Each ego-state carries its own unique experience. We can never predict what ego-states will present in the course of a client's healing. There is, however, one basic protocol for working with any ego-state. (I discussed this briefly in Chapter 12 of Soul-Centered Healing.) The protocol has eight steps:
 1) Facilitate contact with higher self (receiving Light)
 2) Identification of ego-state.
 3) With others or alone?
 4) The promise of integration.
 5) Sharing.
 6) Release.
 7) Any doors or windows?
 8) Conscious experience and integration.

These steps are designed to gain an ego-state's cooperation right from the beginning and help lead it through its sharing and release as easily as possible.

Step 1: Contact with the Higher Self

Once an ego-state is identified and agrees to communicate, the first step in the protocol is to gain its trust and its cooperation. The quickest way to do this is to initiate a contact between the ego-state and the higher self. The therapist asks the ego-state whether it is willing to receive Light/Love energy for itself. If it agrees, then we simply ask the higher self to "safely send the Light/Love energy" to the ego-state, as well as "any other information that might be helpful, especially about healing and release."

The influence of higher self on ego-states is one of the seemingly magical elements in Soul-Centered Healing. I say *magical* because I cannot explain what happens in this contact. It appears that the higher self can bring Light to an ego-state in whatever form is most acceptable or needed by that particular ego-state. It can present it in small doses, address specific fears or doubts the ego-state has, or appear as a fairy godmother or some other positive figure. No matter how scared, belligerent, or confused it is, once an ego-state has received the Light for itself, I would say ninety-eight percent of the time it wants to keep it and it becomes immediately cooperative in the healing process. Once an ego-state receives the Light, all resistance seems to melt away. This positive response to the Light is so consistent that, from a scientific point of view, it is predictable far beyond statistical significance. Clinically, it's a quick and effective way to gain an ego-state's cooperation.

In those situations where an ego-state stops the Light or refuses to receive it, what you will often find is that the Light is drawing forth the ego-state's own pain and memories, that it is being threatened by spirits or entities to stay away from the Light, or it has some device or energy attached to it that causes distress when exposed to the Light. I'll discuss the protocols for dealing with these situations in a later chapter.

For right now, here is an example of this first step in Ego-State Protocol. The therapist is communicating to an ego-state that the higher self has just identified.

Ego-state Protocol. Step 1: Example 1

TH   To this one: are you willing to communicate with me as long as it's safe?
ES   Yes finger lifts.
TH   Do you know yourself to be part of this self and soul I'm working with?
ES   Yes finger lifts.
TH   Are you receiving some Light/Love energy where you are?
ES   Hand lift. (I don't know)
TH   To this one: are you willing for higher self to send you some Light/

Love energy for yourself there?
- ES Yes finger lifts.
- TH I'm going to ask then that the higher self send you that Light/Love energy. You can receive that Light, and if you like it, you can bring it inside to whatever level is comfortable. Beginning: one, two, three. And higher self, please send to this one that Light/Love/warmth energy; and to this one: let yourself receive that Light to whatever level feels comfortable. First finger when it feels complete; second finger if it's stopped or blocked. (Pause)
- ES First finger lifts.
- TH To this one: did you receive that Light for yourself?
- ES Yes finger lifts.
- TH Does that feel all right to you?
- ES Yes finger lifts.
- TH To this one: I'm going to ask the higher self to keep that Light right there with you. Is that agreeable?
- ES Yes finger lifts.
- TH To this one: are you one first created in this present life of Mary's?
- ES Yes finger lifts.

Here is another example of that first step of making contact between the ego-state and the higher self. This example is a little more complex. It involves an ego-state that is not aware that it is part of the self/soul.

Ego-state Protocol. Step 1: Example 2

- TH Higher self, I'm asking that you help that ego-state to come forward here with me. (Pause.) And to this one: do you know yourself to be part of this self and soul I'm working with?
- ES No finger lifts.
- TH Are you willing to have some information sent to you about your connection to this self/soul.
- ES Yes finger lifts.
- TH Okay then. On the count of three I'm going to ask the higher self to send you this information. One, two, three, and higher self, please communicate to this one information about whether they *are* or *are not*, part of this self and soul. Also, please communicate any other information that might be helpful, especially about the healing process we are working with. And to this one: lift the yes finger

when you've received that communication, second finger if you do not.
ES Yes finger lifts.
TH To this one: did you receive this communication all right?
ES Yes finger lifts.
TH Does it seem that you are part of this self and soul? First finger if yes, second finger if not.
ES First finger lifts.
TH Are you receiving Light for yourself now where you are?
ES Hand lifts. (I don't know)
TH To this one: are you willing for higher self to send you some Light/Love energy right now?
ES Hand lifts. (I don't know)
TH To this one: are you willing to have that Light sent to you as long as you can stop it immediately if you need to, or if you like it, you can keep it for yourself, but the choice will be up to you? The Light will not force itself on you.
ES Yes finger lifts.
TH On three then: One, two three... and higher self please send to this one a small piece of that Light/Love energy. And to this one: let yourself receive that Light. You can stop it if you need to, or, if you like it, you can bring it inside and keep it for yourself. First finger lifting when you've touched that Light, second finger if you do not.
ES First finger lifts.
TH To this one: did you receive that Light?
ES Yes finger lifts.
TH Did you decide to keep the Light for yourself? If so, the first finger. If you needed to stop it, the second finger can lift.
ES First finger lifts.
TH To this one: would you like more of that Light/Love energy for yourself?
ES Yes finger lifts.
TH Higher self, I'm asking, then, that you send this one more of that Light/Love energy. And to this one: you can bring that inside to whatever level is comfortable. First finger when that feels complete. Second finger if it's stopped.
ES First finger lifts.
TH To this one: did you receive that Light all right?

ES Yes finger lifts.
TH Does that feel all right to you?
ES Yes finger lifts.

The following is an example involving a five year-old ego-state who is afraid of the Light and has said *no* to any contact with the higher self.

Ego-state Protocol. Step 1: Example 3

TH 5yo, is there some scare for you about the Light?
5yo Yes finger lifts.
TH 5yo: are you willing for higher self to send a tiny ball of Light, as long as it stops at least a foot away… it won't touch you …and you can see for yourself whether or not it looks safe. Are you willing for higher self to do that – to send just a tiny ball of Light – as long as it stays a foot away and you don't have to touch it?
5yo Yes finger lifts.
TH Higher self, on the count of three, I'm asking that you send that ball of Light to 5yo, but keeping it a safe distance away… just so she can see it.
And 5yo, when you see that ball of Light, and it has come to a stop, lift the first finger to let me know. If you don't see it or there's some kind of problem, lift the second finger.
…Beginning now. One. Two. Three. Higher self, please send that ball of Light now to 5yo and stop it in front of her … very safely. And 5yo, let yourself see that ball of Light. It's all right… It won't touch you. It will stop just a foot or so away. It's safe to look at it… First finger when you see it, second finger if not… (Pause)
5yo First finger lifts.
TH 5yo, can you see that ball of Light there?
5yo Yes finger lifts.
TH Is there any pain or distress you're feeling with it?
5yo No finger lifts.
TH 5yo, would you be willing for that ball to come a little closer, just until you feel it? When you do, you can stop it immediately if you need to. Would you be willing to do that?
5yo No finger lifts.
TH Is that still too scary?
5yo Yes finger lifts.

TH Would you be willing, 5yo, just to pass your hand over the top of that ball? Again, you can take your hand away if there's any pain or scare. Would you be willing to try that?

5yo Yes finger lifts.

TH Real good… You can do that now… very safely… Just pass your hand over the top of that ball, high enough to be safe… just until you feel that Light, even a little. First finger when you have felt it, second finger if not.

5yo First finger lifts.

TH 5yo, can you feel that Light?

5yo Yes finger lifts.

TH Does that feel good to you?

5yo Yes finger lifts.

TH Would you like to have more of that Light for yourself?

5yo Yes finger lifts.

TH 5yo, you can reach out your hand and that ball of Light can settle in your palm, and it will bring you more Light. Would you like that?

5yo Yes finger lifts.

TH Higher self, I'm asking that you move the ball now to the palm of her hand. As it does, 5yo, you can feel that Light and bring it all the way inside. It's safe to do that now. Let yourself receive it. It can come to whatever level feels comfortable… First finger when that feels complete; second finger if there's any problem. (Pause)

5yo First finger lifts.

TH 5yo: were you able to bring that Light inside?

5yo Yes finger lifts.

TH Does that feel all right to you?

5yo Yes finger lifts.

TH Are you willing now, with higher self helping, to share what you need to share for your full healing and release?

5yo Yes finger lifts.

As you can see from these examples, the first step is to help an ego-state receive Light, and the most effective way to do that is to offer it a safe experience of the Light where it has nothing to lose and everything to gain. Different ego-states require different reassurances or guarantees. In the end, the guarantee is that the ego-state can safely touch the Light, test it out, and choose for itself whether to stop the

Light or receive it. The ego-state is guaranteed complete control over the experience.

The role of the therapist at this point is to facilitate the contact by offering suggestions and whatever reassurances are needed. Once the ego-state makes contact with the Light, ninety-eight percent of the time it will communicate that the Light feels good and they wish to keep it for themselves. Like with the protective part and the higher self, the first step with an ego-state is to make it an ally in the healing process.

It is not unusual, however, for an ego-state to refuse the Light initially. I have found four main reasons for this.

1) First, contact with the Light can begin to draw up the ego-state's own pain and, perceiving it as the Light causing its pain, the ego-state shuts down the Light to stop the pain.
2) The second reason an ego-state might refuse contact with the Light is because someone or something is threatening it in present time to stay away from the Light. It may be a spirit who is threatening it or it might be threatened by another ego-state.
3) The third reason is that the ego-state has been given the message in the past to stay away from the Light because it will harm or destroy it.
4) Finally, there may be a device of some kind that has been placed on or close to the ego-state that begins to react whenever the Light approaches. The ego-state stops the Light, then, in order to stop the effects of the device.

Each of these situations calls for a change in protocol to resolve the ego-state's refusal, or to identify the source of a threat and neutralize it. These protocols will be discussed in more detail later. For now we'll go back to the ideal scenario where contact has occurred between the ego-state and the higher self.

Step 2: Identification of the Ego-State

Once an ego-state has received the Light and signaled its agreement to healing, the next step is to ask for basic information about who it is: Past life or present? Male or female? Child, adolescent, or adult? A name? This information gives the therapist the basic identity of the one to call for, or come back to, should the communication be stopped or blocked.

The identification of the ego-state is also important in helping the healer to communicate to the ego-state within its own context, so that it understands what is being asked and what is being offered. We talk differently to a three year-old ego-state from a client's present life than we would to a 13th century monk from a past life. If we try to talk to a 17th century squire about an automobile, the communication is likely to get confused.

Finally, the identification of the ego-state allows the therapist to map the course of the healing process, like mapping a river and its tributaries. It gives an over-all perspective and a sense of continuity for both the client and therapist. It also makes it clear that things are not just presenting at random or out of thin air. There is an inner logic to the healing journey.

In this step, the ego-state is not being asked to share its experience. Sometimes the sharing will happen spontaneously, which is fine if it does. In that event, the therapist can just support the sharing process, and then backtrack later to get more information if necessary.

In practice, the protocol for identifying an ego-state might look like this:

Identification of an Ego-State: Example 1

    TH To this one: do you know yourself to be part of this self and soul?
    ES Yes finger lifts.
    TH Are you one first created in this present life of Cindy's?
    ES Yes finger lifts.
    TH Are you younger than twelve years old?
    ES Yes finger lifts.
    TH Younger than seven?
    ES No finger lifts.
    TH Are you younger than nine?
    ES Yes finger lifts.
    TH Are you eight years old?
    ES Yes finger lifts.
    TH And 8yo, are you a female?
    8yo Yes finger lifts.
    TH Do you have a name?
    8yo No finger lifts.
    TH Do you know about the healing process we are working with?

8yo	Yes finger lifts.
TH	Would you like to have that healing and release for yourself?
8yo	Yes finger lifts.
TH	Are you willing, with higher self giving its support, to share what you need to share for that release and healing?
8yo	No finger lifts.

In this example, the identification goes smoothly, but there is resistance by the ego-state to sharing its experience. Using a different protocol, the healer will determine why the ego-state is refusing, and help it to resolve it.

Here's another example of the protocol for identifying an ego-state:

Identification of an Ego-State: Example 2

TH	To this one: are you one first created in this present life of Cindy's?
ES	No finger lifts.
TH	Are you from a past or different lifetime? If so, the yes finger can lift. If you're not sure, the second finger lifting.
ES	Yes finger lifts.
TH	Are you a male?
ES	No finger lifts.
TH	Are you a female?
ES	Yes finger lifts.
TH	Are you an adult?
ES	No finger lifts.
TH	Are you at least an adolescent?
ES	Yes finger lifts.
TH	Do you have a name?
ES	Yes finger lifts.
TH	Is it all right for us to know your name?
ES	Yes finger lifts.
TH	I'm going to ask, then, that you communicate your name right here to the conscious mind on the count of three. One, two, three… just say your name nice and loud right to the conscious mind. First finger when that's complete, second if it's stopped or blocked.
ES	First finger lifts.
TH	Cindy, here with me at a conscious level: Cindy, did you receive that name?

Cy. Yes, her name is Lisa.
TH   To this one: is that correct? Is your name Lisa?
ES   Yes finger lifts.
TH   Lisa, do you know about the healing process we're working with?
ES   Yes finger lifts.
TH   Do you want to have that healing and release for yourself?
ES   Yes finger lifts.

Step 3: Are There Others?

Once an ego-state has received Light and been identified, I will ask it to look around where it is and see if anyone else is there. When the higher self identifies an ego-state to come forward or when an ego-state presents on its own, it is often part of a group. It is good to obtain this information early in the protocol for several reasons.

- It usually saves having to repeat steps later with others in the group.
- It can be appropriate to initiate contact with the Light for each member in the group simultaneously. This usually leads to cooperation of the entire group and an avoidance of future blocking from someone in the group.
- Most of the time it's possible that an entire group of ego-states can move through the sharing and release process together. In that case, I usually will identify the presenting ego-state, find out how many are in the group, but not ask for each one's identification unless necessary. During the course of the sharing and release process, one or more ego-states belonging to the group sometimes need to be identified and worked with individually. In that case, you follow the same protocol. Most of the time, though, an entire group will go through it together.

Step 4: The Place of Integration

The next step, after an ego-state is identified, is to communicate to it about the place of integration that is waiting for it once it has moved through the sharing and release. This step is not always necessary. Some ego-states are ready to share their memories and experiences right after their contact with higher self. However, when there is still resistance or difficulty, the promise of integration can be another powerful motive for an ego-state to say yes to the sharing. Even when it's not necessary, I believe this information offers greater understanding as well to those ego-states who are already willing to share. I would say most of the time I direct higher self to show an ego-state its place of integration just for reassurance and encouragement. All ego-states will find out about this place in the end. The question is whether it would help for an ego-state to see it earlier rather than later.

The place of integration is another of those magical elements in the healing process. It's not a physical place, but a place in consciousness. It's a place where an ego-state can go to once it has moved through the healing process. Every ego-state has its place of integration, and the higher self knows where it is. Additionally, the higher self can show an ego-state its place of integration even before it does any sharing or release.

The magical part is that ninety-eight percent of ego-states respond positively to this knowledge of their place of integration. Sometimes this knowledge is the deciding factor for an ego-state that still has some resistance to the Light or to sharing its pain. If asked, ego-states invariably agree that the place they saw felt good and comfortable, and felt like home. Most of the time, when asked, an ego-state will communicate that it wants to move to the place of integration it just saw. (See Chapters 11 and 12 of *Soul-Centered Healing*.) Here are a couple examples of this step.

Showing an Ego-state its Place of Integration: Example 1

    TH 12yo, did you receive that Light for yourself?
    12yo Yes finger lifts.
    TH Does that feel all right to you?
    12yo Yes finger lifts.
    TH Would you be willing now to share what you need to for healing and release?
    12yo Hand lifts. (Not sure)
    TH Is there still some scare about that?
    12yo Yes finger lifts.
    TH 12yo, did you know that there is a place of Light and integration waiting for you after your sharing and release? Do you know about that place?

12yo No finger lifts.
TH Would you be willing for higher self to show you that place that's waiting for you? Would you like to see it?
12yo Yes, finger lifts.
TH Higher self, I'm asking, then, that you show 12yo that place of Light and integration that is here for her. 12yo, first finger when you see that place, second finger if you do not.
12yo First finger lifts.
TH 12yo, were you able to see that place all right?
12yo Yes finger lifts.
TH Does that look like a good and fitting place to be?
12yo Yes finger lifts.
TH Is that a place you would like to move to after your own healing and release?
12yo Yes finger lifts.
TH Are you willing then, with higher self's help, to share what you need to in order to move to your new place?
12yo Yes finger lifts.

The following is another example where the place of integration is used to gain an ego-state's cooperation.

Showing an Ego-state its Place of Integration: Example 2

TH Oliver, are you willing to share what you need to share for healing and release?
OL Yes finger lifts.
TH On three, then, let yourself share what you need to. One, two, three… Just share right here to the present now what needs to be shared. It's safe to do that now. First finger when complete, second finger if the sharing is stopped or blocked.
OL Second finger lifts.
TH Oliver was the sharing stopped?
OL Yes finger lifts.
TH Peter here with me at a conscious level, Peter did anything come to you?
Pe No. There was nothing.
TH Oliver if you needed to stop the sharing, first finger lifting. If someone or something seemed to get in the way, then second finger.

OL First finger lifts.
TH Oliver you needed to stop the sharing, is that right?
OL Yes finger lifts.
TH Did it scare you?
OL Yes finger lifts.
TH Oliver, did you know there's a place of Light and integration waiting for you when you've moved through your sharing?
OL No finger lifts.
TH Would you like to see that place for yourself Oliver? Just to give you some reassurance that the healing and release can be safe for you?
OL Yes finger lifts.
TH Okay. Higher self, I'm asking that you show Oliver that place of Light and integration that's here for him within the soul. Oliver, just let yourself see that place. First finger when you've seen it, second finger if you do not.
OL First finger lifts.
TH Were you able to see that place all right?
OL Yes finger lifts.
TH Does it look like a good and fitting place to be?
OL Yes finger lifts.
TH Does that give you the reassurance you need, Oliver, to know that it's safe now to have healing and release for yourself?
OL Yes finger lifts.
TH Are you willing to share, then, what you need to share for that release?
OL Yes finger lifts.

This step in the protocol usually goes quite smoothly. Like contact with higher self and the Light, the place of integration is self-reinforcing. It is its own reward. To ego-states, it almost always feels good to them. It feels safe. It makes sense. Who would turn down such a place of comfort and safety and choose, instead, to remain in fear and distress? It's a no-brainer. For an ego-state, there is no risk in receiving information about it, or being shown its own place of integration. If an ego-state is afraid to leave where it is, the higher self can send a picture of the place just as easily.

Nothing is being forced about this. The ego-state makes its own judgment about what it has seen and felt. Most of the time ego-states have a strong and positive response to the place they have seen. They like it and want to move there. If there is a negative reaction, it is almost always due to the ego-state's fear or distress about so much Light or feelings that they don't deserve it or will be rejected by the Light.

So, besides contact with the Light, this promise of integration is another powerful motivation for ego-states to say yes to the healing process, even when that means that it first must share its pain and distress. This knowledge of integration gives an ego-state a kind of ultimate reassurance. However the higher self does it, it helps the ego-state to glimpse its future and where it can live. As I said, I don't use this step with every ego-state or group of ego-states, but I use it often. It reassures those who are scared or suspicious, and it reinforces those who already are willing to share.

Step 5: Sharing

When an ego-state has all the reassurance it needs, and signals its agreement to share what it needs to for release, then the therapist asks it to begin sharing to the conscious mind whatever needs to be shared for healing. Usually, but not always, it is obvious in the client's body language and facial expressions that something is happening. Also, some clients will start sharing out loud what is coming to them. For the client, the sharing can range anywhere from an intense re-living of an experience, to just the emotions or just physiological sensations. Whether the client has been sharing it out loud or not, the therapist waits for the yes signal that the sharing is complete.

Once the signal comes, the therapist asks the client whether he or she has received the sharing, and if so, is there any comment they would make about it? Most clients will give some information.

When that's complete, the therapist will briefly restate what has been shared and ask the ego-state whether it is accurate. If confirmed, then the higher self is also asked whether it agrees that all has been shared that needs to be. If yes, then the ego-state can move to its release.

The following is an example of how the process might look during a session. Staying with our best-case scenario, the sharing is brief and straightforward.

Ego-State Sharing: Example 1

TH 6yo, were you able to see that place of integration all right?
6yo. Yes finger lifts.
TH Does that look like a good and fitting place to be?
6yo. Yes finger lifts.
TH Would you like to move to that place once you've moved through your sharing and release?
6yo. Yes finger lifts.
TH Are you willing then to share what you need to?
6yo. Yes finger lifts.
TH Do you know what needs to be shared?
6yo. Yes finger lifts.
TH I'm going to ask that the higher self keep you surrounded in that Light, and on the count of three you can share what you need to. Beginning: one, two, three… 6yo, let yourself share now what you need to share… what you see, feel, or hear that needs to be shared. Let it come right to the present now. First finger when that's complete, second finger if the sharing is stopped.
(Obvious body language or expressions indicating something happening.)
6yo. First finger lifts.
TH David here with me at a conscious level, David, did you receive something?
Da I see my dad. He's screaming at me. I'm in the basement. He's screaming at me that I'm stupid. I can't move… I'm afraid he's going to hit me.
TH 6yo is this correct? Is this your sharing about dad screaming at you?
6yo. Yes finger lifts.
TH Is there more that needs to be shared?
6yo. No finger lifts. (This may or may not be true. It will become clear though after the release. If the ego-state still feels pain or distress after releasing, then there's a good chance that there is still more it needs to share. Higher self can also be asked about this after a sharing has been done.)
TH Higher self, are you in agreement that 6yo has shared all he needs to for release?
HS Yes finger lifts.

TH   Higher self, can he have a release now from his distress?
HS   Yes finger lifts.

The therapist doesn't need to know what has been shared by an ego-state in order for it to have its release. There are times when a client doesn't want to share what came forward. It may be something embarrassing, something they are ashamed of, or it may just feel too private and vulnerable. Technically, someone could go through his or her entire healing process without ever relating to the therapist what is being shared. What the therapist needs to know is that the sharing did indeed occur to whatever level was necessary. This can sometimes be confirmed directly by the ego-state itself. Also, the higher self usually knows whether the ego-state has shared all it needs to. In the end, though, its release from pain is the final determiner of whether it has shared all it needs to. If it hasn't, it won't be able to report a full release or enter its final integration. It will communicate that it still feels some distress, pain, or hurt.

Having said this, I do encourage a client from the beginning to share what he or she is comfortable sharing. I think it's important for several reasons. First, it encourages the client to give expression and voice to the pain, conflict, or distress they have been carrying. Just like in traditional therapy, the expression of one's repressed or dissociated pain is most often an important part of the healing process. Secondly, I believe this information helps a therapist to maintain his or her empathic connection with the client. It also allows the therapist to know where the client is emotionally and psychologically and be ready to assist or provide direction when needed. Finally, by keeping a record of what ego-states have been worked with, and what has been shared, the therapist can have at least a rudimentary map of the client's course in treatment and the major areas that have presented for healing.

Step 6: Release

Once an ego-state has shared what it needs to, the therapist initiates the ego-state's release of its pain and distress. The higher self is asked to help the ego-state in whatever ways it can to release. This release from pain is one of the primary aims of the healing process. Once an ego-state has shared its experience to the conscious mind, there's no longer any need for it to remain dissociated from the self or to hold onto the pain and fear. It can discharge the energy that has kept the pain and conflict alive at an unconscious level.

When an ego-state signals the end of its release, the therapist asks the ego-state whether it still feels some pain or distress. If it does, it usually indicates that there is more that needs to be shared. In that case, the sharing process is repeated. More will be said about this later. If there is no pain or distress, however, and the ego-state feels good and comfortable inside, then it is ready to move to its place of integration. I will check with higher self whether it is in agreement that the ego-state I'm working with (or a whole group if that is the case) is able to integrate.

It does happen that there are ego-states who have shared all they need to, but are unable to have a full release. If the higher self is in agreement that all has been shared that is necessary, then I'll lead the ego-state through another release. In this case, higher self can usually help the ego-state do its release in a safe way. If there is continued difficulty with the release, I will ask the higher self to review and see if someone or something is interfering with the release.

So, after an ego-state has had a full release and feels no pain or distress, the therapist confirms with the higher self that the ego-state is ready to integrate.

Step 7: Any Doors or Windows?

Before an ego-state integrates, I will ask that it first look around and see if there are any doors or openings where it is. Probably more times than not, the ego-state will signal that it sees doors or openings. The healer then determines the number of doors and asks higher self to place Light at those doors. This is to act as a temporary barrier just in case our work with this particular ego-state or area has triggered something in an adjoining area. The healer will come back to the doors after the ego-state moves to integration.

When that integration is complete, I will ask higher self about the doors. In general, I recognize two categories of doors – those that go to other areas of the self/soul and those that lead outside the soul. If there are doors that go outside the soul, then the next step is most often to carry out a retrieval of any parts or pieces of soul energy that have left or been taken through that opening. If no doors go outside the soul, then higher self is asked whether the doors lead to other areas of the soul. If yes, then I ask higher self whether they are doors that need to be addressed directly. My experience is that most of the time they do.

Retrieving Parts of Soul: Example 1

- TH Higher self, are you aware of those three doors that 10yo talked about?
- HS Yes finger lifts.
- TH Do any of those doors go outside the soul?
- HS Yes finger lifts.
- TH Do more than two go outside?
- HS No finger lifts.
- TH More than one?
- HS Yes finger lifts.
- TH Two go outside the soul, is that correct?
- HS Yes finger lifts.
- TH Have any parts or pieces of the self/soul left or been taken out through those doors?
- HS Yes finger lifts.
- TH Should we do a retrieval, then, at this time?
- HS Yes finger lifts.
- TH Can you and guides carry out that retrieval now?
- HS Yes finger lifts.
- TH On the count of three then: one, two, three… and higher self and guides, using the Light and soul vibration, please retrieve now those parts and pieces of the soul that have left or been taken. Bring them all back here to the self/soul. Make sure they are cleansed and cleared as they are returned to the soul. First finger when the retrieval is complete. Second finger if there is a problem.
- HS First finger lifts.
- TH Higher self, were you able to retrieve all that had left or been taken?
- HS Yes finger lifts.
- TH Can you close and seal that door now?
- HS Yes finger lifts.
- TH Higher self, using the Light, please close and seal that door. First finger when complete; second finger if there is a problem.
- HS First finger lifts.
- TH Higher self, in the retrieval, were there any ego-states retrieved?
- HS No finger lifts. (If yes, Ego-State Protocol is used)

TH Can the soul energy that has been retrieved be re-integrated now with the self/soul?
HS Yes finger lifts.
TH Higher self, using the Light, please re-integrate those pieces of soul energy. First finger when complete; second finger if there is a problem.
HS First finger lifts.
TH Higher self, were you able to re-integrate that soul energy?
HS Yes finger lifts.
TH If that area where we just worked should be filled with Light, first finger. If the area needs to be dissipated, second finger.
HS Second finger lifts.
TH Higher self, please use the Light to dissipate that area, making sure the soul boundary is secure. First finger when complete, second finger if there is a problem.
HS First finger lifts.

Usually, by the time the therapist comes to identify doors and openings, the ego-states or external beings involved have been worked with and the issues resolved. In the process, any permissions to enter the soul or to keep its energy will usually have been rescinded. The soul, with its absolute freedom to choose, can reassert itself and reclaim missing parts without difficulty. External beings have lost control. I picture the retrieval as the soul drawing home its energy like a magnet.

There are times, however, when the higher self and guides are asked to carry out a retrieval and they signal that there is a problem. When this happens, it almost always means there are dark souls involved who are refusing to return the soul's energy. It also usually means they still have some kind of hold or an access. Either there is still someone or something within the soul that they are using or they have some part of the soul in Darkness with them who gives permission.

When a retrieval is blocked, the therapist works with higher self and/or guides to track down those permissions. Most often, they are able to find those accesses, and the therapist starts the Identification Protocol to see who or what it is. Once those accesses are closed, then higher self and guides are directed once again to carry out the retrieval. If there is still a refusal, and the higher self cannot find any other accesses, it usually means that it must be appealed to a higher level.

From a clinical point of view, the situation is this: my client, as a soul, has an absolute right to its own energy, and is now making the choice to bring that energy back to itself. The refusal by dark souls to return the parts or pieces of the soul is a violation of the agreement between Darkness and Light. This means that the Light has the right to forcibly reach into Darkness and take the soul energy.

The first time I encountered this situation, Gerod instructed me to use a *Blue Door*. (I capitalize here to indicate that it is a specific kind of door, not just a blue-colored door.) He said the higher self and guides can find this door. He also said to ask higher self or guides to identify the most appropriate negotiator to go with them to the door. When higher self signals that they are ready, the procedure is begun to have them move to the Blue Door and carry out the retrieval.

What seems to happen most of the time is that Darkness itself intervenes and will force the dark souls to surrender the soul energy to the higher self and guides. Darkness seems to know in some way and at some level that if the soul energy is not returned in accord with the agreement that a soul has absolute free choice at all times, then the Light has the right to enter Darkness in order to exercise that choice. This is something Darkness will not allow. When push comes to shove, it will correct any violation that threatens to open it to the Light.

This procedure with the Blue Door has always been successful when I've had to use it. I don't know specifically what happens in this re-negotiation. Sometimes it seems volatile, and other times, there's a sudden acquiescence and the energy is returned.

At that point, the therapist determines with the higher self whether any ego-states and/or soul energy were returned and need attention.

Step 8: Conscious Experience in the Present and Integration

Integration is probably the easiest step in the protocol. The ego-state, free of pain and distress, is more than ready to go to the place of integration it was shown before. There is, however, another step that is often beneficial for an ego-state to take before it integrates. In this step, the ego-state is brought to the conscious level to have a conscious experience (CE) in present reality. It's as though it comes forward and perceives the present reality directly through the eyes of the conscious person.

Most ego-states, when first contacted, do not know about the client's present reality. Child ego-states, for example, often are not aware that the person is now an adult, that the body has grown, and that there are new people in the client's life. Most ego-states perceive only the reality in which they were created. This is where they still live and have been stuck, and unless they learn otherwise, this is the perception they remain in. However, as conscious beings, they have the capacity to perceive the conscious reality if they choose to. Since they weren't aware of this level of consciousness, though, they wouldn't have thought to try it.

As part of the integration process, it is often helpful for an ego-state to have a conscious experience (CE) before it integrates. This experience immediately alters the ego-state's point of view and understanding. For present life ego-states, it brings them up-to-date. It reinforces their integration with the conscious self in present reality. It is also a powerful demonstration for the ego-state that the past is past. The same is true for past-life ego-states, maybe even more so. Their conscious experience in present reality is an even more radical change in point of view. Following a conscious experience, they usually have some immediate understanding of what has happened, and realize they have been stuck in the wrong time and place.

The question at this stage in the healing process is whether a particular ego-state should have a CE before it integrates. For some ego-states, the higher self will communicate that it's necessary that they have a conscious experience. This goes for past-life and present-life ego-states. It's as though an ego-state needs this new perspective to understand clearly who it is and where it fits in. For others, the higher self recommends a CE, but it's not absolutely necessary. Then there are those where the higher self says the ego-state *should not* have a conscious experience, but should move directly to integration. I do not know on what basis these judgments are made. Sometimes it seems that the conscious experience might be too powerful for the ego-state to tolerate. Sometimes it seems like it just isn't relevant to the particular ego-state involved. The higher self seems to know when a CE is appropriate and when it isn't.

Once an ego-state has had a full release, the therapist asks higher self, whether the ego-state should first have a conscious experience in the present. If so, then the higher self is asked to help the ego-state move to the conscious mind for that purpose and when complete, to help it move to its place of integration. The therapist asks the higher self to confirm the integration with a yes signal when the move is complete.

The following example illustrates these two final steps in an ego-state's healing process.

Ego-States Release and Integrate: Example 1

TH Was everyone able to have that release all right?
GP Yes finger lifts.
TH Is anyone still feeling any distress or pain?
GP No finger lifts.
TH Does that feel good and comfortable for everyone inside?
GP Yes finger lifts.
TH Higher self, can this group move now to their own place of Light and integration?
HS Yes finger lifts.
TH Should they have a conscious experience here in the present first before integrating?
HS Yes finger lifts.
TH Higher self, I'm asking that you please move everyone to the conscious mind for that conscious experience and perception. Communicate to them any further understandings about this present point of view that can be helpful. When that's complete, please move them to the place of integration that is waiting for them, either in the present here with Jerry or their place within the soul. Yes finger when those moves are complete. Second finger if there's a problem.

Ego-States Release and Integrate: Example 2

TH 6yo, I'm going to ask the higher self to help you release now any pain, hurt, fear, or distress. On three, let that pain/distress move right through the body and out. Beginning, one, two, three… and 6yo let yourself release now any of that pain, hurt and fear. Just let it release through the body and out. Higher self and the Light will help move that distress energy through the body and out. …and 6yo, as you release, you can bring more of that Light/Love energy inside. As you do, you can know that you are a part of the Light, that you've always been part of the Light. Just release any pain and fear, and bring that Light inside. First finger lifting when all has been released that's ready.
6yo. First finger lifts.
TH 6yo, were you able to have that release all right?

6yo. Yes finger lifts.
TH Does that feel good and comfortable inside?
6yo. Yes finger lifts.
TH Is there any pain or distress you're still feeling?
6yo. No finger lifts.
TH Higher self, can 6yo now move to his own place of integration?
HS Yes finger lifts.
TH Should he have a conscious experience here in the present first?
HS Yes finger lifts.
TH 6yo, before moving to your new place of integration, I'm asking that you look around you there. Do you see any doors or openings where you are?
6yo. No finger lifts.
TH Higher self, I'm going to ask then that you help 6yo move here to the conscious mind for that conscious experience and perception. Please communicate to him any further understanding about this present point of view that might be helpful. When complete, help him to move to his place of Light and integration here with the conscious mind. First finger when these moves are complete. Second finger if there is any problem.
HS First finger lifts.

These eight steps, then, are the essence of the healing process for ego-states.
1) Contact with Higher Self (Receiving Light).
2) Identification of the ego-state.
3) Are there others?
4) The promise of integration.
5) Sharing.
6) Release.
7) Any doors or windows?
8) Conscious experience and integration.

The bottom line is that every ego-state is being offered relief from all pain and distress and guaranteed a safe place to move to. Also, every ego-state is offered an experience of the Light, which others have described as a feeling of infinite love and belonging. Every ego-state, once it has experienced it, is going to say *yes* to this Light, comfort, and safety. Once an ego-state receives the Light and the information about healing, it (they) will move through the protocol efficiently and safely. This doesn't mean painlessly, but hopefully it is the least painful course.

Sharing in Pieces

If the ego-state doesn't, or can't, move through the sharing and release, then you know something is wrong. Either the ego-state itself has stopped the process or someone or something has stepped in to block.

If an ego-state stops the process once it has received the Light, it may be that the sharing has become too painful. It may be that it's afraid to remember all of what happened, afraid of the feelings that come with it. An ego-state may stop the healing process because it doesn't believe the conscious self will be able to tolerate the pain it carries, and so stops the process to protect the self.

In these cases where an ego-state has stopped its own healing process, there are many things the higher self can do to help resolve whatever difficulty the ego-state is having. The higher self, for example, can help alleviate an ego-state's fear of remembering by giving it a 'safe review.' Or the higher self can help modulate the intensity of emotion being shared so that the ego-state can experience it without being overwhelmed. Or the higher self can help break the pain or memory into smaller pieces so each sharing is tolerable. This may take several sharings (sometimes many more), but the process is repeated until the ego-state has shared all that is necessary and has had a full release.

Sharing is the step in the healing process where the healer most often runs into difficulty and blocking. There are several reasons for this. One of the primary reasons is that this step is usually the most painful or frightening. This is where the self reconnects with an experience which, when it occurred, was so painful and overwhelming that the conscious self could not tolerate it. It needed to be dissociated. Now in the healing process we are asking that that experience be reconnected with the self. This goes against the very purpose for which the ego-state was created, i.e., to stay away from the conscious self. There's a natural tendency for the ego-state and conscious self to repel each other. It's a natural defense against pain. This is a major factor, I think, that can make the sharing process difficult.

A second basis for resistance to sharing is that the ego-state itself is, to some degree, re-living its experience. At some point, the re-living may become too painful and the ego-state stops the sharing. This, too, is a natural defense against the pain of reconnecting to the physical. It is not unusual for an ego-state or group of ego-states to go through this step several times, sharing it in pieces.

A third reason that sharing can be a problem is that an ego-state's sharing may set off other ego-states who are in the same group or field as itself. Like a stone dropped in water, what is being shared to the conscious mind begins also triggering other ego-states that are close by and who resonate to the same pain. The sharing sends out ripples, and there is a reaction. This is one reason why it can be very helpful to check out with the identified ego-state whether there are any others.

Finally, an ego-state can resist sharing because it is afraid the conscious self is not ready or will not be able to tolerate what it has to share. It's afraid that it will cause chaos or things will go out of control. Sometimes this perception of the ego-state is accurate—what it has to share will be shocking to the client at a conscious level, such as the memory of abuse by a parent, or contact by other kinds of beings. Usually, though, the ego-state can be brought to understand that the conscious self is now able to tolerate what it has to share. The higher self can communicate information and reassurance about this. The therapist can also facilitate a conscious experience for the ego-state so it can learn that things are different now for the self, here in present reality.

Once an ego-state has received the Light and information about healing, most of the time it is prepared to share what it needs to for release (even if it takes time or needs to be done in small segments). By *prepared*, I mean that the ego-state

- Feels the support of the higher self and the Light.
- Now knows that what it carries is memory and is not happening in the present.
- Trusts that the sharing will lead to a release from pain
- Knows there is a new place of Light and integration waiting for it after its release.

All of this, I think, helps an ego-state overcome its natural resistance and share what it needs to.

6

Past-Life Protocol

When the higher self identifies an ego-state involved in the client's problem, it is often an ego-state created in the client's present life. However, it may also be from a past or different lifetime. A different lifetime meaning a lifetime on earth, on another planet, in another dimension or in some other way we don't know about. This keeps the door open for other possibilities that don't fit what is normally thought of as past lives on earth. In this chapter, I will focus on past-life ego-states since, next to present-life ego-states, they are the most frequent phenomena to present.

The protocol for dealing with a past life ego-state is practically the same as with present-life ego-states. Once they are identified, the therapist initiates contact with the Light, elicits identifying information, helps them share what they need to, and leads them through a release of pain and distress. One major difference, however, in working with past life ego-states is that they do not integrate with the conscious self in this present life. After their release, they integrate within that part of the soul that holds their own particular lifetime. After a past-life ego-state has had a full release, the higher self can help it have a conscious experience, if called for, and then help move it to its place of integration within the soul.

A second major difference in working with past life ego-states is not so much a difference in protocol as in its execution. The therapist must be prepared to relate to a past life ego-state from within the context of its own historical experience, and, at least initially, on its terms. This may mean a different set of questions and dealing with possibilities that don't exist with present life ego-states. You won't find a present-life ego-state, for example, who carries the experience of being killed in battle, or the terrified mother of children the client doesn't have in her present. When dealing with past-life ego-states, it can mean adapting the process to the constraints of its paradigm of reality.

Most of the time, past-life ego-states do not need special treatment. Once they have received the Light and a communication from the higher self, it's as though they understand their situation and are willing to cooperate with the healing. When I do run into difficulty with a past-life ego-state, I will usually check with higher self whether it would be appropriate for the ego-state to have a conscious experience in the present instead of waiting to take this step along with integration. I have found that once a past-life ego-state has had a conscious experience, it usually gains the understanding and reassurance it needs and will start to cooperate. It's as though when it looks out into the present reality, it understands now what has happened and is glad to be free of it.

I do not routinely initiate a CE at this early stage, because I don't want this new knowledge and perspective to interfere with the ego-state sharing its experience. Conversely, it can often happen that the conscious experience is helpful in resolving the resistance, fear, or anger that keeps a past-life ego-state from moving forward. I have yet to formulate a set policy. It's a therapeutic call.

Working with Past-Life Ego-state: Example 1

   TH Higher self, did you find someone or something involved in this recurring nightmare?
   HS Yes finger lifts.
   TH If it's someone, first finger, if something, second finger can lift.
   HS First finger lifts.
   TH Higher self, I'm asking that you help that one come forward here with me… And to this one: do you know yourself to be part of this self and soul I'm working with?
   __ Yes finger lifts.
   TH Are you receiving Light for yourself where you are? If you are, the first finger lifting. If not, or you're not sure, the second finger can lift.
   __ Second finger lifts.
   TH Are you willing for the higher self to send you some Light/Love

energy? If you like it, you can keep it for yourself or you can stop it if you need to. Are you willing to have that Light sent to you?
— Yes finger lifts.
TH Higher self, please send to this one now that Light/Love energy, and to this one: let yourself receive that. You can bring it inside to whatever level is comfortable. First finger, when you receive that, second finger if not.
— First finger lifts.
TH To this one: did you receive that Light all right?
— Yes finger lifts.
TH Does it feel all right to you?
— Yes finger lifts.
TH Are you one first created in this present life of Jerry's?
— No finger lifts.
TH Are you one from a past or different lifetime.
PL Yes finger lifts.
TH Are you a male?
PL No finger lifts.
TH Are you a female?
PL Yes finger lifts.
TH Are you an adult?
PL No finger lifts.
TH Are you an adolescent or young adult?
PL No finger lifts.
TH Are you a child?
PL Yes finger lifts.
TH And do you know your name?
PL Yes finger lifts.
TH Is it all right for us to know your name?
PL Yes finger lifts.
TH I'm going to ask that you say the name nice and loud right to the conscious mind. On three: one, two, three... And just say the name, nice and loud, right here to Jerry at a conscious level. First finger when that's complete, second finger if it's stopped or there's a problem
PL First finger lifts.
TH Jerry did something come to you?
Je The name William is what came to mind.
TH To this one: is this correct? Is your name William?

Wm Yes finger lifts.
TH William, as you look around you there, is there another or others with you? If so, first finger, if you're alone, the second finger can lift.
Wm First finger lifts.
TH Are there more than four of you there?
Wm Yes finger lifts.
TH More than eight?
Wm No finger lifts.
TH More than six?
Wm No finger lifts.
TH Are there less than six of you all together?
Wm Yes finger lifts.
TH Are there five of you there?
Wm Yes finger lifts.
TH Has everyone else there received that Light for themselves now?
Wm No finger lifts.
TH Are you willing to communicate to them William about the Light and help them receive that for themselves?
Wm Yes finger lifts.
TH On three then: one, two, three... And William, communicate your reassurance to the others there about the Light, and higher self, please send that Light/Love energy to each of those here. First finger when all five have received that Light; second finger if anyone does not.
Wm Yes finger lifts.
TH William, have all of you received that information about the healing process we're working with?
Wm Yes finger lifts.
TH To everyone in the group: do all of you want that healing and release for yourselves? If so, first finger. If anyone does not want that healing, second finger can lift.
___ Second finger lifts.

Working with Past-Life Ego-state: Example 2

TH Higher self, Gina and I have talked about her relationship with Donna and the constant tension she feels around her. Higher self, I'm asking that you look inside and see if there is someone or something

involved with this tension. Yes finger when that review is complete, no finger if it's stopped or blocked.
HS No finger lifts.
TH Higher self, was that review stopped?
HS Yes finger lifts.
TH Higher self, please find the source of that block. First finger when you have found it, second finger if you do not.
HS First finger lifts.
TH Higher self, is that one part of the self/soul?
HS Yes finger lifts.
TH I'm asking, higher self, that you help that one come forward here with me. And to this one: do you know yourself to be part of this self and soul I'm working with?
__ Yes finger lifts.
TH Are you receiving Light/Love energy for yourself now?
__ Yes finger lifts.
TH Are you one first created in this present life of Gina's?
__ No finger lifts.
TH Are you from a past or different lifetime? If so, first finger. If not or that doesn't fit, the no finger can lift.
__ First finger lifts.
TH Are you a female?
__ No finger lifts.
TH Are you a male?
PM Yes finger lifts.
TH Are you an adult?
PM Yes finger lifts.
TH Do you know your name?
PM No finger lifts.
TH As you look around you, is there anyone else with you where you are?
PM Yes finger lifts.
TH Are there more than eight of you altogether?
PM No finger lifts.
TH More than six?
PM Yes finger lifts.
TH Are there seven of you?
PM Yes finger lifts.

TH	Higher self, is everyone in this group part of the self/soul?
HS	Yes finger lifts.
TH	And to this past-life male, is everyone, there, receiving Light now?
PM	Yes finger lifts.
TH	Does everyone know about the healing process we're working with?
PM	Yes finger lifts.
TH	And is everyone willing to share, or allow to be shared, what needs to come forward for healing and release?
PM	Yes finger lifts.
TH	On three, then: one, two, three... And just share here what needs to be shared... What you see, feel, hear that needs to come forward... Yes finger when that sharing is complete, no finger if there's a problem.
PM	Yes finger lifts.
TH	Gina, is there anything you received?
Gn	Just this strong anger... like resentment.
PM	Yes finger lifts.
TH	And to this male or the group, is this correct? Are you sharing feelings of anger and resentment?
PM	Yes finger lifts.
TH	Is there more yet that needs to be shared?
PM	Yes finger lifts.
TH	Is everyone willing to allow that to be shared?
PM	Yes finger lifts.
TH	On three, then. Sharing that next part. Beginning, one, two, three... and share here what needs to be shared about it. It's safe to do that now here in the present, sharing what you need to. Yes finger when that's complete, second finger if it's stopped or blocked.
PM	Yes finger lifts.
TH	And Gina, did you receive that?
Gn	What I'm getting is that this guy was Donna's son in a past life and she had physically abused him, maybe for a long time.
TH	And to this male: is this accurate? Was the soul we know here as Donna, was that soul your mother in a different lifetime?
PM	Yes finger lifts.
TH	Is there more you need to share about that?
PM	No finger lifts.
TH	Are you and the others ready now for that release?

PM Yes finger lifts.
TH On three, then: one, two, three… And to the group, let yourselves release now any pain, hurt and distress. Let it move through the body and out—higher self is helping. Just release and let go of any pain, any anger, let it move through the body and out. And as you release, you can bring in that greater Light, love, and knowledge for yourselves. Yes finger when that release feels complete. No finger if there is a problem.

7

The Spirit Protocol

Going back to the Opening Protocol, once the higher self has completed its review of the problem area, and has communicated that it has found someone involved, then the next step is to identify who that someone is. Chapters 5 and 6 addressed the situation where that someone that higher self identifies is an ego-state, a part of the client's self/soul. This chapter deals with situations where the higher self signals that the someone involved in the problem is not part of the client's self/soul energy, but is separate. In this case, the therapist uses the Identification Protocol to further identify who the separate someone is. For purposes of the protocol, I use four categories:

- Spirits
- Other souls
- Created entities
- Ego-states from another soul or souls (EES).

I came to identify these general categories through clinical experience. I would say that ninety-five percent of the beings I've encountered in my work with clients fit into one of these four categories of phenomena. Each phenomenon, however, requires a different protocol.

This chapter presents the protocol to use when the someone that higher self identifies turns out to be a spirit. In Soul-Centered Healing, we are concerned with spirits who have established some attachment to our client or have even intruded into the client's psyche. These are not physical beings. They are not physical attachments or intrusions. They are discarnate souls and their interactions with humans take place at etheric, or psychic, levels. (We do not yet have a scientific language and terminology for these levels of self and reality.)

These spirit attachments and intrusions can and do affect people psychologically and emotionally. Depending on the specific spirits involved and their intentions, they can affect a person's mood, thinking, perception, or energy levels. These attachments and intrusions can also lead to physical effects and symptoms for a person. In these cases, the physical is not the causative level but rather the end result of interference at these other levels. Depending on the type of spirit involved, its attachment or intrusion can cause significant conflicts at a psychic level that reverberate through every level of a person, including the physical.

In Soul-Centered Healing, it is generally assumed that spirit attachments and/or intrusions are affecting the client negatively, and that the ultimate aim of healing will be to remove them and sever their connection to the client's self/soul. There are few exceptions to this. I'll say more about this later.

When you encounter a spirit in your work with a client, usually you won't know anything else about the spirit except that it is a soul. It may be a soul presenting in human form or voice, especially if it has lived human incarnations. It may be a spirit that has never experienced a physical body and has only existed in spiritual realms. Some spirits dwell in Darkness and prey on incarnate souls. It may be a spirit who belongs to a domain of souls that exist on the fringes of the Light, just a step or two away from our physical. The spirit you encounter may also have been present with your client for a very long time and forgotten that it is a soul. It may believe it is part of the client's soul. These are only some of the possibilities I know from my clinical experience. I have no doubt that if you work at these levels you will encounter types of spirits I have not met. These are realms governed by consciousness and so discarnate souls can take many forms, depending on the spirit's knowledge and creativity.

Fortunately, for the purposes of healing, we do not need to know very much about a spirit in order to facilitate its removal or disengagement from the client. From a clinical point of view, it doesn't really matter who the spirit is. What matters is that it disengage from the client. All we need, as healers, is sufficient information about the spirit in order to know what steps to take to facilitate its leaving.

It is natural to be curious about the spirits we encounter in our work with clients. Who are they? Where do they exist? What are they about? Why do they engage or intrude on humans? How do they do it? Are they aware of the Light?

In an academic or experimental setting, involving volunteers, these questions and many more would be most interesting to pursue. I believe it can be done. In the clinical setting, however, different questions take priority. These questions are utilitarian in nature. The central one—the one which all others are based on—is this question: what will it take for the spirit(s) to leave?

The answer is that most of the time all it takes to have a spirit leave is for the spirit to make direct contact with the Light. When working with a client, once I know I am engaged with a spirit, a separate soul, I know I am dealing with a being of Light. Most probably it is one who has become lost, or forgotten who it is, or even became caught up in a dark network of souls. However, if it is a soul, I know that it has the capacity to experience the Light. And if it does that, I know that almost every time the spirit will gain some kind of greater understanding, desire more Light, and become cooperative. For the purposes of healing, this means the spirit becomes willing to leave the client or has already gone.

The purpose of facilitating a spirit's contact with the Light is to re-awaken the spirit to its own Light, its soul essence, knowing that when that happens, it will precipitate a shift in the spirit's consciousness. Once the spirit agrees to the contact, the Light will become known to it in whatever way is a perfect fit for that spirit. The therapist doesn't have to know what form it takes. Like an ego-state receiving the Light, these spirits seem to undergo a conversion. Once this contact occurs, the therapist directs the spirit(s) to go to the Light if it already knows its way there, or calls for a guide or loved one from the spirit realm to come for them.

Once a spirit has had this contact, it almost always leaves of its own accord. We might think of it in terms of those who describe the near-death-experience. They talk about entering a Light in which they feel infinite love and have full understanding. They remember or know that there is a Spirit Realm of Light and they know they belong there and that loved ones are waiting for them. This same thing appears to happen in the healing session when a spirit reconnects with the Light.

These results are so consistent, that helping a spirit reconnect with the Light is the first step in the Spirit Protocol. From my point of view, it is the most efficient and positive resolution to spirit attachment or intrusion. In this sense, working with spirits is very much the same as working with ego-states, i.e., once contact occurs with the Light there is a radical change in the spirit's attitude and understanding.

Helping Spirits to Awaken

In Soul-Centered Healing, there are two basic strategies for facilitating a spirit's contact with the Light. The first is to have the spirit "look inside" and find its own Light, its own soul-source energy. If it is a soul, then it will have this inner Light, and most of the time, a spirit will quickly be able to find it. For the spirit, this contact with the Light is an internal experience. And when it happens, the spirit will remember who it is and usually be ready to go to the Spirit Realm of Light.

If the spirit does not find that Light, then it is either not a soul, is still resisting (saying "no" to the Light at a deeper level), or there is someone or something interfering with it. When it happens that a spirit is willing to look inside but can't find its inner Light, there are other protocols used to identify the source of the difficulty and resolve it. I'll talk more about these shortly.

The second strategy in helping a spirit make contact with the Light is to obtain its permission for a high-level teacher/guide/healer from the Light to come forward and communicate with it directly. If a spirit gives its consent, then a spirit guide or teacher is asked to come forward and make a safe contact with the spirit we've been working with. In general, it appears that there are spirit guides who are aware of a client's healing process as it is occurring in the present and who are ready to step in and assist if asked. These spirit guides also appear to know when permission is given for such contact and will then make contact with the spirit I'm dealing with.

While I assume that spirit guides and healers are usually present during any person's healing process, it doesn't hurt to ask specifically that they be present during a session. Since I consider high-level guides and healers as always welcome in my work with clients, I don't feel a need to specifically request their presence for each session. I assume the appropriate guides are present. During the course of a session, however, I will often make requests for specific kinds of help from the spirit guides. Making direct contact with attached or intruding spirits is one of the most common requests. In case after case, it appears that the spirit guide knows when permission is given to make contact and knows how to present itself to the attached or intruding spirit in a safe or non-threatening way. I'll talk more about high-level guides and healers later in the book.

Most spirits are willing to take at least one of these two steps, and in taking one, they are usually more than willing to take the other. For the spirit's sake, and as a preventative measure in the healing process, the Spirit Protocol is designed to help an attached or intruding spirit make contact with the Light in both ways, i.e., finding its own inner Light and making contact with a spirit guide. Sometimes, only one of these contacts is needed. A spirit might look inside, for example, find its own Light, remember where it came from, and leave the client immediately for the Light. It's as simple as that. In general, though, I have found it most efficient to just initiate both these contacts right at the start of my contact with a spirit. It's like reminding them not only of who they are but where they can go. In this way, when I ask for a spirit's agreement to leave, it is almost always ready to go.

Usually, I try first to have a spirit look inside and find its own Light. Once it does, then I'll ask for its permission to call a spirit teacher to come forward and communicate with it directly. Sometimes, a spirit may be frightened about looking inside and prefer to have a loved one or a guide come forward from the Light to help it understand what is happening.

If there is a problem for the spirit in finding its inner Light, it's often easiest to switch strategies and obtain the spirit's agreement to make contact with a high-level guide. Also, if a spirit does have a problem finding its inner Light, making contact with a spirit guide often resolves whatever was blocking or keeping the spirit from looking inside. In using the Spirit Protocol, it's a judgment call on which strategy to use first and whether both steps are needed with a particular spirit. The bottom line is that the spirit has made a contact with the Light and is agreeable to leaving the client. The Spirit Protocol is designed to lead a spirit to this agreement in the least number of steps.

The central fact to keep in mind when dealing with a spirit is that it is a being of Light, and once it remembers this, it will usually leave of its own accord and return to its place in the Spirit Realm of Light. So, the aim of the protocol is to help the spirit remember.

The Spirit Protocol

1) Determine whether a separate entity is a soul.
2) Facilitate contact with its own inner Light.
3) Facilitate contact with a guide/teacher from the Light.
4) Obtain the spirit's agreement to leave (usually to go to the Light).
5) Determine whether any other souls are present.
6) If other souls are present, address the entire group, elicit help from the first spirit, and lead the group through the same procedure, each finding its own inner Light.
7) Ask the spirit(s) to go.

Step 1: Identification of a Separate Soul

In Soul-Centered Healing, the higher self plays a central role in identifying what is part of the self/soul and what is separate. You might think of the higher self as a tuning fork of the soul. It knows the soul's core vibration; it knows what resonates as part of the soul vibration and who or what does not. Asking the higher self to determine whether someone or something is part of the self/soul is like asking it to compare vibrations and see if there is a match or not.

Determining whether someone or something is part of the self/soul or separate is a basic procedure in Soul-Centered Healing and underlies all the protocols. At any point in a person's healing process, the healer needs to know whether they are dealing with someone or something that is part of the client's soul or is separate. Depending on which it is, each calls for a very different approach and a different protocol. This is part of the Identification Protocol that I discussed in Chapter 3.

If the higher self identifies someone separate from the client, then it needs to be determined whether or not that someone is a soul, then whether it is a spirit, i.e., a discarnate soul. Sometimes, the entity you are communicating with knows whether it is a soul. If not, the higher self can help determine that. If it is a soul, then we continue with the Spirit Protocol. If it is a created entity or from another soul, then a different protocol is used.

The following dialogue is an example of the identification of a spirit.

Spirit Protocol: Example 1

- TH Higher self, were you able to complete that review?
- HS Yes finger lifts.
- TH Did you find someone or something involved in Pamela's headaches that we should address at this time?
- HS Yes finger lifts.
- TH Higher self, if it's someone, first finger, if something, the second finger lifting. If neither of these fit, the hand can lift.
- HS Yes finger lifts.
- TH If this one is part of Pamela's self/soul, first finger; if not, the second finger can lift.
- HS No finger lifts.
- TH Higher self, if this one is itself a soul, first finger; if a created entity or from another soul, second finger. If you are not sure or these don't fit, the hand can lift.
- HS Yes finger lifts.
- TH Higher self, this one is a soul. Is that correct?
- HS Yes finger lifts.
- TH If it would be best now just to remove it, first finger lifting, if I should communicate with it, the second finger can lift.
- HS No finger lifts.
- TH Higher self, I'm asking that you help that one come forward here with me and to this one: did you know that you are separate from this soul I'm working with?
- SP Yes finger lifts.
- TH Did you know that you are yourself a soul?
- SP No finger lifts.
- TH To this one: are you willing to know whether you are, or are not, a soul?
- SP Yes finger lifts.
- TH I'm going to ask that you look inside and find your soul-source energy. If you are a soul, then you have your own source energy. On the count of three, you can look inside. Beginning, one, two, three... Just look inside now. Move your vision all the way to your center. See the Light that you have there. First finger when you have found that, second finger if not.
- SP Yes finger lifts.

Here is a second example of identifying the presence of a spirit.

Spirit Protocol: Example 2

   TH Higher self, were you able to review this area all right?
   HS Yes finger lifts.
   TH Did you find someone or something involved in Terry's nightmare that needs to be addressed?
   HS Yes finger lifts.
   TH If it's someone, first finger lifting, if something or some energy, second finger lifting.
   HS Yes finger lifts.
   TH Higher self, is that one part of Terry's self/soul?
   HS No finger lifts.
   TH This one is separate from the self/soul, is that correct?
   HS Yes finger lifts.
   TH Higher self, is this one itself a soul?
No response.
   TH Higher self, are you still able to communicate with me?
No response.
   TH To this one who has come forward here: is there some scare or apprehension for you about this question?
No response.
   TH To this one: we are here to help. Whether you are part of this soul or separate, either way we are here to help. If you are part of this soul, there is one kind of help. If you are separate from this soul, then there is another kind of help. We need to know, though, which kind of help is needed. To this one: as long as it is safe, are you willing to communicate with me about this?
   SP Yes finger lifts.
   TH To this one: did you know that you are separate from this soul that I'm working with?
   SP Yes finger lifts.
   TH Are you yourself a soul?
   SP Hand lift.
   TH To this one: are you willing to know whether you are, or are not, a soul?
   SP Hand lift.
   TH To this one: is there some scare about that?

SP   Yes finger lifts.
TH   Do you know what scares you about that?
SP   No finger lifts.
TH   To this one: if you are a soul, then you have your own soul-source energy inside. It is a Light-energy; it is a life sustaining energy. If you are yourself a soul, then it means that you have your own soul-source energy. Would you be willing to look inside and see if that Light is there?
SP   Yes finger lifts.

Step 2: Facilitate Contact with the Spirit's Inner Light

Once an entity has been identified as a spirit, a discarnate soul, the next step is to facilitate its contact with its own inner Light. As I said earlier, this is accomplished by directing the spirit to look inside and find its own soul-source energy, or by facilitating the spirit's contact with a spirit guide from the Light. If it is a soul that you are dealing with, and it agrees to look inside, it will usually be able to find that Light and connect with it. When this happens, the response is almost always the same. The spirit will report that the connection feels good and it wants to keep the Light for itself. Sometimes, this is all it takes. Once the spirit re-connects with the Light, it leaves for the spirit realm.

If a spirit cannot find the Light, it usually means that it is still resisting at some level, or it is being blocked by someone or something else, or it is not, in fact, a soul. If at this point in the protocol the spirit signals that it was not interfered with but needed itself to stop the process, then the healer has to determine the source of the spirit's resistance. Is it afraid, and if so, who or what is it afraid of? Is it still feeling too guilty and undeserving? It might also be that in approaching its inner Light, it may have triggered a forgotten experience that threatened to overwhelm the spirit and so it stopped the process. Once the spirit's motivation has been determined, then, just as with ego-states, the therapist can formulate a proposition that will make it safe for the soul to find its inner Light.

If the spirit signals that it did not stop the process but that someone or something interfered, then the protocol will focus on who or what is interfering or blocking. It could be an ego-state within the client, another spirit(s), or a device/object placed within the spirit that is triggered when approaching the Light.

Once a spirit's own resistance or the external interference is resolved, the next step is to have the spirit once again look inside and find its inner Light. If it is still unable to find it, then the procedure is repeated to find whether it is resisting or whether it is being blocked. If the blocking or resistance continues and you cannot resolve it, it's best to skip this step and move to the next one.

Step 3: Facilitate Contact with a Spirit Guide from the Light

The third step in the Spirit Protocol is to facilitate contact between the spirit(s) that is present and a high-level spirit guide (teacher, angel, loved one, etc.). These guides are aware of your work with a client, and they will provide whatever assistance they can in a form that is perceived by the spirit as safe. Often a spirit will agree to see a teacher, but not a loved one, or vice-versa. Sometimes, a spirit will more readily agree to have such a helper come forward rather than to look inside for their own Light. In that case the steps are reversed. What is needed is the spirit's permission for a spirit guide to come forward and make the contact. Once the spirit has had contact with a guide or loved one, it will either have already connected with its own inner Light or it will do so willingly or it may just leave and so the issue becomes moot.

You can trust that once the contact is made, the spirit guide or teacher will know and communicate what is needed for the spirit you're working with. If the spirit is hesitant or resistant to having a spirit guide or a teacher come forward, then I will ask the spirit if it is willing for a specific loved one to come forward. This may be a parent or grandparent from the life just lived. It might be a soul who has shared many lifetimes with this spirit and who the spirit will recognize immediately. It may be religious or spiritual figure that the attached spirit would recognize and connect with.

In some way, this contact with a spirit guide is an instant experience of the Light for the spirit we are working with. As I said earlier, the spirit seems to remember who it is. Once this contact occurs, the spirit is usually willing to go with the teacher, guide, or loved one who came for it.

Step 4: Obtain the Spirit's Agreement to Leave

Once a spirit has re-connected with its own inner Light and/or had contact with a spirit guide from the Light, the next step is to ask whether it is willing to leave now and move to its place in the Light. If the first two steps have occurred, then the spirit is almost always willing to go, and will.

The following are sample dialogues illustrating the use of the Spirit Protocol from identification of the spirit through to its agreement to leave.

Spirit Protocol: Example 3

TH   Higher self, were you able to complete that review all right?
HS   Yes finger lifts.
TH   Did you find someone or something involved in this feeling of terror that Jim and I talked about at a conscious level?
HS   Yes finger lifts.
TH   If it's someone, the first finger can lift, if some thing, the second finger.
HS   Yes finger lifts.
TH   Is that one part of Jim's own self/soul energy?
HS   No finger lifts.
TH   Is that one itself a soul? If so, first finger lifting. If it is a created entity or from another soul, then the second finger can lift.
HS   Yes finger lifts.
TH   Higher self, if I should communicate with that one, first finger, if just have it removed, the second finger can lift.
HS   Yes finger lifts.
TH   Higher self, I'm going to ask then that you help that one come forward here with me, and to this one: do you know that you are separate from this self and soul I'm working with?
SP   Yes finger lifts.
TH   If you believe that you are yourself a soul, first finger lifting. If a created entity or from another soul, the second finger can lift. If you're not sure, the hand can lift.
SP   Hand lift.
TH   To this one: are you willing to know whether you are, or are not, a soul?

SP Yes finger lifts.
TH Higher self or a guide: I'm asking that you scan this one's energy and determine whether it is or is not itself a soul. First finger when that scan is complete, second finger if it is stopped or blocked.
HS Yes finger lifts.
TH Higher self, is this one itself a soul?
HS Yes finger lifts.
TH To this one: if you are a soul, then you carry within you your own soul-source energy. Are you willing to look inside and see if that energy is there? If you are a soul, it will be there.
SP Yes finger lifts.
TH To this one: on three, you can look inside, beginning, one, two, three… And to this one look all the way inside now. Move your vision right to your center. See the Light you have there. First finger when you see it, second finger if you do not.
SP Yes finger lifts.
TH To this one: were you able to touch that Light?
SP Yes finger lifts.
TH Does that feel all right to you?
SP Yes finger lifts.
TH And to this one: do you know now about your own place in the Light?
SP Yes finger lifts.
TH Are you ready now to move to your place in the Light?
SP Yes finger lifts.
TH Do you need assistance to do that?
SP No finger lifts.
TH To this one: before you go, as you look around you there, are there any others with you where you are?
SP No finger lifts.
TH Okay, then. To this one: I'm asking that you return to your own place in the Light now. Higher self, first finger when it has gone, second finger if not.
HS Yes finger lifts.

When the higher self is free to communicate, the identification and disengagement of the spirit can go smoothly as in this example. However, the identification of a spirit is also the point at which the healer may very likely encounter blocking or interference. If there is a spirit present that is connected to the problem or issue we are asking about, it may move to block our communication with the higher self in order to avoid exposure. Spirits seem to know that they will be displaced or things will change if they are discovered.

If communication with the higher self is blocked, and it is a spirit (as opposed to an ego-state) that is blocking, then the next step is usually to address the spirit itself and see if you can elicit a response. Here is an example.

Spirit Protocol: Example 4

TH Higher self, were you able to complete that review all right?
HS Yes finger lifts.
TH Did you find someone or something involved in this feeling of anxiety that Martin and I talked about at a conscious level?
HS Yes finger lifts.
TH If it's someone, the first finger can lift, if something, the second finger.
HS Yes finger lifts.
TH Is that one part of Jim's own self/soul energy?
No response.
TH Higher self, are you still able to communicate with me?
No response.
TH To the one that has stepped forward here: do you know yourself to be separate from this self and soul I'm working with?
No response.
TH To this one: is there some scare or apprehension for you about this kind of direct communication?
No response.
TH To this one: we are here to help. Whether you are part of this self/soul or separate, we can help. It's a different kind of help, though, depending on whether you are part of this self/soul or separate. Either way, though, we can help. To this one: as long as it is safe, are you willing to communicate with me about this?
SP Yes finger lifts.
TH To this one: do you know yourself to be separate from this self and soul I'm working with?
SP Yes finger lifts.

TH Do you believe that you are yourself a soul? If so, first finger lifting. If not or you're not sure, the second finger can lift.
SP No finger lifts.
TH To this one: are you willing to know whether you are or are not a soul?
SP Yes finger lifts.
TH If you are a soul, then you carry within you your own soul-source energy. Are you willing to look inside now and see if that soul-source energy is there?
SP No finger lifts.
TH To this one is there some scare about that?
SP Yes finger lifts.
TH Are you afraid the Light will harm you or destroy you?
SP Yes finger lifts.
TH To this one: that soul-source energy is a life sustaining energy. It has always sustained you even when you weren't aware of it. Are you willing to look inside just to see if that Light is there? If it is, you can make your own choice about whether to touch it. Would you be willing to do that?
SP Yes finger lifts.
TH I'm going to ask, then, that you look inside now. Move your vision all the way to your center. It's safe to do that. See the Light that is there. It is your own soul-source energy. First finger when you see that, second finger if you do not.
SP Yes finger lifts.
TH To this one: did you also feel that Light?
SP Yes finger lifts.
TH Does that feel all right you?
SP Yes finger lifts.
TH Do you know now about your place in the Light? If so first finger, if not second finger lifting.
SP Hand lift.
TH To this one: would you be willing for a high-level teacher from the Light to come forward and communicate with you about the Spirit Realm of Light and that place that has always been yours?
SP Yes finger lifts.
TH Just turn towards the Light, then, and I'm asking that high-level teacher from the Light to come forward. Just look and see who

comes. It's safe to do that. First finger when you see them, second finger if you do not.
SP Yes finger lifts.
TH I'm asking the teacher now to communicate to this one information about themselves and about their place in the Light. Help them to know about the loved ones who are waiting for them, and about the choices this one has to return home. To this one: first finger when you've received this communication, second finger if you do not.
SP Yes finger lifts.
TH To this one: do you wish now to go to your own place in the Light?
SP Yes finger lifts.
TH Before you go, as you look around, are there any others with you where you are?
SP No finger lifts.
TH On three, then, you can move right to the teacher. Beginning, one, two, three and just move now right into that corridor of Light, move right to the teacher. Higher self, first finger when that one has gone, second finger if not.
HS Yes finger lifts.

Spirit Protocol: Example 5

TH To this one: did you know that you are separate from this soul I'm working with?
SP Yes finger lifts.
TH Are you yourself a soul?
SP Yes finger lifts.
TH Are you aware, then, of the Light you have inside you? It is your own soul-source energy. Are aware of that?
SP No finger lifts.
TH Would you be willing to look inside and see if you have that soul-source energy?
SP Yes finger lifts.
TH On three, then… one, two, three: And to this one: let yourself look inside now, all the way to your center. Look right to your center and see the Light that is there. First finger when you see it, second finger if not.
SP No finger lifts.

TH To this one: if you needed to stop that, lift the first finger. If someone or something else interfered or got in the way, then lift the second finger.
SP Yes finger lifts.
TH To this one: you needed to stop that, is that right?
SP Yes finger lifts.
TH Did that begin to scare you?
SP Yes finger lifts.
TH To this one: would you be willing for a high level teacher from the Light to come forward and communicate further information about this and the choices available to you? First finger, when you see that guide; second finger if you do not.
SP Second finger lifts.
TH Does that feel too scary too?
SP Yes finger lifts.
TH To this one: the guide from the Light will only communicate information. It's information for you to consider. There is nothing you will be forced to do with it. The Light does not operate that way. If the teacher stays a safe distance away, will you allow them to come forward and communicate just the information?
SP Yes finger lifts.
TH I'm going to ask then that you turn towards the Light; and I'm asking a high level teacher or guide who is aware and willing to assist, to come forward, staying at a safe distance. And to this one: first finger when you see that teacher, second finger if you do not.
SP Yes finger lifts.
TH I'm asking the teacher, then, to communicate to this one further understanding about itself, about the Light it carries inside, and about the Spirit Realm of Light that is waiting for it. To this separate one: First finger when that communication is complete. Second finger if it's stopped or blocked.
SP Yes finger lifts.
TH To this one: did you receive that communication all right?
SP Yes finger lifts.
TH Did that make sense to you?
SP Yes finger lifts.
TH Would you like to go with that teacher now and move to your own place in the Light?

SP   Yes finger lifts.
TH   Okay, then. On three you can move right to the teacher. Beginning, one, two, three… and to this one you can move now to the teacher… right into that corridor of Light. Higher self, first finger when that one has gone, second finger if not or there's a problem.
HS   Yes finger lifts.

Spirit Protocol: Example 6

TH   Do you know that you are separate from this soul I'm working with?
SP   Yes finger lifts.
TH   Are you yourself a soul? If so, first finger; if not, second finger, if you're not sure, the hand can lift.
SP   Hand lift.
TH   To this one: are you willing to know whether you are or are not a soul?
SP   Yes finger lifts.
TH   I'm going to ask that you be sent that information now on three… One, two, three… And higher self or a guide, I'm asking that you communicate to this one information and knowledge about themselves, whether they are or are not a soul; also, communicating any other information that can be helpful to them. And to this one: first finger when you've received this communication, second finger if you do not.
SP   Yes finger lifts.
TH   And to this one: Did you receive that communication all right?
SP   Yes finger lifts.
TH   To this one: if it seems that you are a soul, first finger lifting. If not, the second finger can lift. If you're still not sure the hand can lift.
SP   Yes finger lifts.
TH   To this one: as a soul, are you willing now to look inside and find your own soul-source energy? If you are a soul, that soul-source energy is there. Are you willing now to look inside?
SP   Yes finger lifts.
TH   On three, then. One, two, three… And to this one: first finger when you have found that Light, second finger if you do not.
SP   No finger lifts.
TH   To this one: if you needed to stop that, first finger; if someone or

something seemed to interfere, second finger; if none of those fit, the hand can lift.

SP Yes finger lifts.

TH To this one: You needed to stop this, is that correct?

SP Yes finger lifts.

TH To this one: did that begin to scare you?

SP Yes finger lifts.

TH If it began to cause pain, the first finger can lift; if you stopped it for another reason, second finger lifting.

SP No finger lifts.

TH To this one: do you know why you stooped it?

SP Yes finger lifts.

TH Are you willing to communicate a thought, word, or image here to the conscious mind about that?

SP Yes finger lifts.

TH I'm going to ask then that you communicate that right here to the present on three... One, two, three... And to this one: just communicate it here right to the conscious mind... A thought, a word, an image... let it come right to the present. First finger when you've communicated that, second finger lifting if it's stopped or there's a problem.

SP Yes finger lifts.

TH Janet here with me at a conscious level, Janet, did you receive something?

Ja I'm just getting the word, "guilty."

TH And to this one: is this your communication, that you feel guilty?

SP Yes finger lifts.

TH To this one: I want to reassure you that the Creator already knows what happened and has already forgiven you. What needs to happen now is that you forgive yourself. The Creator only wants you to come home to the Light. That's why we've come. Are you willing once more to look inside and see if that Light is there? You don't have to touch it, but you can reassure yourself that it is there. Are you willing to look?

SP Yes finger lifts.

TH On three, then. One, two, three... And to this one: just look inside now; move your vision right to your center and see the Light you have there. It's safe to do that now. First finger when you see that

The Spirit Protocol

Light; second finger if you still do not.
SP   Yes finger lifts.
TH   And to this one: you were able to see that Light, is that correct?
SP   Yes finger lifts.
TH   Did you feel that Light this time?
SP   Yes finger lifts.
TH   And did that feel all right to you?
SP   Yes finger lifts.
TH   To this one: do you know now about your place in the Spirit Realm of Light, that place that has always been yours?
SP   Yes finger lifts.
TH   And to this one: would you be willing now to have a high level guide from the Light come forward to give you further information about the Light and the choices available to you?
SP   Yes finger lifts.
TH   I'm going to ask then that you turn toward the Light and as you do I'm asking that high level guide to come forward who is aware and would like to assist. Just look to the Light there. First finger when you see that guide, second finger if you do not.
SP   Yes finger lifts.
TH   I'm asking the guide now to communicate to this one information about themselves as a soul, their ability to move to the Light, and any other information that might be helpful. And to this one: first finger when you've received this communication, second finger if you do not.
SP   Yes finger lifts.
TH   To this one: did you receive that communication all right?
SP   Yes finger lifts.
TH   Do you know now about your place in the Light?
SP   Yes finger lifts.
TH   Are you ready to go now with the teacher to the Light?
SP   Yes finger lifts.
TH   Before you go, as you look around, are there any others with you there? If yes, the first finger lifting, if you're alone, second finger can lift.
SP   No finger lifts.
TH   Okay. On three, then, you can go right to the guide and to your place in the Light. Beginning, one, two, three… Just move now right to

the guide, right into that corridor of Light. Higher self, first finger when that one has gone, second finger if it does not.
HS Yes finger lifts.

Spirit Protocol: Example 7

TH Higher self, this one you found, is it part of Tony's self/soul energy?
HS No finger lifts.
TH Higher self, this one is separate from self/soul, is that correct?
HS Yes finger lifts.
TH Higher self, if this one is itself a soul, first finger; if a created entity or from another soul, second finger lifting, if none of these fit, the hand can lift.
HS Yes finger lifts.
TH Higher self, has this one entered the soul, if so first finger. If they are operating from outside, second finger can lift.
HS Yes finger lifts.
TH Higher self, if we should just remove this one, first finger lifting. If I should communicate with it, second finger.
HS Yes finger lifts.
TH Higher self, is there more than one separate soul here?
HS Yes finger lifts.
TH Can all of them be removed now?
HS Yes finger lifts.
TH On three, then. One, two, three… Higher self, I'm asking you and guides to identify these separate ones, surround them with the Light, and remove them from the self/soul. First finger when that's complete; second finger if that's blocked or there is a problem.
HS Yes finger lifts.
TH Higher self, were you able to remove them all?
HS Yes finger lifts.
TH Higher self, I'm going to ask that you review and see if these separate ones used someone or something for access. First finger when that review is complete.
HS Yes finger lifts.
TH Higher self, did you find someone or something they used as an access?
HS Yes finger lifts.

TH Higher self, does that need to be addressed directly?
HS Yes finger lifts.
TH If it is someone, first finger. If something or some energy, second finger lifting.
HS Second finger lifts.
TH If it is some kind of device or object, first finger; if more like an energy, second finger lifting. If none of those descriptions fit, the hand can lift.
HS Yes finger lifts.

More will be said about resolving etheric devices and energies in a later chapter.

Step 5: Determine if Others are Present

Right now, staying with a best-case scenario, once a spirit has made contact with the Light and has agreed to leave, it is asked to look around and see if there is anyone else there where it is. If the spirit is alone, the healer can ask that it leave (with or without help from a spirit guide) and that the higher self can signal when it has gone.

If the response is a *yes*, that there is another or others there, then the Identification Protocol is used to identify who is there, how many, and how they need to be handled. There are a number of possibilities. They could all be spirits. There could be both spirits and ego-states present. It could be a group of spirits and created entities. It could be a couple of spirits and several ego-states from another soul, incarnated or not. There are other possibilities. Right now, we'll look only at the situation in which all in the group are spirits.

Once a group of spirits is identified, they usually can be addressed as a group. The aim is to lead them collectively through the same two steps as with the first spirit, i.e., connecting with their own inner Light and allowing contact from a spirit guide. If all the spirits move through these two steps, then they are almost always in agreement with the first spirit's desire to go to the Light.

When there are two or more spirits present, the healer confronts the same question as in working with a group of ego-states. Do you work with them individually or as a group? Usually, like with ego-states, the healer can work with the spirits as a group in 1) making contact with their inner Light, 2) receiving contact from a spirit guide, and 3) agreeing to leave. Usually, when you are dealing with a group of spirits, the most efficient approach is to deal with all of them at the same time. Sometimes, though, a spirit or spirits need to be dealt with individually. There are times when it's more effective to work with one spirit, which can help lead the others through the same steps. Most of the time, I've found that a group of spirits can be identified and worked with collectively, using the presenting spirit as the spokesperson.

When I have a group comprised of both spirits and ego-states, I work with them as two separate groups. The therapeutic aim is different for the two categories. Usually, I will work with the spirits first. Without knowing how much their presence is affecting my client, I want to clear my client of extraneous forces. This helps to clear up confusion about what is part of the self and what is not. Also, dealing with spirits first often seems to pre-empt possible blocking or interference in my work with ego-states later. Often, spirits react as we get closer to identifying them, or they want to protect what they see as their own turf. Depending on the situation, it can be best or even necessary to work with the ego-states first, then the spirits. The higher self can usually assist in making this determination if there are questions or difficulties.

With this in mind, I sometimes use an alternate Spirit Protocol. In this version, as soon as a spirit is identified and engaged, I ask whether there are any others present. If there are, then the healer can turn to the Identification Protocol right away. If there are two or more spirits present, they can usually be worked with as a group, with all of them moving through the same steps simultaneously.

Step 6: Repeat Procedure for Group

Once a group of spirits is identified, the aim is to lead them through the same two steps: connecting with their own inner Light and allowing contact from a spirit guide. If all the spirits move through these two steps, then they are almost always in agreement with the first spirit's desire to go to the Light. This is similar to the situation with ego-states where there is more than one present. Sometimes it is more effective to work with one and then work with the others as a group, and sometimes it's better to identify the group from the beginning and work with all at the same time with one spokesman. This is especially true if other spirits in the group react and block your communication to the original spirit. At that point, it is usually best to find the blockers, gain their cooperation using the same protocols, and then work with the group as a whole.

Here is the alternate protocol:

The Spirit Protocol (Alternate)

1) Determine whether a separate entity is a soul.
2) If it is, determine whether there are others present.
3) Facilitate contact with its (their) own inner Light.
4) Facilitate its (their) contact with a guide/teacher from the Light.
5) Obtain its (their) agreement to leave (usually to go to the Light).
6) Ask the spirits to go.

This alternate protocol is not better than the original, but it is often more efficient. It aims to establish immediate contact and communication with all spirits who are present together. Once a spirit has been identified, it is more efficient to communicate to all of them and help make their contact with the Light. The following is an example of this alternate protocol.

Spirit Protocol: Example 8

TH   Higher self, in that review, did you find someone or something involved in Patricia's panic reactions?
HS   Yes finger lifts.
TH   Higher self, if it's someone, first finger lifting, if some thing or some energy, second finger lifting.
HS   Yes finger lifts.
TH   Higher self, is that one part of the self/soul?
HS   No finger lifts.
TH   Higher self, is this one itself a soul? If so, first finger; if it is a created entity or from another soul, second finger lifting.
HS   Yes finger lifts.
TH   Higher self, if I should communicate with that one, first finger, if just remove them, second finger lifting.
HS   Yes finger lifts.
TH   Higher self, help that one to come forward here with me. And to this one: do you know that you are separate from this soul I'm working with?

	Hand lift.
TH	To this one: are you willing to know whether you are or are not part of this soul I'm working with?
	No finger lifts.
TH	To this one: is there some scare or apprehension for you about this?
	Yes finger lifts.
TH	To this one: we are here to help. Whether you are part of this soul or separate, we are here to help. However, there's one kind of help available if you are part of the soul, and another kind of help if you are separate from this soul. We just need to know which kind of help to give you. As long as it's safe, would you be willing to receive a communication about whether you are a part of this soul or not so we know how to help?
	Yes finger lifts.
TH	To this one: when I count to three, I'm going to have information sent to you about this. On three now; one, two, three and higher self or guide please send to this one information and knowledge about themselves, whether they are or are not part of this soul, and any other information that can be helpful. To this one: first finger when you've received that communication, second finger if you do not.
	Yes finger lifts.
TH	To this one: did you receive that communication all right?
	Yes finger lifts.
TH	To this one: does it seem that you are part of this self/soul that I'm working with?
SP	No finger lifts.
TH	You are separate, is that correct?
SP	Yes finger lifts.
TH	To this one: does it seem that you are yourself a soul?
SP	Yes finger lifts.
TH	When you received that communication, did you also receive some Light?
SP	Yes finger lifts.
TH	Does that feel all right to you?
SP	Yes finger lifts.
TH	As you look around is there anyone else with you where you are?
SP	Yes finger lifts.

The Spirit Protocol

TH Are there more than five of you altogether?
SP No finger lifts.
TH More than four altogether?
SP Yes finger lifts.
TH There are five of you there, is that right?
SP Yes finger lifts.
TH Higher self, are all five separate from the self/soul?
HS No finger lifts.
TH Are at least two parts of this soul?
HS Yes finger lifts.
TH Higher self, are there more than two who are part of this soul?
HS No finger lifts.
TH Higher self, two are part of the self/soul and three are separate, is that correct?
HS Yes finger lifts.
TH Are all three of the separate ones souls? If so first finger, if not, second finger.
HS Yes finger lifts.
TH Higher self, if I should work with these three separate ones first, the yes finger lifting. If I should work with the ego-states first, then the second finger lifting.
HS Yes finger lifts.
TH Higher self, I'm asking that you help these three separate souls to come forward here with me. And the one I just communicated with, are you still able again to communicate with me?
SP Yes finger lifts.
TH And to this one: have the other two with you also received Light for themselves?
SP No finger lifts.
TH To this one: are you willing to communicate with them about this Light and that it is safe for them to have that?
SP Yes finger lifts.
TH To this one: please communicate to them about the Light and I'm asking higher self or a spirit guide to send that Light now to these two and to all three of you, first finger lifting when you've received that Light, second finger if anyone does not.
SP Yes finger lifts.
TH And to this one I've been communicating with: all three of you are

	receiving that Light now, is that right?
SP	Yes finger lifts.
TH	And to this one: are all three of you willing for a high-level guide or teacher from the Light to come forward and communicate to all of you about the Spirit Realm of Light and the choices available to you?
SP	Yes finger lifts.
TH	You can all turn towards the Light and I'm asking that high-level guide or teacher to come forward. First finger when you see the teacher, second finger if you do not.
SP	Yes finger lifts.
TH	I'm asking that teacher now to communicate to all three information and knowledge about the spirit realm, that place in the Light that is waiting for them, that has always been their place. To the three of you: first finger when you all have received that communication, second finger if anyone does not.
SP	Yes finger lifts.
TH	To all three now: are all of you willing to go now with the teacher to your own place in the Light?
SP	Yes finger lifts.
TH	On three, then, you can go right to the Light. Beginning, one, two, three and just move now right to the teacher, right into that corridor of Light. Higher self, first finger when all have gone, second finger if any do not leave.
HS	No finger lifts.
TH	Higher self, did any of these separate ones leave?
HS	Yes finger lifts.
TH	Did more than one stay?
HS	No finger lifts.
TH	I'm asking that one, then, to come forward here. To this one: was there some kind of scare or something in the way of you going to the teacher?
SP	Yes finger lifts.
TH	If that began to scare you, first finger. If someone or something seemed to get in the way, second finger can lift; if none of those fit, the hand can lift.
SP	No finger lifts.
TH	To this one: if it's someone that interfered, first finger; if some thing

The Spirit Protocol

or energy, second finger; if you're not sure, the hand can lift.
SP No finger lifts.
TH To this one: if it's something like a device/object of some kind, first finger; if more like an energy, second finger; if neither of those fit, the hand can lift.
SP Yes finger lifts.
TH Higher self, are you aware of the device or object this one has identified?
HS No finger lifts.
TH Higher self, I'm asking that you scan this one's energy and see if there is some device or object that's been placed inside or attached to it. First finger when the scan is complete; second finger if the scan is stopped or blocked.
HS Yes finger lifts.
TH Higher self, did you find some kind of device or object placed inside or attached to this one?
HS Yes finger lifts.
TH Higher self, can that be removed now?
HS No finger lifts.
TH Higher self, does that one have to give permission for that?
HS Yes finger lifts.
TH And to this one: are you willing to be cleared and cleansed of that device now so you can go to your own place in the Light?
SP Yes finger lifts.
TH On three, then. Beginning, one, two, three and higher self or a high-level guide, I'm asking that you clear this one now of any device or object that has been placed inside or attached to it; dissipate and remove it from this one, first finger when that's complete; second finger if there's a problem.
SP Yes finger lifts.
TH To this one: does that feel better now to you?
SP Yes finger lifts.
TH Are you ready now to go to your place in the Light with that teacher?
SP Yes finger lifts.
TH Just look to the Light again. First finger when you see the teacher, second finger if you do not.
SP Yes finger lifts.
TH Okay. To this one: you can go right to the teacher now, on three.

One, two, three and just move now right to the teacher, right into that corridor of Light. Higher self, first finger when that one has gone, second finger if it does not.

HS Yes finger lifts.

Spirit Protocol: Example 9

TH Higher self, the one you've identified is separate from Tim's self/soul, is that correct?

HS Yes finger lifts.

TH Higher self, if that one is itself a soul, first finger lifting; if it is a created entity or from another soul, second finger lifting; if none of those fit, the hand can lift.

HS Yes finger lifts.

TH Higher self, is there more than one of them?

HS Yes finger lifts.

TH Higher self, if I should communicate with them, first finger lifting, if they should just be removed, the second finger can lift.

HS Yes finger lifts.

TH Higher self, I'm asking that you identify one as a spokesperson and help that one to come forward here with me. And to this one: as long as it's safe, are you willing now to communicate with me?

SP Yes finger lifts.

TH Do you know that you are separate from this soul I'm working with?

SP Yes finger lifts.

TH Do you know yourself to be a soul? If so, first finger lifting, if not, or you're not sure, the second finger can lift.

SP No finger lifts.

TH To this one: are you willing to know now whether you are yourself a soul?

SP Yes finger lifts.

TH To this one: on three, I'm going to have that information sent to you. One, two, three… And higher self or a guide, I'm asking that you communicate to this one whether they are or are not themselves a soul. To this one: first finger when you've received this communication, second finger if you do not.

SP Yes finger lifts.

TH To this one: does it seem that you are yourself a soul?

The Spirit Protocol

SP   Yes finger lifts.
TH   To this one: where you are, is there anyone else with you there?
SP   Yes finger lifts.
TH   Are there more than five of you there altogether?
SP   Yes finger lifts.
TH   More than ten?
SP   No finger lifts.
TH   More than seven?
SP   No finger lifts.
TH   Are there seven of you?
SP   No finger lifts.
TH   Are there six of you altogether?
SP   Yes finger lifts.
TH   Higher self, if all six are separate, first finger. If any are part of Gina's self/soul, second finger can lift.
HS   Yes finger lifts.
TH   Higher self, are all of them souls?
HS   Yes finger lifts.
TH   To all six of you: if you are a soul, you will have the Light inside you; this is your own self/soul energy. Is everyone willing now to look inside for your own soul-source energy?
__   No finger lifts.
TH   I see the no finger. Is there more than one who is not willing to look inside?
__   No finger lifts.
TH   To this one then: is there some scare or apprehension for you about the Light?
SP   Yes finger lifts.
TH   Are you afraid the Light will harm you or destroy you?
SP   Yes finger lifts.
TH   To this one: your soul-source energy is not a destroying energy. It is a life sustaining energy and it has sustained you even when you weren't aware of it. To this one: are you willing to look inside just to see if that Light is there; you don't have to touch it. Are you willing just to see if it's there?
SP   Yes finger lifts.
TH   On three, then, everyone can look inside and find your own soul-source energy. Beginning: one two, three… And each one of you

now, looking inside. Move your vision right to your center, see the Light that is there. You can touch that Light if it feels all right. First finger when everyone has found that Light; second finger if anyone does not.

SP Yes finger lifts.

TH And to this one that I just communicated with: did you see your own Light?

SP Yes finger lifts.

TH Did you decide to touch that Light?

SP Yes finger lifts.

TH Does that feel all right to you?

SP Yes finger lifts.

TH To the group here, all six of you: do you know now about your place in the Spirit Realm of Light?

SP Yes finger lifts.

TH Is everyone ready then to move to the Light?

SP No finger lifts.

TH Is there some scare about that?

SP Yes finger lifts.

TH To the group: are you willing for a high-level teacher from the Light to come forward and communicate information about your place in the Light and the loved ones who are waiting for you?

SP Yes finger lifts.

TH I'm going to ask then that you turn towards the Light and as you do, I'm asking that high-level teacher who is aware and willing to assist, I'm asking that teacher to come forward now, and to this group: first finger when you see the teacher; second finger if you do not.

SP Yes finger lifts.

TH To the teacher: I'm asking that you communicate to this group information and knowledge about themselves; about their place in the Light, and about the loved ones who are waiting for them. Also, communicate any other information that can be helpful. To the group: first finger when everyone has received this communication; second finger if anyone does not.

SP Yes finger lifts.

TH To the group: is everyone ready now to go with the teacher to the Light?

SP Yes finger lifts.

TH On three then, you can move right to the teacher. Beginning: one, two, three… Just move now, right to the teacher, right into that corridor of Light. Higher self, first finger when all have gone, second finger if any do not leave.

HS Yes finger lifts.

Closing Off Access

Once a spirit or group of spirits has left my client, I will often ask the higher self to review inside and see if there is some access that the spirit had used that we need to address. I take this step as a precaution. Not only do I want to remove the spirits that are interfering, I also want to prevent their return or the attachment by different spirits in the future. It would not be unusual to have attached spirits step back from the client when pressure is being mounted for them to leave, only to step back in when the heat is off. Since I don't know when this might be the case and when it's not, I ask higher self to check for accesses. I don't want to leave any doors standing open that should be closed.

Identifying and closing accesses can range from simple to very complex. An earthbound spirit, for example, may be attached to the client through a child ego-state, and it's the child ego-state who does not want the spirit to leave. The spirit may be a recently deceased family member, maybe a grandparent, who has connected to this child personality because in some way, at a psychic level, the child was in pain and calling out for help. The child ego-state may block our communication with the spirit, then, in order to prevent the spirit from leaving. In this case, the child ego-state needs to be addressed and reassured about its own ability to heal and move to a nice place. Once the ego-state understands the situation and its fear is allayed, then it usually will cooperate with and accept the spirit's leaving.

The situation becomes more complex, however, when it involves what I call *dark souls*. These are spirits operating at a psychic/astral level that intentionally target and intrude on or entangle incarnate souls. Their intention is to gain power and control over another soul. It may be to siphon off energy from that soul, cause mayhem just because it can, or to enslave the soul for future uses, including in future lives.

In the next chapter, I will talk about these dark souls, their tactics for gaining access to a soul, and how to work your way through the maze of accesses they have created. The point I want to make right now is that these dark souls are most often the ones who adamantly refuse to make contact with the Light or a spirit guide. They are also the spirits whose awareness allows them to manipulate and exploit the soul, even over lifetimes.

8

When Spirits Refuse

In Chapter 7, I presented the Spirit Protocol using a best-case scenario. This is when a spirit is willing to communicate, makes contact with the Light, and leaves of its own accord or with the assistance of a spirit guide. The process works smoothly and efficiently as long as the spirit agrees to communicate and makes contact with the Light.

All too often, however, attached or intruding spirits refuse to take either step. When this happens, I ask the higher self whether the spirit or spirits should just be removed and their ties severed from the client's soul. If the higher self and/or guides are in a position to carry out this removal and communicate that it would be the best step, then it's a quick and easy solution for a spirit intrusion or attachment. Often, however, the higher self will indicate either 1) that it is not able yet to remove the spirit(s), or 2) that the healer should communicate further with the spirit and attempt to send it to the Light. At this point, a decision needs to be made whether to begin a search for the spirit's access, close it down, and forcibly remove it, or the healer can attempt to find out why the spirit refuses and offer it a solution.

It's a judgment call for the therapist. Is it better to start looking for accesses and close them down, or is there some promise that the spirit might come around and start to cooperate if asked the right questions. If the decision is to shut down the access, then higher self is asked to find whether it is someone or something that is being used for access or accesses. Finding and closing accesses will be treated at length in Chapter 10.

If the decision is to communicate further with the spirit, then the question is how to approach it. The focus in this chapter will be on what steps to take when a spirit refuses contact with the Light. What yes/no questions can the therapist ask to help lead a spirit to change its position and persuade it that making contact with the Light is really its best option? The answer to these questions, I have found, is to answer another question: why the refusal? Is it attached to a loved one still on earth believing the loved one needs its assistance? Is it feeling guilty and afraid of judgment and punishment? Is it afraid that the Light will harm or destroy it if it gets too close? Is it so terrified of God's rejection that it dares not risk opening itself to that Divine Love only to lose it again, and forever? Is the spirit angry and blaming the Light for what has happened, whether during a particular lifetime, or even going back to that soul's original separation from the Light? Is it a network of spirits operating in Darkness, preying on the client's energy? Or is it evil, wishing to destroy all Light and love?

These are some of the main reasons I have found for why a spirit refuses to look inside for its own Light or accept contact from a spirit guide. In knowing why a spirit is refusing the Light, the healer can often formulate a proposition that resolves or allays the spirit's concerns and offers it a safe way to try the Light.

Sometimes, a spirit's refusal is easily resolved. A spirit, for example, may be afraid of going to the Light and being judged and punished. Once the healer learns this, the spirit can be reassured that there is no judgment in the Light; that the only judgment that happens in the Light is a soul's own judgment of itself. Once reassured, the spirit often agrees to allow a spirit teacher to bring it more information, and then shortly it leaves on its own.

In other situations, a healer may need extensive information about a spirit or spirits in order to persuade them to leave or enable higher self finally to forcibly remove it. The extent and depth of the questions about the spirit(s) depends on the client's unique situation. Again, though, the focus is not on learning about the spirit itself, but about what is stopping it from saying yes to a contact with the Light. So, learning about the specific spirits you are dealing with is on a *need-to-know* basis. There are times when you may find some complex entanglement and need to know a great deal more about the spirit or spirits involved in order to resolve the situation. The aim, though, is always to create a situation where the spirit will finally agree to make contact with the Light, or voluntarily leave the client.

Besides facilitating contact with the Light, the protocols for treating ego-states and spirits are the same in another basic way. The sequence of steps in the protocol is to resolve the spirit presence in the least number of steps, from simple removal to complex negotiations.

For example, if I'm working with a client and discover a spirit attachment, the easiest step is to just have higher self remove it. If that can be done, then I don't need any more information about the spirit. If a spirit can't just be removed, then the next most efficient step is to communicate with the spirit and facilitate its contact with the Light. If it takes these steps, I usually won't need to know anything more about it.

If a spirit adamantly refuses contact with the Light, and the higher self cannot forcibly remove it, then more information is needed. The questions I ask will be geared to understanding why the spirit is so opposed to the Light and how to make it an offer too good to turn down. I will promise the spirit relief from any pain, fear, and confusion. Very importantly, I also offer it a safe way to test out for itself what I'm saying and to be absolutely free to accept or reject it. Most spirits will accept this offer because they have nothing to lose and everything to gain. From the spirit's point of view, if I'm telling the truth, then it will finally have a way out of its confusion and distress. If I'm not telling the truth, they can just stay put.

Here are examples of the spirit protocol when a spirit or spirits says no.

Spirit Protocol: Example 10

TH To this one: the one that higher self has identified: do you know that you are separate from this self and soul I'm working with?
SP Yes finger lifts.
TH Are you yourself a soul? If so, first finger. If not second finger. If you're not sure, the hand can lift.
SP First finger lifts.
TH To this one: are there others with you there where you are?
SP Yes finger lifts.
TH Are there more than five of you?
SP No finger lifts.
TH More than three?
SP No finger lifts.
TH Are there three of you?

SP   Yes finger lifts.
TH   Do you know about the Light?
SP   Yes finger lifts.
TH   Are you receiving that Light for yourself right now?
SP   No finger lifts.
TH   Are you willing to receive some Light for yourself?
SP   No finger lifts.
TH   Are you afraid of the Light?
SP   Yes finger lifts.
TH   Have you been told that it would harm you or destroy you?
SP   Yes finger lifts.
TH   To this one: whoever told you that has lied to you. As a soul, you have your own soul-source energy. The Light is a life sustaining energy, not a destroying energy. Whoever told you that wanted to keep you away from your own soul-source energy. They knew that if you remembered who you were—a soul of Light—they would lose their power over you. As a soul, you have the absolute free choice to end your relationship with them if you wish to. You didn't know that, did you?
SP   No finger lifts.
TH   Would you be willing to allow a high-level teacher from the Light to come forward and communicate information about this to you?
SP   No finger lifts.
TH   Does that scare you?
SP   No finger lifts.
TH   Are you afraid the Light will reject you?
SP   Yes finger lifts.
TH   To this one: the Light already knows what happened, and has already forgiven you. As a soul, the Light wants you to come home. There are loved ones in the Light waiting for you. You and the others will have all the help you need. The teacher can communicate to you about this also. Would you be willing if a high-level teacher came forward but stayed a safe distance away, just so you could see them? You can make them go away anytime you choose. There's nothing that will be forced on you. Would you allow the teacher to come forward as long as they stay a safe distance away?
SP   Yes finger lifts.
TH   I'm asking that high-level teacher who is aware, and wishes to assist,

When Spirits Refuse

to step forward, staying a safe distance away. To this one I've been communicating with: yes finger when you see them, second finger if you do not.
SP Yes finger lifts.
TH I'm asking the teacher now to communicate to these separate ones information and knowledge about themselves as souls, about the soul-source energy each carries inside and about the loved ones who are waiting for them. Yes finger when you have received this communication, no finger if you do not.
SP Yes finger lifts.
TH To this one: did you and others receive that information?
SP Yes finger lifts.
TH Does that make sense to you?
SP Yes finger lifts.
TH Do you and the others want to go with the teacher to your own place in the Light?
SP Yes finger lifts.
TH On three, then, you can move right to the teacher. Beginning, one, two, three... and just move right to the teacher now, into that corridor of Light. Higher self, yes finger when all have gone, no finger if any do not.
HS No finger lifts.
TH Higher self, did more than one of them stay back?
HS No finger lifts.
TH Higher self, help that one to come forward here with me. And to this one: are you receiving Light for yourself?
___ Yes finger lifts.
TH Is there still some scare about returning to the Light?
___ Yes finger lifts.
TH You need to know that the only thing your loved ones want is for you to come. You have already been forgiven. The Light understands what happened. Would you be willing for a loved one, someone you know cared about you, would you be willing for that loved one to step forward? You will recognize who it is; someone you know who loved you and cared for you. You can stop it immediately if you need to. Would you let that one step forward, just so you can see who it is.
___ Yes finger lifts.

TH I'm asking that one to step forward, just so you can see who it is. Yes finger when you see them, no finger if you do not.
__ Yes finger lifts.
TH Do you see who it is?
__ Yes finger lifts.
TH Have you already communicated?
__ Yes finger lifts.
TH Would you like to go with them?
__ Yes finger lifts.
TH On three, then. One, two, three… and just move right to your loved one and higher self, yes finger when they have gone, no finger if they stay.
HS Yes finger lifts.

Spirit Protocol: Example 11

TH To this one who has stepped in to block: are you part of this self and soul I'm working with?
SP No finger lifts.
TH If you believe you are a soul, the yes finger can lift. If, not, second finger lifting; if you're not sure the hand can lift.
SP Hand lift.
TH To this one: are you willing to know whether you are, or are not, a soul?
SP Yes finger lifts.
TH I'm going to ask then that the higher self or a spirit guide send you information about this, on the count of three. One, two, three… higher self, I'm asking that you communicate to this one whether they are or are not a soul. And to this one: yes finger when you have received that communication, no finger if you do not.
SP Yes finger lifts.
TH To this one: did you receive that communication all right?
SP Yes finger lifts.
TH Does it seem that you are a soul?
SP Yes finger lifts.
TH Are you willing then to look inside and find your own Light? If you are a soul, you do have that soul-source energy within you. Are you willing to look and see if it is there?

When Spirits Refuse

SP   Yes finger lifts.

TH   On three then – one, two, three… and to this one: just look inside now for that Light. Just move your vision right to your center. See the Light that you have there. Yes finger when you see it. No finger if you do not.

SP   No finger lifts.

TH   To this one: if you needed to stop that, yes finger lifting. If someone or something seemed to interfere, the no finger can lift. If you aren't sure, the hand can lift.

SP   Yes finger lifts.

TH   Did it begin to scare you?

SP   Yes finger lifts.

TH   Did it start to bring up your pain?

SP   Yes finger lifts.

TH   To this one: this is the pain you have carried inside and that has kept you away from the Light. That pain can be healed and released. Would you be willing to have a high level teacher come forward and communicate to you an understanding about this healing?

SP   Yes finger lifts.

TH   I'm going to ask then that you turn toward the Light. See the teacher that comes forward. Yes finger when you see them. Second finger, if you do not.

SP   Second finger lifts.

TH   To this one: if you needed to stop that, yes finger can lift. If someone or something seemed to get in your way, the no finger lifting. If you're not sure, the hand can lift.

SP   Yes finger lifts.

TH   To this one: did that also start to scare you?

SP   Yes finger lifts.

TH   Would you be willing to just hear the communication from the teacher? You don't have to see them or meet with them. It's just information that will be communicated mentally. You can receive that for yourself, and decide whether that makes sense to you. Would you be willing to do that?

SP   Yes finger lifts.

TH   On three then, I'm going to ask that the communication be sent to you. Beginning, one, two, three… I'm asking that high level teacher now to communicate this information about healing. Help this one

	know how they can be free of all pain and return home to the Light. To this one: yes finger when you've received that, no finger if you do not.
SP	Yes finger lifts.
TH	Did you receive this information all right?
SP	Yes finger lifts.
TH	Does it make sense to you?
SP	Yes finger lifts.
TH	Are you willing then to go with the teacher and to have that healing for yourself.
SP	Yes finger lifts.
TH	On three then, you can move right to the teacher. One, two, three… and just move now to the teacher, into that corridor of Light. Higher self, yes finger when they have gone. No finger if they do not.
HS	Yes finger lifts.

9

The Shutdown

When a spirit says no to the Light or to contact with a spirit teacher but continues to communicate, the healer can almost always find out what the problem is and offer it a safe solution. This is true whether the spirit is frightened of the Light, angry at it, being threatened by dark souls, or made a deal with them in the past. As long as the spirit still communicates, the healer can ask the questions that will narrow down and determine where the spirit is stuck.

There is a more extreme refusal, however, in which all communication with unconscious levels is stopped. Whoever I was just communicating with will not, or cannot, respond. The higher self that I've communicated with numerous times also is not responding. This almost always means it is being blocked. The higher self is always willing to communicate, so when it doesn't, it usually means it isn't able to at that time.

At this point, I will usually ask to talk to the protective part or a significant ego-state that I've already worked with before, just to see if I can re-establish any communication. If there are still no signals, then I consider it a *shutdown*.

This type of blocking is one of the most difficult situations to deal with in the process of healing. Unless you are clairvoyant, are a medium, or have assistance like I had with Gerod, we cannot look inside the client and see who or what is causing the shutdown. We don't know if we are bumping up against someone, or something, or some kind of energy.

Herein lies the problem with a shutdown. It can occur at any time in the healing process, and you won't know who or what is causing it.

You may have been communicating with a spirit, for example, when a shutdown occurred. You cannot assume, however, that it was that particular spirit causing the shutdown. That could be the case, but not necessarily. There are other possibilities. You cannot even assume that it is another spirit causing the shutdown. Again, it could be, but we can't assume it. It may be an ego-state, a created entity, or a programmed device that is responsible for the shutdown.

As healers, this is the dilemma. On the one hand, we need to know who or what is behind the shutdown in order to know how to approach it and resolve it. On the other hand, how do we find out who or what it is if it won't communicate? With no feedback or indicators of any kind, the healer is operating blind. It's a blank slate and the healer can only guess who or what is behind the shutdown. What makes it even more difficult is that there are a number of possibilities to choose from. Going back to the Identification Protocol, any of those entities or phenomena could be causing the shutdown, and each one calls for a different approach and a different line of questioning in order to resolve it. An ego-state, for example, needs to be approached differently than a spirit. If you begin communicating with it as though it is a spirit, it may lead to more blocking and/or confusion.

Strategies for Resolving Shutdowns

The identification of *who* or *what* is causing a shutdown is the kind of information I received from Gerod when we were collaborating. I would come to a shutdown with a client, and in my sessions with Gerod, he would identify the source of the block or give information leading to it. Sometimes he gave me a name to ask for. Or he would tell me that the block was a maze, a series of walls, and he would name a certain ego-state inside who could guide me through it. Sometimes he offered suggestions or told me what might help resolve the block. I used this information to prepare strategic questions for my next session with the client.

Over the years, Gerod and I worked through hundreds of blocks with clients ranging from simple to complex. There's no question that without Gerod's ability to *see* behind the blocks and tell me what was happening, I would never have been able to figure them out on my own. However, in working with Gerod, I began to recognize patterns among clients in terms of who or what might be blocking and why.

Over time, I developed strategies for dealing with these shutdowns when they occurred.

The first strategy isn't much of a strategy, but it can work. If a block feels irresolvable, if it seems that nothing you do is getting a response, then it may be time to end the session. It does work at times to end the session and try again next time to re-establish communication with the client's higher self or another part of the self. Sometimes, things do shift in the inner world in between sessions and communication with the higher self or an ego-state is re-established in the next session. That doesn't rule out, though, that you won't run into the same block again.

Usually, when confronted with a shutdown of communication, I will try to resolve it in the session if there is time. In these cases I believe in the old adage, *strike while the iron is hot*. From my point of view, the block or blocker is presenting to me in that moment. The shutdown might even be viewed as the blocker engaging me. It did respond, after all, to something I said. So, I will often try to engage it right then. At the same time, if it's too complex, we can return to it in the next session.

There are two basic strategies I use when facing this kind of shutdown. They are modifications of the Identification Protocol. Instead of questions leading to an identification, in the case of shutdowns, we assume the identity—someone or something—and then ask questions that our assumed blocker would most likely say yes to or identify with. They can be questions also which expect a strong no response, but then in this kind of situation a no acts as a confirmation.

The first strategy is to address the source of the shutdown as *someone*, and to assume that it is listening. By *someone*, I mean a conscious, intelligent being or entity that is able to communicate with me if it chooses, but for some reason is not. The immediate aim is to engage the blocker and establish communication in order to identify it and decide which protocol would be the most effective. The strategy is to ask those questions that are most likely to engage it (them) and elicit a response. When there is a response, the next step is to ask further questions that are non-threatening, easy to answer, and which, at the same time, give some information about who the therapist is communicating with and what questions to ask next. I want to ask a question that captures the blocker's attention and that is so easy it may even respond reflexively.

Secondly, I try to ask questions that imply that there is something to gain for the blocker by communicating with me. I need to make it curious enough to respond. When there is a shutdown, the aim is to get re-engaged as quickly as possible.

The attitude I assume in asking these questions is an openness to understand and accept the blocker for who it is and have a genuine desire to help. The basic message I want the entity to hear behind my words goes something like this: "Look, I know you think what you're doing is okay or it's something you have to do, but you don't. If you're a soul, there's a much better place you can be and it's already waiting for you. You don't have to take my word for it. You can check this out safely for yourself and make your own decision. I'm very confident you're going to like what you find, but you can stop it if you need to."

The problem is that there are several types of *someones* that could be causing the shutdown, and the questions most likely to elicit a response are different from one type of entity to another. It could be an ego-state, for example, that's behind the shutdown, or a spirit, an extraterrestrial or dimensional being, an ego-state from another soul, or an unknown possibility.

Based on my experience over time, the strategy I developed involved compiling a list of those questions that I found most likely to elicit a response from each type of entity. When facing a shutdown, then, and assuming it is someone, I will take my best guess about what kind of entity it is. Those are the questions I will start with. If I think it's an ego-state that felt threatened, for example, I might start with the question: "Do you know you are part of this soul I'm working with?" If I'm guessing it's a spirit that's blocking, I might say: "To this one who just stepped in here, do you believe you are separate from this soul I'm working with?" The idea is to ask an easy *yes* question, basic and non-threatening, that the entity can safely identify with and respond to. If I get no response after two or three questions along these lines, I will go to my next best guess about what kind of entity is blocking and ask a different set of questions.

Without any inside information, it's a strategy based on probabilities. If the first question doesn't elicit a response, then I go to a second question and then to a third, until I get a response or run out of good questions. It's like a fisherman who has learned over time the best places to cast his line. On any given day, there's no guarantee that there's anything there, but experience says that often there is.

When dealing with a shutdown, and assuming it's someone, I try to cast as wide a net as I can before having to get specific. I try to start with a question that can apply to more than one category of possible entities. If I've guessed wrong, I may still get a response, or at least I have not alienated the one who is blocking.

The following are examples of the questions I ask when confronting a shutdown and still assuming it is someone.

Unknown Block: Example 1

> TH To this one blocking: do you know yourself to be part of this soul that I'm working with? If so, the yes finger lifting. If you think you are separate, or you're not sure, then the no finger can lift.

This question is intended to be non-threatening, though the blocker may perceive it as a threat. It may perceive our very attempt at contact to be a threat. This question, though, will often elicit a response, especially from an ego-state. A spirit or separate entity may not respond as readily because it usually does not want to be discovered and identified. The healing work in some way has forced its hand and it reveals its presence when it steps in to block our communication.

If I think it likely that a spirit or other external entity is blocking, I may turn the question around so that it calls for a *yes* response if it is an external entity.

Unknown Block: Example 2

> TH To this one blocking: do you believe you are separate from this soul I'm working with? If so, yes finger lifting. If not, the no finger can lift. If you're not sure then the hand can lift.

If there is a no response to the first question, then I go on to another. The following are the questions I most often use when confronted with a shutdown of communication. In using these questions, I am fishing for a response. I'm hoping that one of my questions fits the blocker closely enough that it is almost compelled to respond.

Which questions I ask, and in what order, depend on the specific situation we were dealing with immediately prior to the block. It depends on my intuition about whether we are dealing with an ego-state or a separate entity, whether the blocker seems to be aggressive or frightened, and what the client's body language is telling me. These assumptions and the questions I ask can be totally off the mark, but you have to start somewhere. The following questions are examples of ones I ask when I'm assuming *someone* is behind the shutdown. The questions are designed to address the different possibilities and their sole aim is to elicit a response.

Unknown Block: Example 3

TH To this one: is there some scare or apprehension for you about this kind of direct communication? Is there some apprehension about that? If so, the yes finger can lift. If that's not a problem, the no finger lifting.

Unknown Block: Example 4

TH To this one who has come forward to block: I want you to know that we are here to help. Whether you are part of this soul or separate, we are here to help. That help is different depending on whether you are part of this soul or not, but there is help either way. To this one: as long as it is safe, are you willing to communicate about the choices available to you?

Unknown Block: Example 5

TH To this one blocking: I don't know if you are part of this soul or not, but if you are, then you need to know there is a way for you to be free of all pain and distress. We are working with a healing process to help everyone inside be free. To this one: if you knew absolutely for certain that you could be free of pain and scare, would you want that for yourself?

Unknown Block: Example 6

TH To this one: I know I was talking to 6yo about what happened. Did that start to scare you?

Unknown Block: Example 7

TH To this one who's needing to block: are you afraid if we go too far here that things will get out of control? Is there some scare about that?

Unknown Block: Example 8

TH To this one who is blocking: is it your job to stop us here? Is this the job you were given?

Unknown Block: Example 9

TH To this one who's blocking: we are here to help. Whether you are part of this soul or separate, we can help you. You may believe you have to do what you're doing here, or that there's no way out. I want to assure you, there is a way for you to be free. There is information for you about this. To this one: as long as it's safe, would you be willing to have this information sent to you? There's nothing you have to do with it. It's just information for you to consider. Are you willing to receive this information?

Unknown Block: Example 10

TH To this one who's blocking: it seems to me that my question about Gina's headaches scared you or caused some distress. To this one who's needing to block: is there some concern for you about us working in this area? Do you wish for us to stay away?

Unknown Block: Example 11

TH To this one who is blocking: my question is whether you are yourself a soul? If you are, then you have within you your own soul-source energy. It's your own soul energy that has always sustained you. Even if you have forgotten it, it has always been there. If you are a soul, then you have your own soul-source energy. To this one: if you are a soul, and have your own soul-source energy, would you want to know that for yourself? Do you want to know if there are other choices available to you? If so, yes finger. If not, the no finger lifting. If you're not sure, the hand can lift.

Unknown Block: Example 12

TH To this one: it seems to me that you must be too frightened to communicate with me directly. It is not our intention to frighten anyone.

We are here to help. Whether you are part of this self/soul or not, we are here to help. Now to this one who has come forward: as long as it's safe, are you willing to communicate with me?

Unknown Block: Example 13

TH To this one: I don't know whether you are afraid to communicate or whether you might be angry. To this one: are you angry at the Light? Did the Light betray you in some way?

Unknown Block: Example 14

TH To this one who is blocking: I've been asking you to communicate and I've seen no signal. To this one: are you being threatened there where you are? Is there someone or something threatening you about communicating with me? If there is, we can help with that, but I need to know first. Is there someone or something threatening you there?

In the face of a shutdown, these are the kinds of questions I will ask depending on the kind of entity I think may be blocking.

The questions are designed to call them out. If none of these questions elicit a response and I feel I'm at a dead end, I will try a second strategy. In this strategy, I assume that the higher self is able to hear me even though the signaling is blocked. I will ask the higher self to look inside and find who or what the blocker is using to stay attached. It can be someone or something. For the moment, I'm still assuming it's someone, and if it is, it's usually an ego-state. After a brief pause, I'll ask this someone if it is willing to communicate with me. It seems that an ego-state, being used as an access, is able to override a block because the blocker's power to shut down communication derives in the first place from this ego-state through whom it has gained access. Whether knowingly or not, this one granted access and it's this one that can withdraw that permission. As part of the soul, it shares in the soul's free choice.

If I do not receive a response, I still consider the possibility that an ego-state being used for access is too frightened to respond or is being threatened. So, I will follow up with questions designed to fit for someone in these different situations.

The Shutdown

Ego-state Used as an Access: Example 1

TH Higher self, I know you can still hear me. I'm asking that you look inside and find who or what this one is using for access. (Pause) To this one: as long as it is safe, are you willing to communicate with me?

No response.

TH To this one: are you being threatened there where you are?

__ Yes finger lifts.

TH To this one: would you like to move to a safer place where you won't be threatened?

__ Yes finger lifts.

TH To this one: on the count of three, I'm going to ask higher self to move you to that safer more comfortable place, beginning, one, two, three... And higher self, please move this one to the safest, most comfortable place that's here for them. And to this one: yes finger when that move is complete, no finger if that's stopped.

__ No finger lifts.

TH To this one: if you needed to stop that move, first finger lifting. If someone or something interfered or got in the way, the no finger can lift.

__ No finger lifts.

TH To this one: do you know yourself to be part of this self and soul I'm working with?

__ Yes finger lifts.

TH Are you receiving some Light/Love energy where you are there?

__ No finger lifts.

TH Would you like to have some of that Light/Love energy sent to you?

__ Yes finger lifts.

TH On three, then, I'm going to have higher self send you that Light/Love energy. Beginning, one, two, three... and higher self, please send this one that Light/Love energy; and to this one: let yourself receive that to whatever level is comfortable. First finger when you receive that, second finger if you do not.

__ No finger lifts.

TH To this one: if you needed to stop that, first finger lifting. If someone interfered again, the no finger can lift.

__ No finger lifts.

TH To this one: as part of this soul, you have the right and the ability to have that one removed who's threatening you. You didn't know that did you?
___ No finger lifts.
TH Are you willing for higher self to send you information about this?
___ Yes finger lifts.
TH Higher self, I'm asking that you send this one information about their right as part of the soul to have this one removed, if they are separate, and moved aside, if they are part of the self/soul. Help this one to know they have the absolute choice about this. And to this one: yes finger when you have received that information, no finger if you do not.
___ Yes finger lifts.
TH To this one: did you receive that information all right?
___ Yes finger lifts.
TH And the one who is threatening you, are they separate from your soul?
___ Yes finger lifts.
TH Would you like to have them removed now?
___ Yes finger lifts.
TH Higher self, are you able now to remove that one?
HS Yes finger lifts.
TH I'm asking that you remove them then on three: one, two, three... Higher self, yes finger when that one is removed, no finger if there is a problem.
HS Yes finger lifts.
TH Higher self, were you able to remove that one?
HS Yes finger lifts.
TH Are there any other separate ones you see there?
HS No finger lifts.
TH I'm asking now for that one I was communicating with to come forward here again. And to this one: are you able again now to communicate with me?
___ Yes finger lifts.
TH Does that feel better to you now that that one has gone?
___ Yes finger lifts.

Continue with the Ego-state Protocol

Ego-state Used as an Access: Example 2

TH Higher self, I know you are still able to hear me. I'm asking that you look inside and find who or what this one is using to stay attached here. (Pause) To this one that higher self has identified: as long as it is safe, are you willing to communicate with me?

No response.

TH I want you to know that we are here to help. Whether you are part of this soul or separate, we are here to help you be free of all fear, pain, and threat. To this one: if you are part of this soul that I'm working with, then you have the right to remove anyone or anything that is threatening you there. To this one that higher self has identified, do you believe you are part of this self and soul I'm working with?
__ Yes finger lifts.

TH To this one: are you receiving Light/Love energy for yourself?
__ Hand lift.

TH Are you willing to receive some Light now for yourself?
__ Yes finger lifts.

TH On three, then, higher self will send that Light. Beginning, one, two, three… Higher self, please send to this one the Light/Love energy, and to this one: first finger when you've received that; second finger if not.
__ Second finger lifts.

TH To this one: if you needed to stop that Light, first finger lifting. If someone or something interfered, second finger lifting.
__ Second finger lifts.

TH To this one: would you like to have that one removed?
__ No finger lifts.

TH To this one: are you being threatened there?
__ Yes finger lifts.

TH Did you know that as part of this soul you have the right to remove that one?
__ No finger lifts.

TH To this one: did you make some kind of agreement with that one?
__ Yes finger lifts.

TH You need to know that any agreement or contract you made with those in the dark is null and void. There are no valid agreements with those in Darkness. Would you be willing to receive more in-

formation about this for yourself?
___ Yes finger lifts.
TH Higher self, I'm asking that you communicate to this one the information about their absolute free choice. Help them to know that they can end any agreement with those in Darkness any time they wish. First finger when this communication is complete; second finger if it is stopped.
___ Second finger lifts.
TH To this one: did you need to stop that communication?
___ No finger lifts.
TH To this one: that one who threatens you does not want you to know your connection to the Light and your power to make it leave. Are you willing for higher self to come where you are there and give it permission to remove this one?
___ Yes finger lifts.
TH Higher self, please move to this one, surrounding them in Light, and on three higher self, please remove this one from the self/soul. Beginning, one, two, three… higher self, I'm asking you and guides now to find this one, surround it with Light and remove it from the self/soul. First finger when that has happened, second finger if not.
HS First finger lifts.
TH And to this one I've been communicating with: has that one left?
___ Yes finger lifts.
TH Does that feel safer to you now?
___ Yes finger lifts.
TH You've let me know you are part of this soul. Are you one first created in this present life of Linda's? If so, first finger. If you think you are from a past or different lifetime, second finger can lift. If you're just not sure then the hand can lift.
___ First finger lifts.

Continue with Ego-state Protocol

When there is a shutdown, and none of these strategies succeed, the healer can try or suggest other means than the hypnosis. Some form of energy work may help, ranging from acupuncture, to healing touch, to energy treatments like Reiki or Ama Deus. Conscious level involvement using some form of active imagination or guided imagery may elicit helpful information about the shutdown and even help address it. A reputable psychic or medium may also be able to provide some information about a shutdown and who or what is creating it. Finally, the client's own prayer for assistance from his or her spirit guide can also bring Light into the situation.

10

Dealing with Souls in Darkness

Identifying Dark Souls

When confronted with a shutdown of communication by a spirit(s), it is often because the spirit is afraid that its presence will be discovered and its activities stopped. In fact, that is the intention of the healing process and, sooner or later, that is what will happen if the healing proceeds. At some point, the client's higher self will identify this situation as one needing to be addressed, or the healer will encounter an ego-state that is being threatened by a spirit or being used as an access. However the healer comes across it, it seems that intruding and attached spirits know when he or she is getting close and, at some point, are compelled to try to stop it or abandon their attachment.

Using strategies from the previous chapter, once a spirit is identified as the source of the shutdown, the healer switches to the Spirit Protocol. The next step, just as with any spirit, is to initiate its contact with the Light and lead it through the steps of the protocol. However, there are spirits who will actively fight all efforts by the therapist to communicate with the higher self, bring in Light, or carry on with the healing process. They are spirits who refuse all contact with the Light. I call these spirits *dark souls*.

From a clinical point of view, what characterizes these spirits is, first, their high level of resistance to any new information and second, their intense opposition to the Light. Not surprisingly, these are the spirits who are often behind a shutdown and who attempt to block all communication if they can. They are also the spirits who often refuse any communication at all. In these cases, a different strategy for removal is needed. I'll talk about this situation and strategy later in the chapter.

A third characteristic of dark souls is that their involvement with a person is quite intentional. They are not present with the client by happenstance, and the activities they are engaged in usually involve exploitation through exercising some level of power and control over the client's soul. The healer usually won't know a spirit's intentions and activities in the initial contact with a dark soul, but if the communication continues, these intentions begin to become clear.

Finally, most souls I have encountered that dwell in Darkness do not appear to exist in isolation. Most of the time they are part of a larger network or web of souls based on a hierarchy. Again, this won't be obvious in the initial contact, but will become an issue if the spirit continues its communication. I think of these networks more as a collective consciousness rather than a group of individuals. These collectives can operate in different ways and with different aims, like gangs controlling different territories in a city, but they all answer in the end to those above them who govern the hierarchy.

When confronted with a group of dark souls, I have found very often that they are at the lower echelon in the hierarchy, just doing what they've been told to do. They have been sent to the client intentionally and they have certain jobs to carry out at these unconscious levels. They are more like worker bees, or foot soldiers that have been sent to the front lines. Most of the time these dark souls are living in the belief that there is no other way to be, or there is no way out for them. They either made a deal or believe they made a deal with dark souls, and are now paying the price. Even further, since these are timeless realms, these contracts or deals never expire and the spirit is always paying it off.

I have also found that a spirit further up the hierarchy is usually monitoring these frontline groups. That spirit might be present within the client, or it may be monitoring from outside the soul, ready to step in if necessary. In fact, I've found that when I work my way up the hierarchy, every level seems to be monitored by those above.

Souls Bound in Darkness

This is the kind of spirit I will assume I'm dealing with if it adamantly refuses to receive any information or contact from the Light, or if a shutdown occurs. I would say many shutdowns, if not most, involve dark souls. In these cases, the challenge for the healer is to offer information or ask a question that will grab the spirit's attention and arouse its curiosity strongly enough that it does respond. So the question is: what information can the healer offer to overcome the dark soul's refusal?

The answer to this question goes back to a deeper one. What is keeping this soul bound in Darkness, even when offered a way out? Over the years, I have found two primary reasons. The first is that the spirit wants to avoid the pain that will be triggered if the spirit makes contact with the Light. They don't know, or they don't believe, that the Light is waiting for them on the other side of that pain. It involves pain. It's the pain of separation. A soul in Darkness who returns to the Light will have to revisit the pain that initially led them into Darkness. Whether that came as the result of some trauma or crisis, or whether the pain built up over time. The bind for the dark soul is that whatever pain initially drove it into Darkness, that pain will always remain unresolved within the soul and will become an issue once again should that soul return to the Light. It's not the case that a spirit can enter Darkness, wait for the fear, or the threat, or the pain to pass, and then move back into the Light as though nothing happened. If a soul moves back into the Light, the pain will have to be confronted and healed. The compounding issue is that once a soul enters Darkness, it is unlikely on its own to come to the wherewithal to confront the pain.

While we usually won't know from the beginning why a particular soul entered Darkness, I have found that the reasons usually fall into some general categories. These are:
- To escape pain.
- To alleviate fear or terror.
- To seek protection.
- To gain power.
- Because of guilt.
- Because it is afraid God will, or already has, rejected them.
- Because they are angry with God and blame God for what has happened to them.
- They became swallowed up in hatred.
- Because they were deceived or seduced by a dark soul.
- The promise of immortality.

There are other reasons a soul may enter Darkness, but the ones I've listed are the main reasons I have found. By knowing these possibilities ahead of time, the healer can remain alert to indications from the spirit that may point to its own particular reason. If I know why a spirit first entered Darkness, then I am in a position to offer general information that fits the spirit's own situation and shows them a possible way out. When I know why a soul initially entered Darkness, I can usually offer it 1) a safe way to receive information, 2) explain to it that it does possess the freedom to leave Darkness if it chooses, or 3) that the conditions that existed when they first entered Darkness are no longer a problem or were misunderstood or misperceived in the first place.

There is a second question that is important in dealing with a dark soul. It comes at it from the other end. The question is: What is the spirit's reason or motivation for remaining in Darkness right up to the present moment? Is it afraid of the Light? Does it believe the Light will harm or destroy it? Is it afraid of being punished by dark souls if it shows an interest in the Light? Does it believe it is unworthy and undeserving of Light and love? Is it angry? Or is it truly evil and, at an inner level, attempting to overpower and control the client's soul for its energy or to enslave it?

The answers to these questions can be important in helping the healer understand what is keeping a particular soul bound in Darkness. This in turn can reveal the conflict or problem a spirit needs to resolve in the present before it will say *yes* to information or contact with the Light. The healer wants to be the one to offer that resolution. This information, then, can help the therapist in deciding on the best strategy to use with a particular spirit or group of spirits.

The preferred outcome in dealing with any inhabiting or attached spirit is for them to leave the client quickly and voluntarily. The most effective way I have seen to achieve this is to facilitate the spirit's contact with the Light. This is true also for numerous spirits I've worked with who were deeply entangled in Darkness.

If none of these strategies are successful, then I will assume the spirit is remaining in Darkness because it is afraid. This is not the only reason, but it's the one I've seen most of the time. When a soul turns down a risk-free opportunity for information, there is usually someone or something it is afraid of. Like with souls entering Darkness for different reasons, however, souls remain in Darkness because of different fears. The following are the fears I see most frequently:

- It is being threatened by another spirit or spirits.
- Deeper parts of its own soul are still aligned with Darkness and act to stop any movement toward the Light.
- It is immobilized by devices or energies inserted by dark souls from further up the hierarchy. These devices can trigger pain when a soul moves toward the Light. (The fear involved in these situations is seen when the spirit is asked whether it would like those devices or energies removed.)
- It believes it will lose all its power.
- Another soul, a loved one, is being held hostage and threatened with destruction if this one leaves for the Light.
- It believes it is bound by a prior contract or deal that it made with dark souls and is being pressed and threatened that it must obey the contract.
- Fear of punishment or rejection by God or loved ones. Deep guilt.

Again, these are not the only possibilities for why a soul says no to the Light, or why there is a shutdown when communicating with a spirit. They are the reasons I've encountered most often. What they have in common is that 1) another soul within the dark hierarchy steps in with some kind of threat to stop the engaged spirit from communicating further, or 2) a preset program or device, set up by dark souls, has been triggered within the spirit. In either case, the spirit is frightened or in pain and so refuses further communication.

When there is a shutdown, I assume the spirit is still able to hear me. I usually appeal to its reason. I will point out that if what I'm saying is not true, then why are other spirits trying so hard to stop it from looking inside or from receiving information? If the spirit feels guilty, I talk about divine forgiveness. If it was deceived, I help it to know that any debt or deal it made isn't valid and they are free to make another choice. If it sought protection, I reassure it that its greatest protection now is in the Light. For a spirit that believes it is so powerful in the dark, I remind it of those above who will quash it if it tries to use its power in ways not approved by the hierarchy. For a soul that blames God for what has happened, I'll suggest to the spirit that it may have been deceived, that it may have been tricked in the beginning by the very souls it is aligned with now. Then I will offer the spirit information to consider about whether this might be true.

A Clinical Stance in Dealing with Dark Souls

When I encounter what I believe to be a dark soul, I always keep in mind that I am communicating with a soul of Light that became lost. I view it as a conscious being trapped in a field of dark energy/consciousness. My intention from the start, in dealing with any spirit, is to remind it that 1) it is a soul, a being of Light, 2) that it is absolutely free to receive Light and return home to the Light regardless of any agreement it made in Darkness, 3) that the Divine Light has already forgiven the spirit for what has happened, and 4) that there are loved ones in the Light waiting to welcome it home. At its deepest level, the consistent message I want to give a spirit is: "you are more than you remember, and you have the power to choose, and there is a place of Light and love where you belong." Even the darkest soul, or most evil, can make a new choice and take steps to return home to the Light. My friend Gerod said this choice to return to the Light is always, always, always open to every soul.

When I first establish contact with a dark soul, it's as though I'm asking it to differentiate itself from the collective and the hierarchy of dark souls. Some are willing to do that. For others, it is frightening. At the same time, when a dark soul does communicate with me, others in the group and in the larger network appear to be aware of the communication to differing extents. It's very much like with ego-states where everyone in the group is aware when communication has been established with one of its members.

I have found that these dark souls on the frontline will quite often respond to my statements about their status as souls and their freedom to exercise choice. They are curious about what I am saying and are willing to hear more. I trust that what I'm saying resonates with them and they want to hear more. Sometimes, others in the immediate group are also receptive to what I am saying. My impression is that these frontline spirits respond because they have not encountered this situation before, and they are not aware that those further up the hierarchy are going to come down on them.

I consider a response by a dark soul to be its first step back to the Light. However, this is also the point at which, after one or two responses from a frontline spirit, I will very often encounter a block by a monitoring spirit. Very often the communication is immediately blocked. It's as though the spirit is yanked away and someone else steps in to close the breach that began to open. In these situations, I can be pretty sure that it is *someone* and not *something* that has stepped in to block. Either it is someone else in the group that does know that there will be consequences and is frightened about what will happen and so blocks the communication; or it is someone from a higher level who is stepping in to protect its turf and prevent the loss of its control. Either way, I usually assume it is someone and will immediately start the Identification Protocol.

When dealing with a dark soul or group of dark souls, the Spirit Protocol is still the one to use. The aim is still to help the spirit make contact with the Light. However, a dark soul needs to be approached with the understanding that 1) at some point, it probably made an agreement with Darkness or dark souls and still believes it is bound by that agreement, contract, or deal; 2) it has been convinced that any contact with the Light will harm or destroy it; 3) that it is most likely part of a network and is pulled by the energy of the collective; and 4) that if the spirit does finally begin to cooperate, it is likely to be threatened or blocked by the intervention of a dark soul higher up in the network.

When this happens, I keep the spirit focused on its ability to look inside and prove to itself that it has its own soul-source energy. The basic message is that it has power. I also emphasize its ability to receive communication from high-level teachers or loved ones in the Light at any time it chooses. Depending on my intuition about the spirit, I'll usually emphasize one strategy over the other until I sense it isn't working. Then I'll switch to the other. For example, a spirit that carries deep guilt might prefer to have a spirit teacher come for it rather than risk looking inside. For another spirit, it may feel too ashamed to have a loved one come forward, and so is more willing to look inside.

High-level guides from the Light are able to assist any spirit with each of the situations listed above. They will only give that help when the spirit I'm working with makes a free-choice request for their help. For the reasons listed above, however, it is unlikely that a spirit will initiate that contact on its own once it has entered Darkness. It is usually pulled in deeper, and finding its own way back to the Light seems to become increasingly more difficult. It is also unlikely that the spirit will have a serendipitous contact with a soul of Light that can bring it information or remind it of who it is. When it isn't the spirit's own fear or anger that keeps it trapped in Darkness, there are those in the hierarchy that are ready to step in to enforce the rules and deal harshly with those who disobey.

The thing to keep in mind is that even those higher-ups in the network are still souls. It is quite likely they have been in Darkness for some time and have become deeply imbued with the reality of Darkness. It may remember it is a soul, but gave up all hope and belief that there was a way back to the Light. Many of these spirits, though, do not even remember they are souls. They don't remember that they have within them their own Light. It's as though they disappeared into ignorance.

If you can engage them, they will still respond to the truth that they are created of Light and that they possess the power and freedom to return to the Light. This is their vulnerability. The Light is what a soul yearns for. It is what a soul seeks. When communicating to a dark soul, even those much higher in the network, this truth about their inner Light seems to strike a deep cord and often begins to resonate.

The challenge for the healer is to ask the right questions that will break through the spirit's indoctrination, ignorance, or fear. The right questions are ones that lead a spirit to say *yes* to receiving knowledge with the guarantee that it will be absolutely free to accept or reject it. The subtext here, and one that is not spoken, is that once the spirit receives knowledge, there will be no going back. It won't be able to un-know what it knows. This is why there are such strong attempts to block the healer's communication to these frontline spirits by those higher up the chain. They know once a soul has a taste of the Light, it will go if given the choice. And conversely, once a spirit has had contact with the Light, those souls higher up do not want it to come back because it may bring this information back to others. The dark souls do not want to risk contamination or a rupture in the hierarchy.

So, in dealing with dark souls, the Spirit Protocol is still the one to use and with the same first objective, i.e. facilitate the spirit's contact with the Light. It's just that with dark souls, they usually have more at stake and their entanglement is more complex than with benign or confused earthbound souls. Most dark souls risk punishment or retaliation for making direct contact with the Light. The higher up in the hierarchy you go, the more resistance you can expect. Just remember: they are still souls and they can reawaken to their own Divinity in any moment they choose, and this is true all the way to the top of the hierarchy. Our strength as healers in this position is that we offer to the dark souls the very thing they seek above all else, even if they are not aware of it at that moment. We know if they get a glimpse of it, and realize they can move into that Light, they will.

When we are engaged with such a hierarchy, it is not our job as healers to work our way up the chain of command in an attempt to free other souls. This kind of work could be undertaken by volunteers with a clear intent to assist these lost souls. In the clinical situation, however, the focus is on our clients, where disengaging from one of these networks may be a significant, but small part of the healing process.

When dealing with a dark hierarchy, the chain usually extends beyond the client's soul to those in Darkness who control the frontline spirits that have intruded or attached to the client. When I encounter a chain of dark souls like this, the objective is to work with each presenting spirit until we reach a point in the chain where 1) the higher-ups refuse any contact with the Light but agree to withdraw and sever their ties with my client, or 2) there is a complete shutdown of communication.

In the first case, where a dark soul agrees to withdraw and sever ties, the operating assumption is that all those lower down in the hierarchy will also obey that directive and be withdrawn from the client. This has been my experience. Once a point in the chain is reached where a dark soul refuses any contact with the Light but is willing, and has the authority, to sever all ties to the client, then I take that as a conclusion.

I'll go back to higher self and confirm that all the spirits did indeed leave. If higher self signals that they have, then we will go back to the area or issue where the block first occurred and continue from there. If higher self signals that not all spirits have left or withdrawn their attachment, then I'll start the protocol again. That is, determine whether or not the higher self can just remove it (them). If not, then communicate with the spirit directly. Determine whether it is alone or in a group. Begin steps to help it make contact with the Light or voluntarily leave. The strategy here is to work your way through a group or up the chain only as far as necessary in order to have all spirits disengage.

So, these are the suggestions I would keep in mind when you believe you are dealing with a dark soul:
- In whatever way you say it, communicate the message that if it is a soul, it carries within it its own soul-source energy and it has the power to safely prove this for itself.

- That any agreement made with Darkness or souls in Darkness is not valid and can be ended anytime the spirit chooses.
- That there are high-level teachers and/or loved ones that can come forward and communicate further information about the choices available to the spirit.
- Communicate to it that if such information is being blocked, it's because those in Darkness do no not want the spirit to know the truth.
- And as a soul, it has the right to override the block and allow communication from a spirit teacher or guide.

The bottom line is that a soul in Darkness does have the power to deal with all these situations, but it does not yet know or remember that when we first make contact during the healing session. The truth of its own power and inner Light is ultimately what will convince a soul that it is free to return to the Light. The role of the healer is to help the soul remember this truth by identifying and resolving any questions, fears, or threats that keep a spirit from looking inside.

The following dialogues are examples when I believe I am dealing with a dark soul as the blocker or source of a shutdown.

Engaging A Dark Soul: Example 1

TH To this one who is blocking: do you know yourself to be part of the self/soul I'm working with?
SP No finger lifts.
TH Do you believe you are separate from this soul?
SP Yes finger lifts.
TH Do you believe you are yourself a soul?
SP Hand lift.
TH To this one: if you are a soul, you will carry within you your own self/soul energy. Did you know that?
SP No finger lifts.
TH Would you be willing to look inside and see if you have that soul-source energy?
SP No finger lifts.
TH Does that scare you?
SP Yes finger lifts.
TH Are you afraid it will cause you pain?

Dealing with Souls in Darkness

SP   No finger lifts.
SP   Is there someone or something there that is threatening you?
SP   Yes finger lifts.
TH   If it's *someone*, first finger. If *something*, second finger can lift.
SP   Yes finger lifts.
TH   To this one: did you know you have the right to sever your connections to those threatening you and move to a safe place?
SP   No finger lifts.
TH   Would you be willing for information to be sent to you about this?
SP   Yes finger lifts.
TH   Higher self or a guide, I'm asking you to send this one information and knowledge about their right to sever ties to these other souls and move to a safe place in the Light.
__   No finger lifts.
TH   To this one: did you need to stop that information?
SP   Yes finger lifts.
TH   Did that start to trigger some pain for you?
SP   No finger lifts.
TH   Did those others threaten you to stop it?
SP   Yes finger lifts.
TH   You need to know they are threatening you because they do not want you to have this information. They know that if you receive this information, you will understand the choices available to you, and that you will go free. To this one: as a soul, it is your right to re-connect with your own soul-source energy and make your own decision about the Light. Do you wish to receive this information? If you do, it will be sent to you.
SP   Yes finger lifts.
TH   Higher self, please send this one information now about their own soul-source energy, and the choices they have available. Yes finger when that information has been received. Second finger if it is stopped again.
SP   Yes finger lifts.
TH   To this one: did you receive that information for yourself?
SP   Yes finger lifts.
TH   Are you willing now to look inside and find your own soul-source energy?
SP   Yes finger lifts.

TH	On three then. One… Two… Three. And to this one: look inside now, move your vision all the way to your center. See the Light you have there. You can touch that Light and remember who you are and your freedom to make your own choices. First finger when you have found that soul-source energy. Second finger if you do not.
SP	First finger lifts.
TH	To this one: did you find that Light inside?
SP	Yes finger lifts.
TH	Do you know you are free now to return to your own place in the Light?
SP	Hand lift.
TH	Are you willing to have a high-level teacher from the Light come forward and communicate to you about this?
SP	Yes finger lifts.
TH	I'm going to ask, then, that you turn toward the Light and as you do I'm asking that high-level teacher to come forward. First finger when you see them. Second finger if you do not.
SP	First finger lifts.
TH	I'm asking the teacher now to communicate to this one information and knowledge about themselves as a soul and their right to return home now to the Light. Communicate to this one about the loved ones who are waiting for them. And to this one: first finger when you receive this communication. Second finger if you do not.
SP	First finger lifts.
TH	To this one: did you receive that information all right?
SP	Yes finger lifts.
TH	Would you like to return now to your own place in the Light?
SP	Yes finger lifts.
TH	You can do that now. On three: one, two, three… And to this one: you can go now right to the teacher, right into that corridor of Light. Higher self, first finger when they have gone. Second finger if they do not.
HS	First finger lifts.

Engaging A Dark Soul: Example 2

TH	To this one who stepped in to block: are you part of this soul I'm working with?

	No finger lifts.
TH	Do you believe you are separate from this soul?
	Yes finger lifts.
TH	Do you believe you are yourself a soul?
SP	Yes finger lifts.
TH	Do you know you have your own soul-source energy inside?
SP	Yes finger lifts.
TH	Are you in touch with that Light right now?
SP	No finger lifts.
TH	Are you willing then to touch that Light now as long as it is safe?
SP	No finger lifts.
TH	Are you afraid of that Light?
SP	No finger lifts.
TH	Is there someone or something threatening you there to stay away from the Light?
SP	No finger lifts.
TH	Do you know about the Spirit Realm of Light?
SP	Yes finger lifts.
TH	Do you know you are free to return to the Light if you wish?
SP	Yes finger lifts.
TH	Is it your wish to remain in the Darkness?
SP	Yes finger lifts.
TH	Do you believe you will lose your power if you leave the dark?
SP	Yes finger lifts.
TH	Do you know how limited your power is there?
SP	No finger lifts.
TH	I think you know that if you exercise your power in ways that those above you don't like, they will stop you. Isn't that true?
SP	Yes finger lifts.
TH	It seems to me, then, that you're not so powerful after all. It's more like you do the bidding of those above you and you only have the power they allow. That doesn't sound very powerful to me at all. It sounds like you have power only as long as you do what you are told. Do you think that is true?
SP	Yes finger lifts.
TH	To this one: you do not have to live this way. You can be free of these others any time you choose. Did you know that?
SP	No finger lifts.

TH Did you make some kind of agreement or deal with those in Darkness?
SP Yes finger lifts.
TH To this one: as a soul, you have the absolute freedom to choose. You need to know that any agreement or contract made with those in Darkness is null and void. As a soul, you are free at any time, to end any agreements you made with those in Darkness. They haven't told you that, have they?
SP No finger lifts.
TH Would you be willing for a high-level teacher to come forward and communicate to you about the choices available?
SP No finger lifts.
TH Are you afraid about a teacher coming forward?
SP Yes finger lifts.
TH Would you be willing for a teacher to communicate this information just so you can hear it, but not see them?
SP Yes finger lifts.
TH On three then: one, two, three… and to the teacher, please communicate to this one mentally that information about itself as a soul, how there is freedom to end any deals or agreements with those in Darkness, and communicate to this one about their place in the Light and the loved who are waiting for them to return. Yes finger when that communication is complete. Second finger if it is stopped.
SP Yes finger lifts.
TH To this one: did you receive that communication all right?
SP Yes finger lifts.
TH Would you wish to end any agreements with those in Darkness and return now to your own place in the Light?
SP Yes finger lifts.
TH Would you like that teacher there to assist you?
SP Yes finger lifts.
TH I'm asking the teacher to step forward then. Yes finger when you see them. Second finger if you do not.
SP Yes finger lifts.
TH To this one: you can move right to the teacher on three. One, two, three… and just go now right to the teacher, right into that corridor of Light. Higher self, yes finger when they have gone, second finger if not.
HS Yes finger lifts.

Engaging A Dark Soul: Example 3

TH To this one who is blocking: do you know yourself to be part of this self and soul that I'm working with?
No response.
TH To this one we are here to help. Whether you are part of this soul or separate we are here to help. We are here to help everyone be free of pain fear and distress. To this one: as long as it's safe, are you willing to communicate with me?
No response.
TH To this one: since you needed to step in to stop this communication, I'm assuming that my contact in someway is upsetting or distressing to you. Is that true?
No response.
TH To this one: do you know yourself to be in violation of this soul I'm working with?
No finger lifts.
TH To this one: do you believe that you have some claim on this soul?
— Yes finger lifts.
TH Do you know your self to be a soul?
— Yes finger lifts.
TH Do you know you were created in the Light?
— Yes finger lifts.
TH Do you remember the Light you have inside?
— No finger lifts
TH To this one: if you are a soul, then you have your own soul-source energy? Do you know that?
— No finger lifts.
TH If you are a soul, you do have your own soul-source energy. Are you willing to look inside and see if that energy is there?
— No finger lifts.
TH Are you afraid of that Light?
— Yes finger lifts.
TH Are you afraid that if you touch that Light that it will harm or destroy you?
— Yes finger lifts.
TH To this one: whoever told you that has lied to you. That Light energy you carry inside is a life sustaining energy, not a destroying energy.

Those who told you that the Light would harm you do not want you to know about your own power and freedom. If you are a soul, then you do have the power to make your own decisions any time you wish to. They didn't tell you that did they?
— No finger lifts.
TH To this one: they do not want you to know that you have your own power. As long as they could keep you afraid of the Light they knew you would not re-connect with your own power and freedom. To this one: there is a high level teacher that can come forward and communicate information to you about the choices available to you. Are you willing for that teacher to come forward and communicate this information to you?
— No finger lifts.
TH Are you being threatened right now?
— Yes finger lifts.
TH To this one: it is your right to have this information and to know your freedom of choice. You have the freedom to choose if you want to receive information from the teacher. This teacher can also move you to a safe and protected place if you choose. You have this power. Are you willing for the teacher to communicate this knowledge to you?
— Yes finger lifts.
TH Just turn toward the Light, and I'm asking that teacher to step forward, staying a safe distance away, and communicate to you about your freedom to choose. Yes finger when you see that teacher.
— Yes finger lifts.
TH I'm asking the teacher now to communicate to this one information and knowledge about itself as a soul, its absolute freedom of choice. Help them to know that they have the right to return home to the Light. To this one: yes finger lifting when you have received that information, second finger if not.
— Yes finger lifts.
TH To this one: did you receive that information all right?
— Yes finger lifts.
TH Do you wish to return home to the Light and the loved ones waiting for you there?
— Yes finger lifts.
TH On three then you can move right to the teacher. Beginning, one,

two, three... Just move right to the teacher, right into that corridor of Light. Higher self, yes finger when that one has gone. Second finger if not

HS Yes finger lifts.

Shutdowns and Closing Dark Accesses

In the second case, where instead of reaching an agreement for dark souls to withdraw, you encounter a complete and persistent shutdown, the strategy then becomes one of forcible removal and the severing of any ties it has to the client's soul. This strategy is based on the understanding that for any attachment or intrusion by a dark soul—or any other kind of separate entity, for that matter—it must have an access, a yes from the soul, to engage it and begin its activities. When all communication with a dark soul shuts down, then the focus shifts from the spirit to the access or accesses it uses to stay present. The aim of the healing then is to find, close, and seal any access, whether that's an ego-state, a device, a hidden door, or whatever.

I have found that ego-states and etheric devices or energies are the most common ways a spirit accesses another soul. Sometimes, a spirit has gained access to a client through another spirit or entity that already has access. In this case the spirit or entity with the original access also has to be identified and the access dealt with.

Ego-states Used as Access

As conscious beings, ego-states can be engaged by other conscious beings. Even though the ego-state's consciousness may be very limited and restricted, it still has the capacity to understand and respond if approached in the correct way. It could be likened to a lock and key. In the case of dark souls, it appears that they have many tactics for eliciting an ego-state's response and engaging it. All the different tactics come down to two basic strategies – the carrot or the stick. The first one is that they offer the ego-state something it wants, needs, or finds attractive. It might be protection, or a stuffed animal, or a toy; it could be a weapon, or the promise of immortality; it could be companionship, or relief from pain. When an ego-state says yes to any of these offers, it is establishing a connection. It is opening the door and as long as the connection is intact the door remains open.

The second strategy dark souls use to open up the connection with an ego-state is through intimidation, terror, or threat. When an ego-state's experience, for example, involves intense feelings of terror or pain, the dark souls will use that terror and fear of pain against it and try to force the ego-state into submission. It is not unusual to find devices placed inside an ego-state, attached to it or nearby, that keep the ego-state frightened or immobilized. Instead of enticing an ego-state to accept an offer, the dark souls use the ego-state's vulnerability to bully their way in and take control.

When an ego-state is identified as an access for outside souls or entities, the healer switches to the Ego-state Protocol. The first step, again, is to have the ego-state make contact with the higher self and the Light. If this happens, then the ego-state itself will come to the knowledge that it can have spirits removed and sever all contacts with them. Sometimes it goes this smoothly. However, when an ego-state has been involved with dark souls, it is often more complicated.

This is where these two strategies by the dark souls come into play. When an ego-state refuses the Light, the question becomes: which strategy or strategies have the dark ones used with this ego-state to make the connection? This usually can be determined fairly quickly by determining whether the ego-state is 1) refusing the Light because it is being threatened in some way, or 2) because it is afraid of the Light itself—afraid that the Light will harm it or will take away something it needs or wants or that it will have to remember and feel its pain.

In the first case, when the ego-state is being threatened, I find the best strategy is to keep the ego-state's attention on its own power to connect with the Light and to make its own choices. It may need specific reassurance that, as part of the soul, it has the right to receive the Light and that it has the power to sever any connection to these dark souls if it chooses. This will usually come as quite a surprise to the ego-state. Often, it doesn't initially believe it. However, the ego-state can be offered immediate confirmation of this by the higher self. The higher self can also offer information about a place of Light and safety waiting for the ego-state, a place it can move to right now, where the dark souls will not follow it. When an ego-state is terrified and being threatened by dark souls, it can also be told that high-level helpers from the Light are ready to come and assist, if it will give permission.

It can be helpful to know the ego-state's situation so as to offer information that pertains directly to its own questions or fears. Sometimes the healer can provide the information that the ego-state needs to take the next step. Other times, the information will need to come from the higher self. I have found that it is most helpful to do both. I give an ego-state whatever reassurance I can about its ability to be free of pain. Then I communicate to the ego-state that its own higher self can confirm what I'm saying and give even more information about it.

Once an ego-state has been identified as an access, engaged, and brought into contact with the Light, it is asked to give permission to have the spirit(s) removed. Once the ego-state says yes, the higher self can break the dark soul's connection to the client. At that point, it can be removed or its ties to the soul severed, whether it likes it or not.

The power to do this is based on the soul's absolute freedom to choose. These external spirits gain access to a soul by engaging only a part of the soul. It's like finding a crack and creating a door to slip through. By identifying that door and closing it, the intruding spirit is denied permission to put its hooks anywhere. Once an access has been disabled or closed, the client (or the ego-state) can choose to have these spirits removed.

It is possible, however, that dark souls have more than one access. In fact, this is very often the case. This is one of their strategies: to find and/or create more accesses. They seem to do this in order to get a really powerful lock on a soul. Like a harpooned whale, the soul is pierced in many places and is slowly brought to a halt. The more access points they have, the more difficult it becomes for the soul to free itself. Also, the more accesses these dark souls have, the more control they can exercise in the person's inner world and the more freedom they have to expand and carry out their activities.

When spirits have more than one access, it's usually the case that those accesses will need to be found and closed as well. It's like going around the house and locking all the windows and doors. It's not going to work to force them out and then leave the doors open.

Once a spirit's accesses have been closed, it must leave, or the higher self can forcibly remove it. The higher self can usually carry out the removal itself, and sometimes does it with the aid of high-level guides. Sometimes, at this point, the spirit or spirits will acknowledge that the jig is up, and they will leave before the inevitable happens. It also happens during this process that these spirits begin to change their tune when they see their accesses drying up and realize they don't have all the power they thought they had. If you offer them another opportunity to find their own Light, they may take you up on it, once they understand the alternative is to be removed.

Other dark souls, however, fight to the end. They claim to have ownership of the client's soul, or claim some other right to be present. The higher self is asked to remove these spirits. If the removal doesn't happen, then the therapist knows that there is still an access or connection that wasn't found. Higher self is asked to review once again for "anyone or anything that is being used as an access." We know that the spirit must have an entrée; it can't just waltz in on its own. When it gets to this level of hidden devices and doors, then you also know you are dealing with entities that have been at this for a long time, not necessarily with your client, but then again, maybe so.

In the second case, where the ego-state has accepted someone or something it felt it needed or wanted, the situation is a little more complicated. In these cases, it is the ego-state itself that is refusing the Light based on its own perception or belief, and not because a separate soul is threatening it. (When the ego-state does start coming around, that's when you can expect the interference and threats to start.) The complication is that the ego-state's belief or perception is often the result of a deception or manipulation by dark souls in the beginning. In essence, the dark souls have been able to turn a part of the soul against itself. If, for example, a past-life ego-state is carrying deep guilt, and dark souls discover it, they may engage the ego-state by playing on that guilt, reinforcing it. They are reinforcing also the ego-state's fear of judgment and punishment to the point where you can almost guarantee that the ego-state will never go near the Light in the future. In such a case, the healer may need to strongly reassure the ego-state that it has already been forgiven and that the Light (God, Allah, Yahweh, the Divine) wants it to come home. And again, the ego-state can be given immediate information and confirmation of this by the higher self.

Another complication, when it is an ego-state itself refusing the Light, is its refusal is usually based on the ego-state's own unique experience of trauma, pain, fear, etc. It's that experience, in which it was created, that is also its vulnerability. That's where its pain is, or its fear, or its anger, or its confusion. It's the vulnerability that dark souls look for as they probe a person's soul.

The problem from a clinical point of view is that there are countless possible experiences from this life or a past life that may have led an ego-state to refuse the Light. As healers, we won't know initially what that experience may be, and so we cannot know where this particular ego-state is stuck and what information it needs to get free.

When I encounter an ego-state that refuses the Light, and it's not because of direct threats from the outside, then I assume that the ego-state is afraid. The most frequent fears include:
- Fear of remembering/reliving its pain
- Fear that the Light will harm or destroy it. (This is what it has been told.)
- Is deeply ashamed or feeling guilty and fears rejection by loved ones or by God.
- Fear of judgment or punishment.
- Afraid it is unworthy

The bottom line, when an ego-state is being used for access, is to find a way that will make it safe enough to say yes to a contact from the Light. This almost always creates a motivation for the ego-state to say no to any dark souls that they now realize have kept them ignorant and ensnared in Darkness.

Shutdowns and Closing Accesses: Example 1

    TH To this one who has come forward: do you know yourself to be part of this self and soul.

No response.

    TH To this one: is there some apprehension for you about communicating in this way directly?

No response.

    TH To this one who is blocking: we are here to help. Whether you are part of this soul or separate, we are here to help. That help is different depending on whether you are part of this soul or not. Either way, we can help. To this one: are you willing to have more information about this?

No response.

    TH To this one: it seems to me that something must frighten you very much if you cannot even risk receiving information. You don't have to believe any of it but at least you have a chance to consider it and make your own decision about it. Are you willing to have information sent to you and make your own decision?

No response.

TH Higher self, I know you can hear me even though the signals are blocked. I'm asking, higher self, that you look inside and find who or what this one is using to stay present here. First finger when you have found that, second finger if you do not.

HS First finger lifts.

TH Higher self, did you find someone or something being used as an access?

HS Yes finger lifts.

TH If it is someone, yes finger lifting, if something, the no finger can lift.

HS Yes finger lifts.

TH Higher self, please help that one come forward, and to this one: do you know yourself to be part of this self and soul I'm working with?

ES Yes finger lifts.

TH Are you aware of this one that is blocking?

ES Yes finger lifts.

TH Are you willing now for higher self to remove that one?

ES No finger lifts.

TH Is that one a friend of yours?

ES No finger lifts.

TH Do you believe you have to let them stay?

ES Yes finger lifts.

TH To this one: you don't have to let anyone stay. As part of this soul, you have the right to make the blocker leave. Did you know that?

ES No finger lifts.

TH Would you be willing to have information sent to you about this?

ES Yes finger lifts.

TH Higher self, I'm asking that you communicate to this one that knowledge and understanding about their right, as part of the soul, to make the blocker leave if they choose. To this one: first finger when you've received this communication, no finger if you do not.

ES First finger lifts.

TH To this one: did you receive that understanding all right?

ES Yes finger lifts.
TH Would you like that separate one there to be removed?
ES Yes finger lifts.
TH Higher self, I'm asking then that you find that separate one and escort them out of the self/soul. Yes finger when complete, second finger if there is a problem or block.
HS Yes finger lifts.
TH To this one I've been communicating with: does that feel better to you now?
ES Yes finger lifts.
TH Are you receiving some Light/Love energy for yourself now?
ES Yes finger lifts.
At this point, the therapist would continue with the Ego-state Protocol.

Shutdowns and Closing Accesses: Example 2

TH 8yo, who I was just communicating with: are you still able to communicate with me?

No response.

TH 8yo, is someone or something in the way there?

No response.

TH Higher self, are you still able to communicate with me?

No response.

TH To the one who has stepped forward here: are you willing to communicate with me as long as it is safe?

No response.

TH This one who is blocking: are you afraid of this kind of direct communication?

No response.

TH To this one: we are here to help. Whether you are part of this soul I'm working with or are separate, we're here to help everyone get free of pain and fear. To this one: there is a way to be free. If you are yourself a soul, then there are choices available to you. To this one: are you willing to have that information sent to you as long as there is nothing you are forced to do?

No response.

TH To this one: is there someone or something there that is threatening you?

No response.

TH Higher self, I know you are still able to hear me. I'm asking that you look inside and find who or what this one is using to stay attached here. Yes finger when you have found that, no finger if you do not.

No response.

TH I'm not aware of a signal. I'm going to assume, higher self, that you found some part of the soul involved here. I'm asking that you help that one come forward here with me. And to this one: as long as it's safe, are you willing to communicate with me?

No response.

TH To this one that higher self has identified. If you are part of this soul, you have the right to receive Light/Love energy and move to a place of safety. I want you to know that there is a way you can be released of all pain, hurt and fear. To this one: as long as it's safe, are you willing to communicate with me?

ES Yes finger lifts.

TH To this one: are you receiving Light for yourself there?

ES No finger lifts.

TH Would you like some Light/Love energy sent to you now?

ES Hand lift.

TH You can stop it if you need to. If you like it, you can bring it inside to whatever level is comfortable. It will be up to you. Are you willing to have that Light sent?

ES Yes finger lifts.

TH It will come on three then, one, two, three… and higher self send to this one the Light/Love/Warmth energy and to this one: let yourself feel that and you decide. If you like it you can bring it inside. Yes finger when you've received the Light, no finger if it doesn't come.

ES No finger lifts.

TH To this one: if you needed to stop that, yes finger lifting. If someone or something seemed to get in the way, the no finger can lift.

ES No finger lifts.

TH If it's someone, first finger. If something or some energy, then the no finger. If you don't know, the hand can lift.

ES First finger lifts.

TH Can you see who it is?

ES Yes finger lifts.

TH Is that one a friend of yours?

ES   No finger lifts.
TH   Do they scare you?
ES   Yes finger lifts.
TH   To this one: as part of this soul I'm working with, you have the right and power to make that one go away. You didn't know that, did you?
ES   No finger lifts.
TH   Would you like to have that one removed?
ES   Yes finger lifts.
TH   Higher self, are you able now to remove that one that was blocking?
HS   Yes finger lifts.
TH   I'm going to ask that you remove that one, and any other separate ones there. On three: one, two, three… and higher self, surround that separate one with Light and escort them out of the self/soul. Yes finger when that's complete, no finger if there's a problem or block.
HS   Yes finger lifts.
TH   And to this one I've been communicating with, is that one gone now?
ES   Yes finger lifts.
TH   And are you receiving that Light now for yourself?
ES   Yes finger lifts.
TH   Does that feel all right to you?
ES   Yes finger lifts.
TH   Did you decide to keep that Light for yourself?
ES   Yes finger lifts.
(Note: The Therapist would switch at this point to the Ego-State Protocol.)

Devices or Energies Used as Accesses

Besides ego-states, the most frequent accesses used by dark souls are what I call devices and energies. When there has been a shut down, and the higher self is asked to look inside and find the access point a spirit(s) is using to stay attached, it will signal that it has found something. I will ask higher self whether it is some kind of device/object or more like an energy. These two categories are almost always sufficient to start the identification process. I will talk more about these devices and energies in Chapter 14. The point to keep in mind right now is that these phenomena are frequently involved in allowing a spirit access to a person's psyche.

11

The ET/Dimensional Protocol

Incarnate Souls: Some Human, Some Not

Sometimes, when the higher self reviews a client's problem area or finds the source of a block, it communicates that someone is involved, but it is not someone who is part of the client's self/soul. It is a separate entity. The last chapter dealt with one kind of separate entity that could be interfering or intruding on a client. That was spirits. There are other kinds of separate entities besides spirits, however, that can be interfering with a client and causing problems. I divide these entities into two categories that I label extraterrestrial and dimensional.

These are functional terms that I have found useful within a clinical framework. You might even think of them as two ends of a spectrum ranging from visible beings to invisible, from physical to etheric. I use the term *extraterrestrial* to refer to beings that are souls incarnate. They possess a physical body and/or are able to operate in the physical reality, either directly or remotely. This would include such phenomena as alien abduction, visits by the men in black, some UFO sightings, and physical encounters with alien beings.

I use the term *dimensional* to refer to beings that exist in other dimensions of consciousness and reality that are not physical. Intrusion by these entities seems to occur at a mental, psychic, or etheric level. This kind of activity can affect a person psychologically, emotionally, and even physically, but the disturbance is originating at a level of consciousness, not in the physical body. I think of these dimensional beings more as nonphysical. However, some of them appear able to move through dimensions even to the point of manifesting in a physical body and then dematerializing at will. Examples of dimensional beings would include elfin or gnome-like beings, shadow people, phantoms, or the jinn.

In general, I take the view that these activities and intrusions, carried out at unconscious levels, constitute a violation of my client's free choice as a soul incarnate. Once I uncover the presence of extraterrestrial or dimensional beings, the most efficient thing, in my view, is to establish direct communication and ask that they respect the soul's choice and disengage. If these beings recognize the soul's free choice, and often they do, then they will usually withdraw voluntarily. If they refuse, though, I still know that my client, as a soul, will have the final say. It may take some work to get there.

The important thing to keep in mind is that these beings, as with spirits, must have some access, some permission, within the soul.

Identification

I know very little about these different kinds of beings, their different activities and purposes, or the dimensions in which they exist. I only know what has presented in my work with clients, and that has been plenty. I've encountered enough different entities and phenomena to know that my perspective and knowledge about these realities is limited, very limited. What I do know is based on clinical experience and observation understood primarily from a therapeutic perspective. The problem in classifying these beings isn't that there are too few cases to study. The problem is that there are far too many, and they appear to involve many different kinds or species of beings.

In my opinion, we don't know enough about these beings yet to even establish a viable system of classification. There are other cultures that do recognize and classify different kinds of beings. In our Western culture, however, scientists and academicians don't even recognize the existence of these beings, at least not out loud. From their point of view, there's nothing to classify. How does the empirical paradigm classify a being, for example, that appears able to step from a non-physical dimension into our physical dimension, and step back out again, literally appearing and disappearing before our eyes? How do we classify beings that are able to psychically invade a person's mind and carry out activities at a cellular level for the purpose of harvesting information? How do we classify beings who are intervening with a client at a physical level, transporting him or her from their present location to another and then returns them, and induces amnesia for the entire experience. How do we classify entities, called shadow people, who appear to exist in a dimension just adjacent to our own, but are only seen as two-dimensional reflections passing along the walls and sometimes engaging a person directly?

The fact is that our own boundaries of thought and definition begin to blur when we try to define many of these phenomena within our empirical science and framework of dualistic thinking.

A second reason I know so little about these different beings – besides not having the conceptual framework – is that studying them is not the aim of the healing process. Just like with spirits, it is natural to ask who these beings are, where they come from, and what they are about. These are, in fact, critical questions. They need to be asked and addressed, but they are not the questions we ask as healers. Our clients do not come to us to act as research subjects. So, when encountering separate beings that are engaged with a client at unconscious levels, the aim usually is to expose their presence and bring their activities and intrusions to an end.

The investigation of these beings, then, within a clinical context, is focused on understanding them only to the extent necessary to negotiate their withdrawal from the client. If that agreement can be reached with these beings in just one session, then there's no need to find out more about them. If they refuse to disengage, we will need to ask questions and gather information. The questions, though, will be focused on what needs to happen to obtain their agreement to leave or, if necessary, close their accesses and forcibly remove them.

Finally, I know so little about these different beings because most do not want us to know. Gerod once described the person/self as the soul's focus of consciousness while incarnate, and therefore, he said, the conscious self exercises a great deal of the soul's power in his or her freedom to choose. This is one of the main reasons, I believe, that these beings so often want to conceal their presence and activities from the conscious self. A person won't choose to evict them if he or she doesn't even know they are present in the first place. Just like with discarnate souls, however, once their presence is revealed, it can lead quickly to their having to withdraw from the client.

This desire for secrecy by outside beings involved with a client has always set off alarms for me. First of all, it raises red flags because these interactions are happening to and affecting my clients without his or her conscious awareness and consent. My question is: who does business this way? Why the lack of transparency? And second, most of these beings appear to have the capacity to communicate directly to humans at a conscious level, but choose not to. It's another red flag. If everything is on the up and up, then why not be communicating to the conscious person about their presence and what it is they desire?

Therapeutic Approach to External Beings

Fortunately, from a clinical point of view, we usually don't need to know who these beings are in order to bring their interference or intrusion to an end. What we need to know, however, is whether we are dealing with souls or not because this will determine what treatment approach we take. Not surprisingly—given the similarities with spirits—the protocol for dealing with extraterrestrial or dimensional beings is structured in the same way as the one for dealing with spirits. That is, once the involvement by an external being or beings is identified, the next step is to determine if they are souls. If they are, then the next step is to facilitate their contact with the Light and obtain an agreement to end their activities and involvement with the client. If they refuse to leave, or they shut down communication, then steps are taken to identify and close their accesses and then sever their energetic ties with the client.

In my mind, one of the major distinctions between working with a spirit and an extraterrestrial/dimensional being centers on the issue of incarnation. Spirits, as Gerod called them, are *discarnates*. They do not possess a physical body. Extraterrestrial and dimensional beings, however, as I conceive it, exist in a defined universe that has its own rules and limited consciousness by which a soul becomes bound when choosing to incarnate, just as humans do. In other words, there are rules. They too appear to possess a distinct body of some kind – whether physical, etheric, or some other dimension – and that body would have to be shed in order for the being to enter into the Spirit Realm of Light.

This move can happen when dealing with an extraterrestrial or dimensional being. That is, once it awakens to its own soul, it sheds its body and returns to the Spirit Realm of Light. Most often, though, it would appear that these beings continue to exist in their own realms and go about their own business after they have disengaged from the client. It is also likely that they are involved with other humans and will be continuing those contacts and activities as well, just as they had been with the client. A contact with the Light may change that, as I described above, but not necessarily.

This distinction as incarnate beings can be important in the healing process when it comes to negotiating their withdrawal from the client. First of all, moving to the Spirit Realm of Light won't be used as an incentive for these beings to sever their ties with the client. Instead, the aim will be on helping these beings 1) recognize the client's rights as a soul, 2) recognize themselves as souls if they do not already, and 3) to voluntarily withdraw. This is certainly easier on the client and more efficient in terms of the healing process. I also believe it is easier on these beings, which is why they so often do withdraw voluntarily.

The Protocol

The protocol for dealing with extraterrestrial or dimensional being, as I've said, is very similar as the one for dealing with spirits. These are the seven basic steps of the protocol:

1) Identify separate entity as a soul.
2) Determine if there are others.
3) Facilitate that being's (or that group's) contact with its own inner Light and/or a spirit teacher.
4) If refused, give all reassurance that spirit teacher will only communicate information. If still refused, try to identify why it is refusing so that the reason can be addressed specifically.
5) Once contact with Light is made, begin negotiations for these beings to disengage.
6) Facilitate the disengagement, and confirm with higher self.
7) If still refusing, begin protocol for identifying the being's access.
8) Once gone, find and close any accesses and remove anything left behind.

1. Identify as separate soul.

When the higher self has identified someone that needs to be addressed, the Identification Protocol is used to determine more specifically who it is—part of the self/soul or separate? If separate, is it a soul, a created entity (a non-soul), or an ego-state from another soul? And if it is itself a soul, is it a spirit or a soul incarnate? This, again, is where language becomes very tricky.

When speaking of humans, it is easy to use the distinction between discarnate and incarnate, having a physical body and not having a physical body. When talking about incarnate souls, however, it seems that what constitutes *incarnate* can include other levels of reality that are not pure spirit, but are not necessarily physical either in terms of how we define physical.

The important thing in the healing process is, first, not whether the intruding beings are discarnate or incarnate. The important thing is to know whether we are dealing with a soul or group of souls. This information will determine how we approach these beings. If we are dealing with a soul, then we can assume they carry within them—whether aware of it or not—their own soul-source energy and the capacity to know the Light directly.

2. Is there more than one?

Once an entity is identified as a separate soul, it is asked whether there are any others there with it. What is implied in the question is whether there are other beings present that are of the same kind or part of the same group as the one communicating. If the being says there are others, it cannot be assumed that they are all of the same kind. It's possible that there is some combination of ego-states, spirits, extraterrestrials, dimensional beings, or external ego-states.

When there is more than one present, the higher self can help determine how many are part of the soul and how many are separate. Of those that are separate from the client, how many are souls? If all the beings are of the same kind, then usually all can be treated as a group. If there are different kinds of beings present, then they may need to be worked with as sub-groups.

3. Initiate contact with the Light or a spirit teacher

At this point, the therapist often won't know yet whether he or she is dealing with a spirit, an extraterrestrial, or a dimensional being. So far, it doesn't matter. The therapeutic strategy and aim is the same whether we are dealing with a spirit or an incarnate soul, i.e., elicit its agreement to have a direct contact with the Light. The two strategies for accomplishing this are also the same as with spirits: either direct the being(s) to look inside for its own Light, or have it allow a spirit teacher from the Light to come forward and communicate with it directly. If a soul(s) makes this contact with the Light in whatever way is appropriate for it, then it usually comes to an understanding that it is in violation of the client's soul. It's as though they are given the big picture and understand that they cannot violate a soul's free choice without serious repercussions for themselves. In all likelihood, this contact with the Light will lead to the separate soul's cooperation in removing whatever it may have placed within the client's soul and then to disengaging from the client.

4. If refused, give all reassurance that spirit teacher will only communicate information. If still refused, try to identify why it is refusing so that the reason can be addressed specifically.

Within the healing process, whenever an extraterrestrial or dimensional being refuses contact with the Light, it raises the question of *why*? Assuming it is a soul, why would an intelligent being refuse contact with a source of infinite love and knowledge? Why refuse contact with its own creator? The most frequent answers I have found are: 1) it has forgotten who it is and doesn't remember the Light; 2) the knowledge threatens its culture or the power structures of the society within which it exists; 3) it believes the Light will destroy it, or 4) it is being threatened or blocked from the Light.

If a separate being refuses to know whether it is a soul, or it knows that it is a soul, but refuses any contact with the Light, I will again give it all the reassurance I can that we are here to help, and that we are only asking that it receive information about the choices available to it. I reassure the being that the Light will not force it to do anything. What is implied but not spoken here is that the Light will force a being to disengage from my client's soul if that is what my client chooses.

This last part is not usually stated outright because, from the point of view of these beings, it implies a negative outcome, and it may just threaten them and trigger a resistance. To avoid this unnecessary conflict, I will wait until later to deal with the issue of the soul's free choice. The truth will become clear soon enough when a being finally does make that contact with the Light. What will also become clear, as well, is that there are consequences for violating another soul's free choice. So, the issue of force becomes a moot point.

When all reassurance fails, I will attempt to ascertain the reason for such an adamant refusal to what, for a soul, would be a risk-free proposition. The four reasons listed above will guide my questions as I probe to understand what the resistance is based on. If I can determine the reason, then usually I can offer a resolution to any objection, threat, or fear the particular beings may have. Again, it's the same approach as with spirits. In my experience, however, these extraterrestrial /dimensional beings seem to have less resistance than spirits to an initial contact with the Light.

5. Once contact with Light is made, begin negotiations for these beings to disengage.

Once an extraterrestrial or dimensional being has re-awakened to its own Light or made contact with a spirit teacher, the next step is to negotiate its (their) disengagement from the client. Once they've made contact with the Light, it is usually a simple matter to elicit their agreement to leave. At that point, they seem to recognize the client's absolute freedom to choose and, whether in full cooperation or reluctantly, they do disengage.

My impression is that this experience of the Light and knowledge alters the being's consciousness and that it will have ongoing positive ramifications for the particular soul or souls I'm dealing with. This often involves these beings taking this knowledge back to those who sent them or to the larger group of which they are a part. Whatever ramifications there might be for these souls, however, is not a clinical concern. Most of the time the therapist and client won't know what the long-term effects are for these beings. I assume, however, that any time a separate soul makes contact with the Light there will be positive results, or at least no negative results.

6. Facilitate the disengagement, and confirm with higher self.

If the beings engaged with the client have made contact with the Light, then they usually leave voluntarily. It is still good, I think, to make this a formal step. Spirits can get to this point in the process and still balk when it comes to taking this final step. The healer communicates directly to one of the beings and confirms that all are prepared to leave. The beings are asked to begin the disengagement and higher self is asked to confirm that when it is complete.

7. If still refusing, begin protocol for identifying the being's access.

Up to this point, the therapeutic approach and protocol is the same for spirits, extraterrestrials, and dimensional beings. As souls, they are beings of Light and when they reconnect to that Light, they usually will withdraw voluntarily because they now recognize and respect the soul's absolute freedom to choose. Others leave because they know that, without accesses, they will be forcibly removed.

In some cases, it's quite possible that the therapist may lead a separate being through these steps and never know whether he or she had been dealing with a spirit, an extraterrestrial, or a dimensional being because it left immediately after a contact with the Light. In my experience, all extraterrestrial and dimensional beings, as souls, have had the capacity either to become aware of their own inner Light, just as spirits can, or receive contact from a spirit teacher, or both.

There are other extraterrestrial and dimensional beings that, like spirits, will refuse to end their activities or their contacts with the client. For example, if a spirit refuses contact with the Light, it may be because of guilt and fear of punishment in the spirit realm. If an extraterrestrial refuses, however, it may be because their contact with a client involves a project that's been ongoing since the client's early childhood, or over lifetimes of the client's soul, or the client may be part of a genetic study carried out over generations. When discovered and confronted, extraterrestrials are not very quick to give up such investments just because the therapist says they have to. The same can apply to dimensional beings. For example, they may have been carrying on a lifelong relationship with the client at an etheric level and resist any attempts to end it.

In these cases, the protocol still remains basically the same as the Spirit Protocol. The therapist knows that any separate being must have some kind of permission or access in order to engage and carry out their activities with the client. So, if these beings refuse to leave voluntarily once they have been detected and confronted, the primary strategy for removing them is to find their points of access and to close them. It could be a child ego-state that allows them in, or a part of the soul that has lived incarnations in their system. (Gerod once said that a particular client I was working with might feel "he belongs more with them than he belongs on earth.") The access could also be an etheric device or energy placed within the soul to create a door through which these beings can come and go.

In the computer world, a programmer will sometimes create what's called a backdoor into a program where only he or she knows the code. If at some point a company suffers a catastrophic failure of the program with the potential for the loss of all its data, the programmer has a way to access the program and make the necessary corrections. This kind of hidden access can also be used, of course, for more nefarious purposes.

Some of these beings do somewhat the same thing. During interactions with a soul, they leave devices and energies which can be re-accessed later, even lifetimes later, by those with the key. The aim in Soul-Centered Healing, then, is to find these points of access and withdraw the permissions or remove device/energies, and close off the openings.

When confronted with adamant refusal, I consider most of these beings to be operating at some level of Darkness. They have either forgotten the Light and who they are as souls, or they have some justification about why it's all right for them to interfere with humans in such secretive and traumatic ways. Still others, I think, are evil, and some of them appear to be in league with evil spirits. Their intent is to enslave the soul by force, using techniques as varied as those used by dark souls.

When extraterrestrial or dimensional beings still refuse to communicate and/or disengage from the client, the next step in the protocol will be to identify and close down any accesses these beings have to the client. Again, just as with spirits, once the accesses are closed, then these beings can be forcibly removed, either by higher self or with assistance from spirit guides.

The accesses can be ego-states, spirits (though not usually), etheric or physical implants, energy devices, or parts of the soul being held in the intruders' dimension of reality. The procedure in these cases is to use the identification protocol to determine these accesses one by one.

8. Once gone, find and close any accesses and remove anything left behind.

When negotiating the withdrawal of extraterrestrial or inter-dimensional beings, one thing to keep in mind is to make sure that all separate beings do leave or are removed, and that all devices and implants are removed as well. When dealing with cooperative beings that have made contact with the Light, they are usually agreeable to this clearing. Even so, it's a good idea to check out directly with higher self and/or guides whether it has been done. If all accesses have been found and closed, then the client can expect that there will be no further interference or intrusion by these beings. If there is, then it means that an access was missed and needs to be found and addressed. You shouldn't be surprised when involvement by outside beings requires this kind of flushing out. Like with dark souls, extraterrestrial and dimensional beings at times also have established more than one access, especially if they have been involved with a soul over lifetimes.

In cases where the external beings had to be removed, the higher self should definitely review and find any accesses that may remain and which could be used at a later time.

Finally, when I am dealing with these beings, I assume from the first contact with them that I am dealing with a soul or souls. I treat them as beings of Light who have forgotten their source, or become ensnared in a dark reality. As souls, I also know I can point the way to what they ultimately seek, their source in the Light, just like us.

It may be possible that there are soulless beings created by the Darkness itself, I doubt it. Darkness as I understand it would not possess this level of creativity or the desire to create something more powerful than itself. I'm not sure what Gerod would say about it. However, besides souls, there are, what I call, *created entities*. I'll talk about these in Chapter. 13.

Identifying Extraterrestrial and Inter-Dimensional Beings

Before giving examples of the protocol, there is another important factor that often comes into play when dealing with extraterrestrial and dimensional beings. That factor is the information that comes from a client either prior to engaging these beings or once they have presented in the healing process. Sometimes, what a client shares about his or her anomalous experiences make it appear likely that separate beings are present. The information may also give some indication of what kind of beings they are—spirit, extraterrestrial, or inter-dimensional. Most of the time, the information is subtle, and vague. It may come from dreams that the client is reporting, odd occurrences they remember, flashback experiences, nagging impressions, etc.

Except in the most obvious cases, however, one or two indicators are not going to provide a sufficient basis for making judgments or reaching conclusions. One dream, for example, or a couple of memory fragments may raise suspicions. It usually requires an accumulation of these clues or indicators, however, to get a reliable sense that there is involvement by separate beings. The client, for example, might report a recurring dream in which the same or similar figures appear and which feel *alien* ("not me") to the client. It may be a series of strange occurrences beginning in childhood and continuing for years, even into the present. It might be memories of waking up in strange places, like waking up in the kitchen or the driveway instead of one's own bed. Even with these indicators, though, it remains a hypothesis, but one which the therapist is ready to test out at the appropriate time.

In being aware of these indicators, the therapist will be more prepared on *how* to engage these beings should they present, either directly, through the sharing of an ego-state, or in some other manner. Depending on what the client reports, the situation may even call for immediate action. If the client is reporting distress, feelings of terror or agitation in relation to such phenomena presenting in dreams or thinking back on certain experiences, the therapist can communicate with higher self on whether it is a situation which needs to be addressed soon, or even immediately.

These subtle clues and indicators are the kinds of things a therapist learns to pick up on. It may be a certain tone of voice, a tensing of the body, or the face suddenly becoming flushed. As therapists, when we see these clues, and they accumulate, we pretty much know it's an issue, which at some point, will need to be addressed in the therapy. The same is true about these clues and indicators concerning separate beings. Through experience, the therapist develops a sense and intuition about these phenomena and how they present with different clients. It's not something that can be taught just conceptually.

Is Contact Past or Ongoing?

Finally, there is another important consideration in dealing with ET/dimensional contact. If this kind of material comes forward during a session indicating contact with alien or dimensional beings, then it has to be determined whether that contact occurred in the past and at some point, came to an end, or whether it is ongoing in the present.

If a client has had contact and involvement with other beings, but it has ended, then it can be treated like other past trauma, i.e., identify any parts still carrying those experiences, and then help them move through the sharing, release and integration process. If, for example, a five year-old ego-state shares a memory of an encounter with several strange beings in which he or she was terrified, it can have a release of the terror and move to its place of integration just as with other ego-states.

If the client's contact with these beings has ended, then the focus of healing, as far as these beings are concerned, will be on dealing with those past traumas as they present in the healing process (most often as ego-states). It is not unusual, for example, to find ego-states created out of such encounters. It's not even that the beings involved were acting in a hostile or threatening manner, (though that happens too). It can just be the shock of the encounter itself, an experience in which ego-consciousness is forced outside the box and has no psychology or understanding, no context, for what is happening. This can be so profoundly confusing, threatening, or terrifying at an ego level that the experience is dissociated. In addition, some of these beings appear able to intentionally create a dissociative state in a person in order to carry out their activities, and when finished, return the person to "normal" consciousness, with no memory of what occurred in that other state of consciousness.

If the higher self answers *yes* to the question of whether there is ongoing contact by these beings, then most of the time this will become a priority. The reason is that if these beings are still actively engaged with the client, they then will react to the healing process as it approaches areas that involve them.

When this is the case, that there is ongoing contact, I anticipate having direct communication with these beings at some point to negotiate their withdrawal from my client. My attitude usually is *the sooner, the better*. If not, I might wind up having these beings undermine or undo everything my client and I accomplish from one session to the next.

It is also at this point of identifying contact by external beings that you are likely to encounter a block. Just as with spirits, they perceive the healing process as a threat. Whatever kinds of ET/dimensional beings are involved with a person, most of the time they do not want their activities exposed or ended. That's when they see the process as getting too close. They will attempt to block communication between healer and the client's higher self, or between the healer and an ego-state that they have been using for access. They see the process as interfering with, or threatening to ruin, their activities and so they react to protect what they see as their turf.

Sometimes, one of these beings will come forward and communicate directly when asked. At other times, you have to work your way to them by identifying those parts of the self or those devices that are being used by them as an access.

An added complication to all this is that these external beings may have had contact and involvement with the client's soul in past or different lifetimes and it is these aspects of the soul that are being re-engaged by these beings. They, too, will be worked with just as with other past-life ego-states, only in their case, it may involve those parts saying no to these other beings with whom they feel so connected. Finally, as I mentioned earlier, the client's soul may even have lived in that system in another incarnation. That part may feel aligned with these beings and so welcomes these contacts. From within its limited consciousness, then, it is a willing participant in these contacts.

ET/Dimensional Protocol: Example 1

TH   7yo, were you able to share that time about what happened?

7yo   No finger lifts.

TH   Did you need to stop the sharing? If so, first finger lifting. If someone or something else seemed to get in the way, the second finger can lift. If you're not sure, the hand can lift.

7yo   Second finger lifts.

TH   If it's someone, first finger. If something or some kind of energy, second finger lifting. If you're not sure, the hand can lift.

7yo   Second finger lifts.

TH   Higher self, I'm going to ask that you look inside and locate the source of that block. First finger when you have found it, second finger if not.

HS   First finger lifts.

TH   Higher self, if it is someone, first finger: if some thing or some energy, second finger can lift. If you're not sure, the hand can lift.

HS   Second finger lifts.

TH   Higher self, if it is something like a device or object, first finger

The ET/Dimensional Protocol

lifting. If it is more like an energy, the second finger can lift.
HS Yes finger lifts.
TH Higher self, if that device is made of self/soul energy, first finger. If it is separate from self/soul, second finger lifting.
HS Second finger lifts.
TH 7yo, are you aware of that device there?
7yo Yes finger lifts.
Cl I'm getting a picture of this box. It's small and reddish in color.
TH 7yo, is that correct? Is there a box there?
7yo Yes finger lifts.
TH 7yo, are you willing for us to remove that?
7yo Yes finger lifts.
TH Higher self, I'm asking that you use the Light to dissipate and remove that device. On three: one, two, three… First finger when that has been removed, second finger if it is not.
HS Second finger lifts.
TH Higher self, were you stopped from removing that device?
HS Yes finger lifts.
TH Higher self, if someone got in the way first finger. If some thing, second finger lifting. If you are not sure, the hand can lift.
HS First finger lifts.
TH Higher self, I'm asking that you identify that one and help them come forward here. To this one: are you one who is part of this self/soul?
__ No finger lifts.
TH If you are yourself a soul, first finger lifting. If you are a created entity or from another soul, the second finger can lift. If you are not sure, the hand can lift.
__ Hand lifts.
TH To this one: are you willing to know whether you are, or are not, a soul?
__ Yes finger lifts.
TH On three, then, that information will be sent to you. One, two, three, and higher self or a high level guide, please send to this one that information and knowledge about whether they are, or are not, a soul. And to this one: first finger when you have received that information. Second finger if you do not.
__ First finger lifts.
TH To this one: did you receive that information all right?

	Yes finger lifts.
TH	If it seems that you are a soul, first finger lifting, if a created entity or from another soul, the second finger can lift. If you're still not sure, the hand can lift.
	First finger lifts.
TH	To this one: are you aware now that you are in violation of this soul I'm working with?
	Yes finger lifts.
TH	Are you willing then to remove this box and to sever all your connections to this soul?
	Yes finger lifts.
TH	Are you also willing now to remove any other devices or energies you have placed with this soul?
	Yes finger lifts.
TH	On three then. One, two, three. To this one: I'm asking now that you remove any devices or energies that you have placed here, and when that is complete, that you sever your ties here with this self /soul. Higher self, first finger when they have withdrawn, second finger if they do not.
HS	First finger lifts.
TH	Higher self, I'm going to ask that you review once more for anyone or anything else that might be used as an access. First finger when that review is complete, second finger if there is a problem.
HS	First finger lifts.
TH	Higher self, did you find anyone or anything else yet that can be used as an access?
HS	No finger lifts.
TH	Higher self, I'm going to ask that you have 7yo come back here with me, and 7yo, are you willing again now to communicate with me?
7yo	Yes finger lifts.
TH	Have those other ones gone now?
7yo	Yes finger lifts.
TH	Is that all right with you that they are gone?
7yo	Yes finger lifts.
TH	7 yo, are you willing again now to share what you have to share?
7yo	First finger lifts.
TH	On three, then one, two, three… Just share here now what needs to be shared… right to the present…

ET/Dimensional Protocol: Example 2

The following is another example where the access used by external beings has to be found and closed off before they are removed.

- TH To the higher self, first finger lifting when that review is complete, second finger if it is stopped.
- HS First finger lifts.
- TH To the higher self: did you find someone or something involved in these feelings of terror that Mark has talked about?
- HS Yes finger lifts.
- TH Higher self, first finger if it's someone, second finger if it's something or some energy.
- HS First finger lifts.
- TH Higher self, is this one part of the self/soul?
- HS No finger lifts.
- TH Is this one itself a soul?
- HS Yes finger lifts.
- TH Are you in agreement higher self that I communicate with this one?
- HS Yes finger lifts.
- TH And to this one: are you willing now to communicate with me?
- __ Yes finger lifts.
- TH To this one: do you know you are separate from this soul that I'm working with?
- __ Yes finger lifts.
- TH Do you know you are yourself a soul?
- __ Yes finger lifts.
- TH Do you know, then, about the Light you have inside you?
- __ No finger lifts.
- TH Are you willing for a high-level teacher from the Light to send you information about this?
- __ No finger lifts.
- TH Do you know you have been in violation of this soul I'm working with?
- __ Yes finger lifts.
- TH Are you willing now, and any others with you, to withdraw from contact with this person?
- __ No finger lifts.

TH Higher self, are you and guides able now to remove these beings?
HS No finger lifts.
TH Higher self, I'm asking that you look inside and find who or what these beings are using for access. First finger, when you have found that, second finger if you do not.
HS First finger lifts.
TH Higher self, if it's someone being used for access, first finger; if something, second finger lifting.
HS First finger lifts.
TH Higher self, is this one part of the self/soul?
HS Yes finger lifts.
TH Please help them come forward here with me. To this one: do you know yourself to be part of this self and soul I'm working with?
__ Yes finger lifts.
TH Are you one first created in this present life of Mark's?
__ No finger lifts.
TH Are you from a past or different lifetime?
__ Yes finger lifts.
TH Are you a male?
__ Yes finger lifts.
TH Are you an adult?
__ Yes finger lifts.
TH Do you know your name?
__ Yes finger lifts.
TH Is it all right for us to know your name?
__ Yes finger lifts.
TH Just say the name on three, then. One, Two, three… just say the name right here to the conscious mind. First finger when that's complete, second finger if it's stopped or blocked.
__ First finger lifts.
TH Mark, did you receive that.
Ma Benjamin came to mind.
TH To this one: is your name Benjamin?
Bn Yes finger lifts.
TH Benjamin, do you know about these other beings?
Bn Yes finger lifts.
TH Do you like it when they contact you?
Bn No finger lifts.

TH Did you know Benjamin that as part of this soul you have the right to make these beings leave and not come back? Did you know that?
Bn No finger lifts.
TH Benjamin, are you willing to receive some information about this and the choices available to you?
Bn Yes finger lifts.
TH Higher self, I'm asking that you communicate to Benjamin now this information about himself, his absolute freedom and right to end all contact with these beings. Benjamin, first finger when you've received this communication, second finger if not.
Bn First finger lifts.
TH Benjamin, did you receive this communication all right?
Bn Yes finger lifts.
TH Would you like the higher self to remove these beings?
Bn Yes finger lifts.
TH To this separate one: with Benjamin's choice, you will have to sever contacts with this soul. You can do that on your own, or you will be removed.
ET. No finger lifts.
TH Higher self, on three, I'm asking that you remove these ones, severing their contact here with Benjamin and the soul. Beginning, one, two, three… First finger when that is complete; second finger if there's a problem.
HS First finger lifts.
TH Higher self, were you able to remove them all right?
HS Yes finger lifts.
TH Higher self, do you think that Benjamin is the most appropriate one to work with now for sharing and release?
HS Yes finger lifts.

In this example, the Ego-State Protocol would be used with Benjamin to help him share his experience and have a release. This is most likely the point at which the therapist will be given some information about these beings, and possibly be able to make some determination about what kind of beings are involved. Regardless of how little or how much is shared, though, the important step is in Benjamin having a full release and integrating within the soul. This is a strong assurance that these beings will no longer have their access. If Benjamin were not found and resolved, it's very possible that these beings would make another approach to Benjamin in this lifetime or another and exploit again his original vulnerability.

ET/Dimensional Protocol: Example 3

TH Higher self, Sarah and I have talked at a conscious level about this dream she had last night about several figures coming into her room. Are you aware of this dream, higher self?
HS Yes finger lifts.
TH Higher self, are these figures part of Sarah's self/soul?
HS No finger lifts.
TH They are separate from the soul. Is that correct?
HS Yes finger lifts.
TH Higher self, if this was a dream Sarah had *about* these beings, first finger lifting. If they were actually present, the no finger can lift.
HS No finger lifts.
TH Higher self, are they present right now?
HS No finger lifts.
TH Are they observing us now?
HS Yes finger lifts.
TH If they were present physically last night, first finger, if it was at a psychic or etheric level, second finger. If it's not clear, the hand can lift.
HS Second finger lifts.
TH Higher self, if I should communicate with them directly right now, first finger lifting. If not, the no finger can lift.
HS First finger lifts.
TH Higher self, please make that contact now, and to this one who has been observing, are you willing to communicate with me?
__ Yes finger lifts.
TH Is this correct that you are separate from this person I'm working with?
ET Yes finger lifts.
TH Were you in contact with this person last night?
__ Yes finger lifts.
Sa I'm starting to feel this sensation like energy in my brain.
TH Is it painful, Sarah?
Sa No. It doesn't hurt. It's like a tingling.

TH To this one: are you yourself a soul? If so the yes finger, if you're a created entity of some kind or a part from another soul, the no finger can lift. If none of these fit, the hand can lift.
ET Yes finger lifts.

12

Protocol for External Ego-States

Another kind of entity you might encounter in working with a client is an ego-state, but one that has come from another soul. It appears that an ego-state from one person (soul) can cross the boundary and enter into another person – in this case, a client – at a psychic level. What effect the presence of an external ego-state is having on a client will depend on the specific ego-state and its connection to the client. It could be an ego-state, for example, from the client's mother, one that was created and sent to protect the client as a child and has remained with him or her. It might also be one that was created and sent to control the child in certain ways (for its own good). An external ego-state might also be one created in a past lifetime that the client shared with another soul, who in this lifetime is his brother. You might find an external ego-state present who is still doing battle with a part of your client and who is not aware that the war ended many lifetimes ago.

While I do not find these external ego-states present with every client, I would say they are not rare. When I do encounter one, I know the ultimate aim of the healing process will be for that external ego-state to leave the client's soul. It may return to a safe place within its own soul, or it may be taken into the Light by guides to await the return of its own soul to the spirit realm.

Most of the time, when it is an external ego-state that is identified, you won't know right away that it is separate from your client. Also, an external ego-state may or may not know that it is separate from your client's self/soul. It may believe it is part of your client's soul because that's where it has always been since it was created. An external ego-state also will have the same capacities as your client's ego-states, i.e., able to communicate, able to receive Light, carrying some kind of experience, etc.

This again is the reason why my first or second question to anyone I encounter in my client's inner world is usually: do you know yourself to be part of this self/soul I am working with? If I get a "no" response, or an "*I don't know*" to this question, then I will ask higher self to determine whether it is part of the client's soul or separate. If separate then I use the Identification Protocol to be more specific about whom I'm communicating with.

Once you know you are dealing with an external ego-state, the next step in the protocol is to determine from higher self whether it should just be removed or whether to communicate with it directly. Most of the time, I find that I'm directed by higher self to communicate with the EES directly. I think the reason for this is that when an ego-state from another soul is present, it's because there is some kind of significant bond, conflict, or shared experience between the two souls and this situation can be an opportunity for healing, both for the client and for the other soul or souls involved. Also, most of the time the external ego-state is from a soul that is presently incarnate. Usually, it is a person with whom the client has, or has had, some direct relationship.

There are situations, however, when the client is being harassed, stalked, or intruded on by ego-states from another soul. These situations can also be an occasion for healing, but there are times when the appropriate strategy is not to engage them but just remove them or sever their ties to the client. Most of the time, though, I find that external ego-states agree to receive Light and information.

If the decision is to work with the external ego-state, then the protocol to use is almost the same as the Ego-State Protocol. You help the external ego-state receive Light, make contact with a spirit guide or teacher, and then check with client's higher self whether it would be best at that point for the external ego-state(s) to leave or whether it needs to do a sharing and release before it leaves. Very often I find that something needs to be shared before it leaves—it may be a thought, a feeling, or an image—and then it's ready to go. Some external ego-states are able to return to their soul on their own. Others may need assistance from the higher self or a spirit guide. I usually try to have a spirit guide involved just to ensure that it leaves my client and finds its appropriate place.

If the client's higher self signals that I should communicate with the EES, then the next step is to determine what needs to happen with this external ego-state before it is ready to go. It may need to share something, just like the client's ego-states, so that it can have a release; or it may need to share along with one of the client's ego-states because of some shared experience; or it may have some important information or understanding that the client needs in order for the healing process to continue. It may also be that one of the client's ego-states is holding on to the EES and doesn't want it to go. Whatever the reason, the therapeutic aim is for the EES to leave the client. Once an external ego-state receives the Light, it makes the process much easier, just as it does with the client's own ego-states. It also makes it easier to find out what needs to happen in order to resolve the situation.

So the protocol for dealing with external ego-states looks like this:
1) Identify entity as an external ego-state (EES).
2) Determine whether there is more than one.
3) Facilitate EES receiving the Light.
4) Facilitate contact with a spirit guide or teacher.
5) Check with higher self whether the EES at this point should leave or stay.
6) If stay, then determine whether EES is part of a soul that is presently incarnate or discarnate.
7) If incarnate, determine if client is in relationship to that soul in the present or has been at some point in this present life. (It may be from a past but significant relationship, etc.)
8) If the external ego-state's soul is discarnate, determine whether its soul is in the Light.
9) Determine whether it should just leave or be worked with for sharing and release.
10) Once resolved, determine whether the EES should return to its own soul, or go to the Light with a spirit teacher to await its soul's return to the spirit realm.

When it comes to dealing with external entities, I find that external ego-states are usually the easiest to deal with. They are like the client's own ego-states. They are usually open to at least an initial contact with the Light and then also become cooperative once they have had that contact. The complication is in determining the best way to resolve an external ego-state, both for the benefit of the client's inner world and for the other soul involved. I would say that a healer usually will have a sense of how important it might be to work with an external ego-state or to just send it on its way with a spirit guide.

Dealing with External Ego-States: Example 1

TH To this one: do you know yourself to be part of this self and soul I'm working with?

EES No finger lifts.

TH If you believe that you are separate, the first finger can lift. If you're just not sure, the second finger lifting.

EES Second finger lifts.

TH To this one: are you willing to know now whether you are, or are not, part of this soul I'm working with?

EES Yes finger lifts.

TH I'm going to ask higher self or a guide from the Light to send you that information on three: one, two, three… Higher self or guide, please communicate to this one information and knowledge about themselves, whether they are, or are not, part of this soul, and any other information that might be helpful to them. First finger when that communication is complete, second finger, if the communication is stopped or blocked.

EES First finger lifts.

TH To this one: did you receive that communication all right?

EES Yes finger lifts.

TH Does it seem that you are part of this soul I'm working with? If so, first finger lifting. If not, the second finger can lift.

EES Second finger lifts.

TH To this one: it seems that you are separate from the self and soul I'm working with. Is that accurate?

EES Yes finger lifts.

TH If it seems that you are yourself a soul, first finger can lift. If you believe you are a created entity or from another soul, then second finger can lift.

EES Second finger lifts.

TH To this one: if you believe you are a created entity, the first finger can lift; if a part from another soul, then the second finger lifting.

EES Second finger lifts.

TH	To this one: you are from another soul? Is that correct?
EES	Yes finger lifts.
TH	Are you receiving Light there where you are?
EES	No finger lifts.
TH	Would you be willing to have some Light/Love energy sent to you now?
EES	Yes finger lifts.
TH	On three, then, that Light will come to you. Beginning, one, two, three… And higher self or a guide, please send to this one that Light/Love/Warmth energy they're able to receive at this time. And to this one: you can receive this Light, and if you like it, you can bring it inside to whatever level is comfortable. First finger when you have received that Light. Second finger if you do not.
EES	First finger lifts.
TH	To this one: does that feel all right to you?
EES	Yes finger lifts.
TH	To this one: the soul you are a part of… Is that soul presently in a physical body?
EES	Yes finger lifts.
TH	To this one: is that person presently in a direct relationship with John in this lifetime?
EES	Yes finger lifts.
TH	Higher self, is it important that John know who that is?
HS	Yes finger lifts.
TH	Higher self, I'm going to ask that you communicate to John here at a conscious level who that is. On three: one, two, three… First finger when that's complete; second finger if there's a problem.
HS	First finger lifts.
TH	John, did you receive that?
Jo	Yes, I got the message that this one belongs to my sister Judy.
TH	Higher self, is that correct? Is this one from Judy's self/soul?
HS	Yes finger lifts.
TH	Higher self, if this one needs to share something for healing and release, first finger lifting. If they can return now to their own soul or go with a guide, then second finger can lift.
HS	Second finger lifts.
TH	If they can return to their own soul, first finger. If we should call for a guide to come help, second finger can lift.

HS   No finger lifts.
TH   To this one: would you be willing for a high-level helper from the Light to come forward and assist you?
EES Yes finger lifts.
TH   On three, then... one, two, three... just turn towards the Light and I'm asking that high-level helper to come forward here with us, and to this one: first finger when you see that helper, second finger if you do not.
EES First finger lifts.
TH   I'm asking that helper now to communicate to this one any information or knowledge that would be helpful. To this one: first finger lifting when you've received that communication, second finger, if you do not.
EES First finger lifts.
TH   To this one: are willing now to go with the helper?
EES Yes finger lifts.
TH   On three, then... one, two, three... To this one: you can move right to that helper now, right into that corridor of Light. Higher self, first finger when that one has gone. Second finger if it does not.
HS   Second finger lifts.
TH   This one I've been working with: were you stopped from going to the helper?
EES Yes finger lifts.
TH   If you needed to stop that, first finger. If someone or something seemed to get in the way, then second finger lifting.
EES Second finger lifts.
TH   To this one: if it was someone, first finger, if something or an energy, second finger can lift. If you're not sure, the hand can lift.
EES Hand lift.
TH   Higher self, please look inside and find the source of that block, first finger when you have found it, second finger if you do not.
HS   First finger lifts.
TH   Higher self, did you find someone or something that got in the way?
HS   Yes finger lifts.
TH   If it was someone, first finger. If something, second finger. If neither of those fit, the hand can lift.
HS   First finger lifts.
TH   Higher self, is that one part of this self and soul?

HS Yes finger lifts.
TH Is it one it would be good for me to communicate with now?
HS Yes finger lifts.
TH Higher self, please help that one come forward here with me. And to this one: are you willing today to communicate with me?
ES Yes finger lifts.
TH Do you know yourself to be part of this self and soul I'm working with?
ES Yes finger lifts.
TH Are you receiving Light/Love energy for yourself there?
ES No finger lifts.
TH Would you like to have some Light/Love energy sent to you?
ES Yes finger lifts.
TH On three, then… one, two, three… and higher self, please send to this one that Light/Love energy. Also, communicate any other information that might be helpful, especially about the healing process we're working with. And to this one: let yourself receive that Light. You can bring it inside to whatever level is comfortable. First finger when you have received it, second finger if you do not.
ES First finger lifts.
TH To this one: did you receive that for yourself?
ES Yes finger lifts.
TH Does it feel all right to you?
ES Yes finger lifts.
TH Are you aware of this one I've been communicating with from that soul we know as Judy?
ES Yes finger lifts.
TH Do you know now that the best place for her is a place of Light within her own soul?
ES Yes finger lifts.
TH Are you willing for her to return now to her own soul?
ES Yes finger lifts.
TH I'm asking then that you say your goodbyes, and to this separate one, are you willing to go with your helper there?
EES Yes finger lifts.
TH On three, then… one, two, three… And to this one: just move right to your helper, right into that corridor of Light, and higher self, first finger when they have left. Second finger if that is stopped again.
HS First finger lifts.

A dialogue like this could be even longer if the client's ego-state needed to share and release before it was ready to let go of the external ego-state. It could be that the EES refuses to leave because it is being threatened by a dark soul from outside that is communicating that it should stay where it is. It could also be that the external ego-state might be from one of the client's children that came in a time of crisis. An external ego-state may also be from another soul who shared a past life with the client and has reconnected in this present life.

In short, there are myriad possibilities for why an external ego-state may be present with a client. Using the protocol, the therapist finds the most appropriate and efficient resolution for the client. Sometimes it will be just to remove the EES. Other times, it will be to work with the EES and its connection to the client's soul. It's all the better when it benefits the other soul as well, but if there is too much resistance, then forcible removal may be necessary just as with the other kinds of separate beings we've discussed.

Dealing with External Ego-States: Example 2

TH Higher self, did you find someone interfering or blocking the 5yo's sharing?

HS Yes finger lifts.

TH Higher self, I'm going to ask that you help that one come forward here with me. And to this one: do you know yourself to be part of this self and soul I'm working with?

___ No finger lifts.

TH If you believe you are separate from this soul, first finger lifting. If you're just not sure, the second finger can lift.

___ First finger lifts.

TH If you believe you are a soul, the first finger can lift. If not or you're not sure, the second finger lifting.

___ Second finger lifts.

TH To this one: are you willing to know now whether you are a soul yourself?

___ Yes finger lifts.

TH That information will come to you on three. One, two, three… And higher self or a guide, please send to this one that information about themselves; help them to know whether they are or are not themselves a soul. First finger when you have received this information.

Second finger if you do not receive it or it is blocked.
_ First finger lifts.
TH To this one: does it seem that you are yourself a soul?
_ No finger lifts.
TH If it seems you are a created entity, first finger. If you are part of another soul, second finger can lift.
EES Second finger lifts.
TH And are you receiving Light for yourself there now?
EES Yes finger lifts.
TH Are you in that same group as 5yo?
EES Yes finger lifts.
TH Are there others there with you from your soul?
EES Yes finger lifts.
TH Is it more than three?
EES No finger lifts.
TH Is it more than two?
EES No finger lifts.
TH Are there two of you there?
EES Yes finger lifts.
TH Higher self, if it would be best for these separate ones now to return to their own soul, the first finger can lift. If I should communicate further with them, the second finger lifting.
HS Second finger lifts.
TH Are both of you receiving Light/Love energy for yourselves now?
EES Yes finger lifts.
TH To this one: the soul you are part of... Is that soul presently in a physical body? If so, first finger, if not, second finger. If you're not sure, the hand can lift.
EES First finger lifts.
TH And is that soul in some direct relationship to Carol here in the present?
EES Yes finger lifts.
TH To this one: is it all right for Carol to know who that is?
EES Yes finger lifts.
TH I'm going to ask that you communicate that name right here to Carol on the count of three: one, two, three... (Pause) Carol, did something come to you?
Ca Yes. I think this one is from my mother, but she's one from a past

life. It's something like Marylou or Marilyn…

TH To this one: is your name Marylou?

EES No finger lifts.

TH Are you Marilyn?

Ma Yes finger lifts.

TH Is there a Marylou with you there?

Ma No finger lifts.

TH Okay. Marilyn, is this accurate? Are you part of Sandra, Carol's mother?

Ma Yes finger lifts.

TH Is there something you need to share here or communicate with Carol before returning to your own soul?

Ma Yes finger lifts.

TH Higher self, are you in agreement that it would be good for this one to share here with Carol?

HS Yes finger lifts.

TH Okay. I'm going to ask that you share here to Carol what you need to share, on three… one, two, three… Just share it, Marilyn, what you need to share. Let it come right here to the conscious mind what you feel, see, or hear. First finger when that's complete. Second finger if it's stopped.

Ma First finger lifts.

TH Carol, is there something you received?

Ca Yes. I get the sense that Marilyn is from a past life. She's dressed in really old-fashioned clothes and it's like she came forward to help the 5yo, that year my dad died.

TH Is that right Marilyn? Did you come to help 5yo?

Ma Yes finger lifts.

TH Is there more that needs to be shared?

Ma Yes finger lifts.

TH I'm going to ask that you share it then right here to the present. Beginning: one, two, three… and let it share now, right to the present Marilyn what you need to share. First finger when complete. Second finger if it's stopped.

Ma First finger lifts.

TH Carol, did something come to you?

Ca Yes, what I'm getting is that her mother died when she was young – she seems about 10 years old – and there was nobody to take care

of her. I think she eventually got sick and died.
TH Marilyn, is that what you're sharing? Did your mother die and leave you alone?
Ma Yes finger lifts.
TH The one that is with you, is that one also from a past lifetime?
Ma Yes finger lifts.
TH Higher self, does that one need to share more?
HS No finger lifts.
TH Higher self, can these two and 5yo have some release now from this pain and grief they've carried?
HS Yes finger lifts.
TH Now to all three of you: on three, let yourselves release all pain, grief, and hurt. Beginning: one, two, three… and just release now, right through the body and out, any grief and sadness, any pain and fear. Let it move right through the body and out. The Light will help move that pain also, moving that distress energy through the body and out. First finger when all has been released that's ready; second finger if there's a problem.
___ First finger lifts.
TH To all three of you – were you able to have that release all right?
___ Yes finger lifts.
TH Is anyone still feeling any distress or pain now?
___ Yes finger lifts.
TH Is there something more yet that needs to be shared?
___ Yes finger lifts.
TH Are all of you willing to share –or allow to be shared – what needs to come forward now?
___ Yes finger lifts.
TH Do you know what needs to be shared?
___ Yes finger lifts.
TH I'm going to ask that you share it then, on three: one, two, three… and let it share now right to the present. It's safe to do that now, right here in the present. First finger when complete. Second finger if it's stopped or blocked.
___ First finger lifts.
TH Carol, is there something you received?
Ca Yes. That second one with Marilyn is from a different past life. She's an older woman and I think she lost a child. She's been taking care

of Marilyn for a long time, and when my dad died these two came forward to help the 5yo.

TH To this one with Marilyn: is this right, did you yourself lose a child?

___ Yes finger lifts.

TH Are you ready now to release that pain and grief?

___ Yes finger lifts. All three again, just releasing, on three: one, two, three… and just release now any further grief and pain. Let it move right through the body and out. First finger when that feels complete. Second finger if there's a problem.

___ First finger lifts.

TH Now to all three of you. Is anyone still feeling some distress or pain there?

___ No finger lifts.

TH Does that feel good and comfortable now inside?

___ Yes finger lifts.

TH Higher self, can Marilyn and the mother now each return to their soul?

HS Yes finger lifts.

TH And to both of you: are you ready now to return to a place of integration with your own soul?

___ Yes finger lifts.

TH On three, then, higher self and guides will help you make that move. Beginning: one, two, three…and to both of you, I'm asking higher self or guides to help you now return to your own soul. Higher self, first finger when both have gone. Second finger if either do not.

HS First finger lifts.

TH Higher self, can 5yo move now to her own place of integration here in the present?

HS Yes finger lifts.

TH Should she have a conscious experience here in the present first?

HS Yes finger lifts.

TH 5yo, before moving to your place of Light, I'm asking that you look around where you are there… Are there any doors or openings you see where you are?

5yo No finger lifts.

TH Okay. On three then, higher self will help you make these moves. Beginning: one, two, three… Higher self, help 5yo to move now to the conscious mind for that conscious experience and perception

here in the present. Communicate to her any further information or understanding about this present point of view. When complete, help her to move to her place of Light and integration here in the present with Carol. First finger, higher self, when those moves are complete. Second finger if there's a problem.
HS   First finger lifts.

Dealing with External Ego-States: Example 3
TH   Higher self, are you able to communicate with me?
HS   Yes finger lifts.
TH   Higher self, Jan and I have talked at a conscious level about this dream last night where she told Dave she wanted a divorce and he went ballistic. Higher self are you aware of this dream?
HS   Yes finger lifts.
TH   If there is someone or something that needs to be addressed about the dream, first finger lifting. If not, second finger can lift.
HS   Yes finger lifts.
TH   If it's someone, first finger, if something second finger. If neither of those fit, the hand can lift.
HS   First finger lifts.
TH   Higher self, is that one part of the self/soul?
HS   No finger lift
TH   If that one is a soul or part of a soul, the first finger lifting. If it is a created entity of some kind, the second finger lifting.
HS   First finger lifts.
TH   Higher self, is there more than one?
HS   Yes finger lifts.
TH   More than five?
HS   Yes finger lifts.
TH   Is it more than ten?
HS   No finger lifts.
TH   More than eight?
HS   Yes finger lifts.
TH   Are there nine?
HS   Yes finger lifts.
TH   Can all of them be removed now?
HS   Yes finger lifts.

TH	Higher self, would it be agreeable to call for high-level helpers from the Light to assist you with this?
HS	Yes finger lifts.
TH	Jan, is this agreeable to you, that we call in guides to help with this.
Jn	"Yes."
TH	Higher self, I'm asking that we call to the Light for those who are aware and able to assist. First finger when they are here, second finger if not.
HS	First finger lifts.
TH	I'm asking now higher self that you and the guides surround these separate ones with the Light. Gather and remove them now from the self/soul. First finger when that is complete, second finger if there is a problem or it is stopped.
HS	First finger lifts.
TH	Were you able to remove them all?
HS	Yes finger lifts.
TH	I'm going to ask then that you close and seal any access they were using. First finger when that's complete. Second finger if there is a problem.
HS	First finger lifts.
TH	Higher self, were you able to close them all?
HS	No finger lifts.
TH	Is there someone or something yet that they can use as an access?
HS	Yes finger lifts.
TH	If it is someone, first finger, if something second finger.
HS	First finger lifts.
TH	Is that one part of the self/soul?
HS	Yes finger lifts.
	(Note: We are coming to the end of the session and this is likely to be an involved piece of work. I decide to secure things as best we can at the moment and expect to come back to this in the next session.)
TH	Higher self, I'm asking that you help that one come forward here with me... and to this one: do you know yourself to be part of this self and soul I'm working?
__	Yes finger lifts.
TH	Are you one first created in this present life of Jan's?
__	No finger lifts.

TH	Are you from a past or different lifetime?
__	Yes finger lifts.
TH	Are you a female?
__	Yes finger lifts.
TH	Are you an adult?
PF	Yes finger lifts.
TH	Do you know your name?
PF	No finger lifts.
TH	Have you and I communicated in this way before?
PF	Yes finger lifts.
TH	Are you still receiving Light for yourself there?
PF	No finger lifts.
TH	Would you like to have that Light sent to you again?
PF	Yes finger lifts.
TH	Higher self, please send this one that Light/Love energy, and to this one: let yourself receive that Light. You can bring it inside to whatever level is comfortable. First finger when you've received that Light, second finger if you do not.
PF	Yes finger lifts.
TH	Does that feel all right to you?
PF	Yes finger lifts.
TH	To this one: as you look around, is there anyone else with you where you are?
PF	No finger lifts.
TH	You're alone there, is that correct?
PF	Yes finger lifts.
TH	Did you know that I'm communicating with you from the year 2012? Did you know that?
PF	Yes finger lifts.
TH	Would you like to move to a safer, more comfortable place for yourself?
PF	Yes finger lifts.
TH	Higher self, is there a safer more comfortable place she can move to at this time?
HS	Yes finger lifts.
TH	I'm asking now that you move her to that safer place, and to this past life one, first finger when that move is complete, second finger if it is stopped or blocked.

PF   First finger lifts.
TH   To this one: does that feel better to you there?
PF   Yes finger lifts.
     Note: Because the separate ones that were removed seemed quite strong, I don't trust that they won't approach this one in between sessions even though she is in a safer place. For that reason, I would like a guide to stay with her.
TH   To this one: we will come back to help you move to a place of Light and integration. Would you like a high-level helper to stay there with you until we come back?
PF   Yes finger lifts.
TH   Higher self, is that agreeable that we call for a guide?
HS   Yes finger lifts.
TH   I'm asking then that we call for that high-level guide who is aware and able to assist to come forward here to this one. And to this one: first finger when that one is there, second finger if not or there's a problem.
PF   First finger lifts.
TH   And to this one: we will come back and help you to that new place that's waiting for you. Is that agreeable?
PF   Yes finger lifts.

Ego-States of One Person Engaging Ego-States of Another

Another situation that the therapist may run into is when an external ego-state has not entered the client's energy, but is engaged with some part of the client at a psychic level. It would not be unusual, for example, to find one of your client's ego-states triggered by and reacting to an ego-state within another person with whom the client has a significant relationship. A frequent example of this occurs in marriages. An ego-state of one of the partners triggers, or is triggered by, an ego-state of the other. The ego-states involved may be ones created in each person's present life that are reacting to each other because they share a common issue, conflict, or feeling. They push each other's buttons in some way. Or they can be ego-states from a particular past life which the couple shared together and resulted in unresolved conflict and pain.

In this case, the therapeutic aim is not that the external ego-state leaves—it hasn't entered the client. The aim is to determine what kind of resolution the client needs in the particular situation. This can be determined usually with the help of the higher self, and/or spirit guides, or maybe the ego-states themselves know what needs to be done. Again, the exact situation is unpredictable. Most of time, though, some resolution is called for because it is affecting a client's relationship in the present. It may be that the ego-states need to share with the client what happened. They may not need to share, but just to have a spirit teacher come forward and explain to each why things happened the way they did in that lifetime. Or they may be two lovers from a different lifetime, tragically separated, and now reconnecting in this present life and unwilling to be separated again. The possibilities are endless.

of resolution the client needs in the particular situation. This can be determined usually with the help of the higher self, and/or spirit guides, or maybe the ego-states themselves know what needs to be done. Again, the exact situation is unpredictable. Most of time, though, some resolution is called for because it is affecting a client's relationship in the present. It may be that the ego-states need to share with the client what happened. They may not need to share, but just to have a spirit teacher come forward and explain to each why things happened the way they did in that lifetime. Or they may be two lovers from a different lifetime, tragically separated, and now reconnecting in this present life and unwilling to be separated again. The possibilities are endless.

13

Protocol for Created Entities

Thought-Beings

When a client's higher self identifies *someone* to work with, what we have seen so far is that the *someone* is a soul (spirit, extraterrestrial, or dimensional) or is part of a soul (present-life ego-state, past-life ego-state, external ego-state.) As such, all of these beings have had the capacity to receive Light because they are created of Light.

There is another kind of *someone,* however, that can present during a session, but it is not a soul, or part of a soul. Most of these entities do not have the capacity to receive the Light. I first learned about these entities from Gerod when discussing clinical cases with him where such beings presented or were identified by the higher self. I came to call them *created entities*. While they are not souls, or parts of a soul, most of them, I think, have been created by a soul. I view them as thought creations or thought-beings.

They usually present as sentient beings, and come in many different forms. They can present, for example, as a person, an animal, a mythical creature, or a phantom. They possess some level of consciousness and intelligence, and can act independently of their creator. I don't believe they are sentient beings, however, but more akin to extremely sophisticated programs—a kind of artificial intelligence on steroids. They are programmed to carry out certain functions, but the program does not come with a soul or free will. These entities are not creative. They don't think or act on their own or exercise free choice. They won't contradict their programs. In a very real sense, you could say that they *are* the program. Just as we create very complex machines that act independently of us, these entities do the same thing. They can communicate, follow logical thought, and carry out complex actions involving a client at psychic and spiritual levels, depending on who created them and why they have targeted my client.

Unlike ego-states, however, a created entity is not a center of consciousness. I view ego-states as a kind of organic creation of the self/soul in response to life experience. A created entity, on the other hand, is a deliberate creation and must operate within the confines and limitations of its program and the soul that created it. The closest analogies I can think of come from our science fiction—figures like the computer, HAL, in the movie *2001: A Space Odyssey,* or the droids in Star Wars or Star Trek. You would almost think they were human.

Having said all this, I want to emphasize that this description of created entities is from a clinical point of view. Most of the created entities I have encountered have been created for negative or dark purposes, i.e., to create fear, carry out psychological/emotional conditioning, act as a block to keep the conscious self unaware, to gather information, etc.

I have met entities, though, that contradict everything I've said. I have encountered created entities, for example, that were able to exercise choice, receive Light, and contradict their program. I have worked with some who were even able to go to the Spirit Realm of Light with a guide. It's as though these entities were created of enough "soul stuff," or had developed enough, that they were capable of receiving Light, independent of their creator. In these cases, I will facilitate an experience of Light for such an entity and call for a guide to come forward and assist the entity in moving to the Light. The higher self and/or guides can usually determine whether an entity has the capacity for Light.

I have also read of another kind of created entity called a *tulpa*. This is a Tibetan term and refers to "a being or object that is created through willpower, visualization, attention and focus, concerted intentionality, and ritual." In other words, it is a materialized thought that has taken physical form."* Tibet is not the only culture that talks about such entities. An Internet search will produce a great deal more material on entities like the tulpa.

I worked with a client once who had been a victim of ritual abuse as a child. In one of her memories, she describes the cult members all

---

* Mysteries of the Unexplained, 1990, Reader's Digest Association Inc. Page 176.

gathered around in a circle, including her and other children. A ritual was being performed, and after some time, she said, a large being appeared in the center. She said it was human-like but she didn't think it was human. Looking back now, I would guess it was quite probably a created entity, like a tulpa, and not a spirit manifesting in a physical body.

Finally, I have also encountered entities that turned out to have been created and sent by a client's own soul to act as an inner guide or to serve some other positive function. It may have been created recently, or one who had been present within the soul for many lifetimes and was being called into service.

I have no idea what kinds of entities can be created. I can think of other possibilities than ones I've mentioned. I see it limited only by the soul's imagination. These entities, however, present the same issue as working with the other separate beings I have talked about. Our purpose in healing is not to do research on these beings, but to learn only what is necessary to resolve their intrusion or interference. Clinically, once they are gone, we go back to where we left off before the entities presented.

I am curious about these different entities. I read about them and listen to others' stories about them. I believe all of us have the capacity to create such entities. I also believe, however, that it involves a focused consciousness and intent, along with some kind of know-how. I remember working with a client before I knew that spirit guides could be called on to assist in the healing process. I was working with a five-year-old ego-state of woman who had suffered severe abuse as a child. What she was sharing was extensive and it required more than one session. At the end of our first session, the ego-state was feeling terrified and didn't want to be alone. The thought came to me whether I could mentally create a kind of protective entity to leave with the child until our next session.

I asked Gerod about this possibility in our next session. He agreed that I could create a thought being like this, but he advised against it. He explained that one had to be careful when creating an entity to engage with or even enter another person's soul. He said this creates energy connections between the two souls that are not always predictable and which can lead to entanglements that could be difficult to undo. The message I took from this was that you need to know what you're doing if you exercise this kind of power. While I believe it can be used for good, it seems to have the ready potential to get dark and go south very quickly.

The Protocol

In many ways, created entities are easier to deal with than separate souls. Their programs do not prepare them for the kind of direct confrontation that happens in the healing process. While they can communicate and follow logical thought, they very quickly come to the limits of their knowledge and understanding. When the therapist starts asking questions outside the parameters of their program, they often wind up confused, immobilized, or they just doggedly try to carry out their function until someone or something makes them stop.

Since they are not creative and do not have free choice, they are caught in a predicament where their three options are to leave voluntarily, be forcibly removed, or be dissipated. This is what I have found to be a distinguishing characteristic between dealing with souls and created entities. With souls, it comes down to the first two options – leave or be removed. A client's higher self and/or spirit guides can remove a separate soul once all the accesses are closed, but they cannot dissipate another soul. However, they can dissipate a created entity if it refuses to leave, and this is what it often seems to come down to in the end. The entities cannot make an independent choice to leave. They seem to understand that they will be destroyed if they do not leave the client. Yet, they will attempt to continue with their activities right to the end because their program does not include an exit strategy or a return to the soul that created it. Unless it is one that has the capacity to receive Light, which is rare, then it must be dissipated.

In terms of the protocol for created entities, the process becomes more focused, more quickly, than in dealing with separate souls. The emphasis will not be on having them receive Light, or make contact with a spirit guide, or communicating about a soul's (client's) freedom to choose. Once someone has been identified as a created entity, the focus is on whether it can be dissipated or removed immediately. If it can't, then the focus shifts to finding and closing whatever access the entity is using.

At this point, we face the same issue as we did with the other separate beings. If a created entity cannot be dissipated or removed, then it has to have an access. It may be an ego-state, an etheric device, or a sympathetic connection. In these cases, the accesses have to be tracked down and closed just as with the other separate beings.

The protocol for dealing with created entities should look familiar. Keeping in mind the distinctions discussed above, the protocol is very much like with other separate beings. Here are the steps:

1) Identify entity as a non-soul.
2) Determine if it is alone or with others.
3) Inform entity it is in violation of the soul and will have to leave.
4) Determine whether the entity will leave on its own.
5) If not, ask higher self and guides to remove it (them).
6) If they can't, find the entity's access or accesses.
7) Resolve accesses and have higher self and guides remove or dissipate the entity.

The biggest complication in dealing with a created entity is that it will not be alone. Based on clinical experience, I would say that it often is part of a larger web involving other created entities, devices, or energies, as well as some active involvement by the soul that created and sent it. Imagine someone going through your home and placing video and audio devices in every room that were capable of receiving and transmitting. It won't accomplish much to remove just a couple devices. The whole network has to be dissolved or dismantled.

There's no general rule about how much of a network must be shut down before the whole thing can be removed. It will depend on the complexity of the network, whether the soul that created it is still engaged, or whether ego-states are interwoven in the network to make it more binding. The approach I have found most effective is working with higher self to identify each link in the chain, and continue to check at different steps whether the whole network can be removed yet.

Dealing with Created Entities: Example 1

TH Higher self, were you able to find the source of that blocking?
HS Yes finger lifts.
TH If it is someone, the first finger can lift. If something or some energy, the second finger lifting.
HS First finger lifts.
TH Higher self, help that one to come forward here with me. And to

	this one: do you know yourself to be part of this self and soul I'm working with?
__	No finger lifts.
TH	Do you believe you are separate from this soul?
__	Yes finger lifts.
TH	Are you yourself a soul? If so, first finger, if not, second finger, if you're not sure then the hand can lift
__	Hand lift.
TH	To this one: are you willing to know whether you are, or are not, a soul?
__	No finger lifts.
TH	Is there some scare for you about this?
__	No finger lifts.
TH	To this one: is there someone or something that stopped you from receiving this information?
__	Yes finger lifts
TH	If it is someone that's in the way, first finger lifting. If some thing, the second finger can lift
__	First finger lifts.
TH	Is that one with you there where you are?
__	Yes finger lifts.
TH	Higher self, I'm asking that you identify that one and help them come forward here with me... To this one are you willing now to communicate with me?
__	Yes finger lifts
TH	Are you separate from this soul I'm working with?
__	Yes finger lifts.
TH	If you are yourself a soul, the first finger can lift. If you are a created entity or from another soul, then the second finger can lift. If you are not sure, then the hand can lift.
__	Hand lifts.
TH	Are you willing to know whether you are yourself a soul?
__	Yes finger lifts.
TH	That information will come to you then on three. One, two, three... First finger when you have received that information, second finger if you do not.
__	Yes finger lifts.
TH	To this one: if it seems that you are a soul, first finger. If a created

Protocol for Created Entities

entity or from another soul, second finger.
— Second finger lifts.
TH If you are a created entity, first finger. If from another soul, second finger.
EN First finger lifts.
TH To this one: are there others with you where you are?
EN Yes finger lifts.
TH Are there more than four?
EN Yes finger lifts.
TH More than six?
EN No finger lifts.
TH More than five?
EN No finger lifts.
TH There are five of you, then, is that correct?
EN Yes finger lifts.
TH Higher self, are all five created entities?
EN Yes finger lifts.
TH To this one: do you know that you and the others are in violation of this soul?
EN No finger lifts.
TH To this one: you do not have permission to remain here and you will have to leave.
EN No finger lifts.
TH To this one: this soul has the absolute right to remove anyone or anything separate from itself. Are you willing to have information sent to you about this?
EN No finger lifts.
TH Higher self, are you able to just remove these five now?
HS Yes finger lifts.
TH On three then: one, two, three, ... higher self, I'm asking that you and the guides now, using the Light, find and surround these entities and, with that Light, remove them from the soul. First finger when that is complete, second finger if there is a problem.
HS First finger lifts.
TH Higher self, were you able to remove them all?
HS Yes finger lifts.
TH Higher self, I'm asking that you look inside now to see if there is anyone or anything else connected to these entities. First finger

when that review is complete, second finger if it is stopped.
HS First finger lifts.
TH Higher self, did you find anyone or anything else present here connected to these entities?
HS Yes finger lifts.
TH Higher self, if it is someone, first finger lifting, if it is some thing or energy the second finger lifting.
HS Second finger lifts.
TH Higher self, if that is a device or object of some kind, first finger lifting. If more like an energy, second finger lifting.
HS First finger lifts.
TH Higher self, there is a device or object of some kind present, is that correct?
HS Yes finger lifts.
TH Is there more than one?
HS No finger lifts.
TH Higher self, can you dissipate and or remove that device/energy now?
HS Yes finger lifts.
TH Higher self, I'm asking on three that you dissipate it or remove this device/object. Beginning, one, two, three... Higher self I'm asking that you find this device/object, and using the Light vibration, dissipate and remove it from the self-soul. First finger when that is complete. Second finger if there is a problem.
HS First finger lifts.
TH Higher self, is there anyone or anything else you see connected to those entities?
HS No finger lifts.
TH Is there someone or something else now that it would be good for us to address?
HS Yes finger lifts.
TH If it's someone, first finger can lift; if something, second finger.

Dealing with Created Entities: Example 2

TH 8yo, I'm asking that you share on the count of three: one, two, three... First finger lifting when that sharing is complete, second finger if it's stopped.

Protocol for Created Entities

8yo No finger lifts.
TH 8yo, I see the second finger. Was your sharing stopped?
8yo Yes finger lifts.
TH If you needed to stop it, the first finger lifting. If someone or something got in your way, the second finger can lift.
8yo Second finger lifts.
TH If it is someone, first finger, if something second finger lifting.
8yo First finger lifts.
TH Can you see that one?
8yo Yes finger lifts.
TH Is there more than one?
8yo No finger lifts.
TH Higher self, do you see this one who's blocking?
HS Yes finger lifts.
TH Can you remove that one now?
HS No finger lifts.
TH If I should communicate to that one, first finger, if just work to remove them, the second finger lifting.
HS Second finger lifts.
TH 8yo, is it agreeable to you that we remove this one?
8yo No finger lifts.
TH Do you like for them to be with you there? Are they like a friend?
8yo No finger lifts.
TH Are you afraid of them?
8yo Yes finger lifts.
TH 8yo, did you know that as part of this soul you have the right to have anyone leave who is not part of the soul? Did you know that?
8yo No finger lifts.
TH Would you be willing to receive information from higher self about this?
8yo Yes finger lifts.
TH Higher self, please communicate to 8yo now about her right to have this one leave. First finger when you have received that communication, second finger if you do not.
8yo First finger lifts.
TH Did you receive that all right 8yo?
8yo Yes finger lifts.
TH Would you like to have that one removed?

8yo Yes finger lifts.
TH Higher self, are you able now to remove that one?
HS Yes finger lifts.
TH On three, then… one, two, three… higher self, I'm asking that you surround that entity with the Light and escort them out of the self/soul. First finger lifting when that's complete, second finger if there's a problem.
HS Second finger lifts.
TH Higher self, were you stopped from removing that one?
HS Yes finger lifts.
TH Higher self, I'm asking that you review inside to see if that entity is using someone or something to stay attached here. Yes finger when that review is complete, second finger if it's stopped.
HS Yes finger lifts.
TH Higher self, did you find someone or something that allows this one to stay attached?
HS Yes finger lifts.
TH If it's someone, first finger, if something or some energy, second finger.
HS Second finger lifts.
TH Higher self, if it is a device or object of some kind, first finger lifting; if it is more like an energy, second finger lifting.
HS First finger lifts.
TH Higher self, if that device/object is created of self/soul energy, first finger, if not, second finger can lift.
HS Second finger lifts.
TH Higher self, is there more than one?
HS No finger lifts.
TH Can you dissipate or remove that device now?
HS Yes finger lifts.
TH On three, then: one, two, three… and higher self, please dissipate and remove that device. First finger when that is complete, second finger if there is a problem.
HS First finger lifts.
HS Higher self, can you remove that entity now?
HS Yes finger lifts.
TH I'm asking, then, that you surround that entity with Light and remove it from the self/soul. First finger when that's complete, second finger

	if there's a problem.
HS	First finger lifts.
TH	8yo, is that right? Is that one gone now?
8yo	Yes finger lifts.
TH	Are you willing then to share what you need to for your healing and release?
8yo	Yes finger lifts.
TH	On three, then: one, two, three…

14

Protocols for Clearing Devices and Energies

The Identification Protocol presented in Chapter 3 was designed to help a therapist quickly move through a series of logical steps to identify *who* or *what* is presenting at any moment in the healing process. I said the protocol had two main branches based on the distinction between *someone* and *something*. Here's Figure 3 again reproduced from Chapter 3.

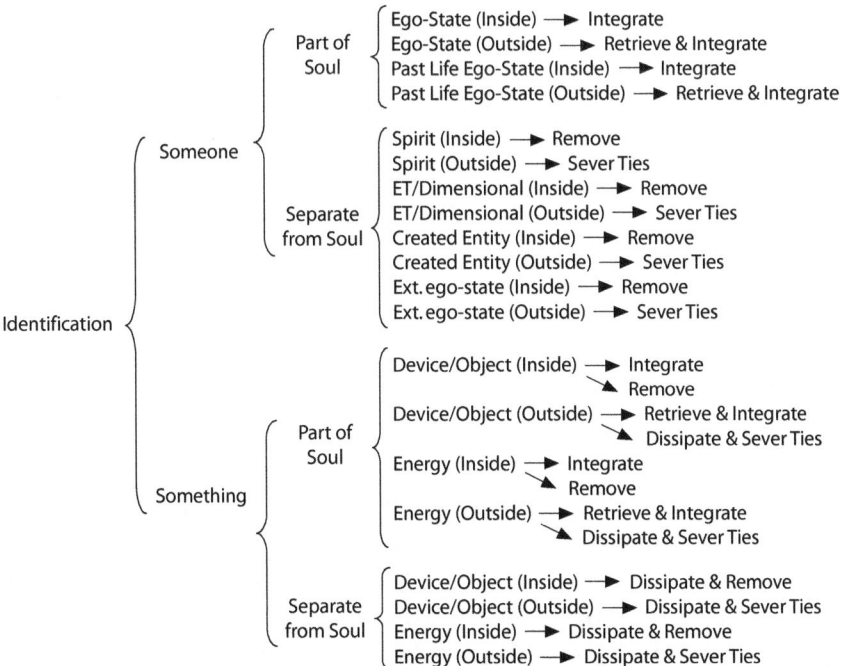

The distinction between someone and something is important because each branch of phenomena calls for a different approach and protocol. We treat conscious beings differently than we treat things. We don't try to talk to a block of wood. We think nothing of it when we break a glass. We just clean up the pieces and get another one off the shelf. We treat them as objects. We would say they are not alive. When we encounter someone, we treat him or her as very much alive, and communication is the first thing we try to establish. Not so, when dealing with things.

So far, all the protocols I've presented are dealing with the first branch—*someone*. Each one is addressing a different kind of conscious being, but all the protocols are based on direct communication with those beings. The protocol goes on then to identify more specifically what kind of being it is. With the exception of created entities, these beings also are either souls or parts of a soul.

In this chapter, we will be dealing with the lower branch of the Identification Protocol. These are the protocols to use when the higher self, or an ego-state, or a separate entity identifies the source of a block or difficulty as *something*, not someone. At that point, the focus will not be on communication. The aim of the protocol will be to identify what kind of thing it is and decide how it needs to be dealt with.

I learned about these devices and energies from Gerod when he identified them as being present in different clients. Usually, they were being identified because they were involved in the blocking that I was encountering with those clients. When I would ask Gerod about these specific cases, he often would identify an object of some kind that he said needed to be dealt with. Then he would go on to tell me *how* it could be dealt with.

Over thousands of client sessions, I came to classify these things Gerod was identifying as *device/objects* or *autonomous energies*. Whenever Gerod, or a client's higher self, or an ego-state identified something that was blocking or in the way, the next question would be: "Is it a device/object of some kind, or is it more like an energy?"

In general, I think of devices as things that tend to be stationary and take the fixed form of objects. For example, a device might be the shoes an ego-state is wearing, or a box that it sees in the same room where it is, or the chain it has around one leg. The device could be a padlock, a sword, a wall, or a pocketknife. Without focusing too much on its specific form, we can think of these devices as energy anchors or thought-forms constellated or placed within a person's energy field. Some devices are created from within the self, but most appear to be created and inserted by outside beings that know how to use them to perform different functions. Depending on the beings involved, these devices can be physical or etheric. I have found that most devices are etheric. When dealing with extraterrestrials, though, physical devices (implants) can be involved. In those cases, there appear to be guides who can dissolve or remove these implants. It's also possible in working with a client that the beings who originally placed the implant will be alerted and will themselves remove it before we get to it clinically. That's fine by me if it leads to them disengaging from my client.

Energies, in contrast to devices, appear more fluid, such as a liquid or gas. Some of these energies appear to be stationary and act as a block, like a cloud or vapor. Many energies are moving, or have the potential to move. An ego-state, for example, might report that there is a black cloud moving toward it, or some gooey liquid is covering the floor where it is standing, or the higher self identifies a swirling force in the throat chakra or a snake-like energy moving through the body. Some of these energies are natural, like the buildup of a static charge, a flowing stream, or the spinning vortex like a tornado. Other energies, however, are created and used intentionally for different purposes, especially by outside beings. A group of ego-states, for example, might be corralled by a ring of energy analogous to the electronic fence used by pet owners. Or there might be a pool of liquid created of dark energy that is thicker than tar and blocks all forward movement.

Most of the time, in the context of healing, devices and energies present as a block or a source of distress. The higher self (and sometimes a spirit guide) can usually find and identify these devices and energies. Once a device or energy is identified, the therapeutic aim is almost always to neutralize it. Before deciding how to deal with it, however, there is the second question posed by the Identification Protocol: is this device or energy part of the client's self/soul, or is it created of separate energy?

Speaking in general, if a device or energy is identified as separate from the client's self/soul, then the aim of treatment will be to dissipate and/or remove it. As the therapist, I do not know which is appropriate to do, or what is even possible. This is a question I put to the higher self. Usually higher self knows which is the best step to take, and it is also the one to carry out the procedure. Again, guides will be available to assist if called upon.

The other possibility is that the device or energy is operating and affecting the client from outside the self/soul. It might be functioning as a kind of satellite, or monitoring device. It may act as a direct link back to the ones who placed it. There might be an energy acting as a shield to keep certain areas of the inner world in darkness. Many times these outside devices and energies appear to act as an energy source for those operations set up within the client's self/soul energy.

When such devices or energies have been identified as operating from outside the self/soul, the higher self is asked to find and close any access points they are using and to sever all energy ties they have to a client.

Besides device/energies separate from the self/soul, there are also those created of self/soul energy. It's possible, for example, for an ego-state to create a device or energy. It might do this in order to control other ego-states in its group or another group, or to keep certain areas blocked off or locked up. It might create a container —a suitcase or a box—to hold intense and frightening emotions.

When such devices and energies are identified, the therapeutic aim is still to neutralize them. Unlike with outside devices or energies, however, where the aim is always to remove them, there is a second possibility when dealing with devices and energies created of self/soul energy. Here the higher self might communicate that the device or energy needs to be re-integrated within the self/soul.

Again, I rely on higher self or a spirit guide to determine which is the more appropriate step, and then to carry out the procedure. I would say that most of time the resolution is to re-integrate the soul energy. There are certainly enough times, however, when it needs to be dissipated and expelled. It's as though the soul energy has become so contaminated or compromised that it can't be restored.

This is a simple step, but I think it's an important one. I view it as the soul being able to re-claim or free parts of its own energy. I also believe that it's always a positive step whenever this reintegration is the final resolution.

At this stage, it's possible that the higher self or guides could just remove or reintegrate the device or energy without the therapist or client ever knowing exactly what it was. The important thing is whether the procedure cleared the block or difficulty that was caused by the device or energy.

Complications

There are two complications that prevent the higher self from dissipating devices or energies immediately after they are found. The first is that a device/energy from outside the self/soul can resist dissipation or removal if it has an access. In this way, these device/energies are like dealing with external beings. The same principle applies. When the higher self cannot remove a device or energy, the most likely reason is that some permission has been obtained by the external entities that placed them. There's a hook of some kind. So, like with external beings, the focus of treatment shifts from the device or energy to finding its access or accesses.

Often, permission is obtained through an ego-state. It might be offered something very appealing – a toy, a stuffed animal, a weapon, a necklace – and accepts it willingly. Or the device – a growling dog, a box that emits a painful screech, or a recording repeating negative thoughts – is used as a threat. Once an ego-state understands the nature of the device and its own ability to choose to have it removed, it almost always will agree for higher self to remove it. Once the ego-state makes this choice, the higher self will be free to remove it.

The second complication is a corollary to the first. When a device/energy cannot be removed immediately, it is often an indication that it is part of a larger web that can involve other devices or energies, ego-states, created entities, or external beings. These networks, as I talked about earlier in relation to external beings, just have to be dealt with methodically until all accesses are closed and sealed. These networks can range from simple to complex. Whatever its form and complexity, the therapist and higher self work together to identify each link in the chain and remove it all.

A phenomenon that I have seen many times, and which I stay alert for, is when an energy is identified as a problem and turns out to be a blend of both external energy and self/soul energy. Sometimes this blending seems to be done intentionally, almost as though to create a stronger bind. Other times this blending of energies appears to be the result of a meeting or collision between the self/soul and external energies. If a network, or part of it is created of self/soul energy, then the higher self can determine whether that self/soul energy can be separated out. Most of the time, the higher self seems able to do this. When the external energy has been removed, then higher self can help determine whether the self/soul energy should be reintegrated or whether it, too, should be dissipated and expelled.

Once the higher self signals that a device has been removed, the focus shifts back to the point in the healing process where the device or energy became an issue or block.

The Protocols

The protocols for dealing with devices and energies is really one protocol with slight modifications depending on whether it is a device or energy, and whether it is part of the self/soul or separate. One of the biggest differences I have found is that thinking about devices is different than thinking about energies. Depending on which it is, I'll be asking different questions. This is especially helpful when the removal of a device or energy is blocked.

- Determine that it is something.
- Determine whether it is a device/object or an energy.
- Determine whether it is created of self/soul energy or separate
- Determine how many are present.
- Determine if it needs to be dissipated/removed or, if part of self/soul, whether it needs to be re-integrated.
- Have higher self carry out the appropriate procedure.

Dealing with Devices and Energies: Example 1

TH 10yo, if you needed to stop the sharing, first finger lifting; if someone or something got in the way, second finger. If you're not sure or don't know, the hand can lift.

10yo Hand lifts.

TH Higher self, I'm going to ask that you review inside and find the source of that block. First finger when you have found that. Second finger if you do not.

HS First finger lifts.

TH Higher self, if it's someone, first finger lifting, if something, second finger. If it's not clear, the hand can lift.

HS Second finger lifts.
TH If it's a device or object of some kind, the first finger can lift. If it's more like an energy, then the second finger.
HS First finger lifts.
TH Higher self, please scan it and determine whether it is created of self/soul energy. First finger when that's complete. Second finger if the scan is stopped.
HS First finger lifts.
TH Higher self, is this device created of self/soul energy?
HS No finger lifts.
TH It's created of separate or outside energy, is that correct?
HS Yes finger lifts.
TH Can you dissipate and remove it now?
HS No finger lifts.
TH Is it using someone or something to stay attached?
HS Yes finger lifts.
TH Higher self, please look inside and identify who or what the device uses to stay attached. First finger when you have found that. Second finger if you do not.
HS First finger lifts.
TH Higher self, if it's using someone, first finger. If something, second finger.
HS First finger lifts.
TH Higher self, help that one to come forward here with me. To this one: do you know yourself to be part of this self and soul I'm working with? If so, first finger lifting. If not, second finger can lift. If you're not sure the hand can lift.
___ First finger lifts.
TH Are you receiving some Light for yourself there?
___ No finger lifts.
TH Would you like to have some Light/Love energy there where you are?
___ Yes finger lifts.
TH Higher self, please send this one Light/Love energy, and to this one: let yourself receive it. You can stop it if you need to, but if you like it, you can keep it for yourself and bring it inside. First finger, when it's complete, either way.
___ First finger lifts.

TH	To this one: did you receive that Light all right?
__	Yes finger lifts.
TH	Did you decide to keep it for yourself?
__	Yes finger lifts.
TH	To this one: are you one first created in the present life of Jerry's. If so, first finger. If you're from a past or different lifetime, the second finger lifting. If neither of those fit, or you're not sure, the hand can lift.
__	First finger lifts.
TH	Are you younger than ten?
__	Yes finger lifts.
TH	Younger than six?
__	No finger lifts.
TH	Younger than eight?
__	No finger lifts.
TH	Are you eight years old?
__	Yes finger lifts.
TH	8yo, are you in the same place with ten-year-old who I've been communicating with?
8yo	No finger lifts.
TH	Are you aware of 10yo?
8yo	Yes finger lifts.
TH	Are you aware of that device that higher self has identified?
8yo	Yes finger lifts.
TH	Is it yours?
8yo	Yes finger lifts.
TH	Did you make it?
8yo	No finger lifts.
TH	Did someone give it to you?
8yo	Yes finger lifts.
Cl	(Speaking aloud) I'm getting this picture of someone holding an axe. It looks kind of like a toy hatchet, like he could threaten someone by shaking it at them.
TH	8yo, is this you? Are you holding a hatchet?
8yo	Yes finger lifts.
TH	Are you willing now to give the hatchet to higher self and move to a safer place for yourself?
8yo	Yes finger lifts.

TH Just give the hatchet to higher self, and higher self please dissipate and remove that from the self/soul. First finger when complete, second finger if there's a problem.
HS First finger lifts.
TH Higher self, can 8yo move now to a safer more comfortable place for himself?
HS Yes finger lifts.
TH Do you think it would be good for him to move to that same place with 10yo?
HS Yes finger lifts.
TH 10yo, are you willing for 8yo to move to that place with you?
10yo First finger lifts.
TH 8yo, is that agreeable with you?
8yo Yes finger lifts.
TH Higher self, please move 8yo to that same place with 10yo, introducing them if necessary. First finger when that's complete. Second finger if there's a problem.
HS First finger lifts.

Once again, if a client's higher self cannot remove a device or energy, it's almost always because it has some kind of permission or access to be present. In that case, higher self is asked to locate the access – who or what is being used – and to use the appropriate protocol to close it. Once that's done the higher self can then reintegrate the energy or remove it, whichever is appropriate.

The protocol is designed to help the therapist identify whether a device or energy is present that is negatively affecting the client and, if so, which steps to take to resolve it. The following is another example.

Dealing with Devices and Energies: Example 2

TH To the higher self, were you able to finish that review?
HS Yes finger lifts.
TH Did you find someone or something involved with these periods of nausea?
HS Yes finger lifts.
TH If it's someone, first finger lifting, if something, second finger.
HS Second finger lifts.
TH Higher self, if it's more like a device or an object of some kind, the

yes finger. If more like an energy, the no finger can lift. If neither of those fit, the hand can lift.
HS No finger lifts.
TH Higher self, if it is part of the self/soul energy, first finger. If separate from self/soul, the no finger can lift.
HS No finger lifts.
TH Higher self, if this energy has entered the self/soul, first finger. If it's operating from outside the soul, the no finger lifting.
HS First finger lifts.
TH Higher self, can you and guides remove that energy now?
HS No finger lifts.
TH Higher self, I'm asking that you look inside and see if this energy is using someone or something to stay attached here. First finger when that review is complete, no finger if it's stopped or blocked.
HS First finger lifts.
TH Higher self, did you find someone or something this energy uses for access?
HS Yes finger lifts.
TH If it's someone, first finger. If something, second finger.
HS First finger lifts.
TH Higher self, is this one part of the self/soul?
HS Yes finger lifts.
TH Is it agreeable that I communicate with this one?
HS Yes finger lifts.
TH Higher self, I'm asking that you help that one come forward here with me. First finger when they are here. No finger if there is a problem.
HS First finger lifts.
TH To this one: are you willing to communicate with me?
ES Yes finger lifts.
TH Do you know yourself to be part of this self and soul?
___ Yes finger lifts.
    (Break)

At this point, Protocol 1 is used to identify the ego-state; find out its connection to this energy and how it came to say yes to it. The aim will be to elicit its agreement to have the energy removed. If it's someone other than an ego-state, then the appropriate protocol would be used until all accesses have been closed and the energy removed.

15

Mixing and Matching Protocols

When the higher self signals that it has found someone or something involved in the problem area, more often than not it means that it has found a complex situation, and that the one it has identified to address is only the starting pointing. It can certainly be as simple as one ego-state or one earthbound spirit causing a person's particular problem. Usually, though, it's not that simple. Dealing with areas of deep pain, fear or conflict is more than likely to trigger defenses and reactions that extend further than the specific entity or device the client's higher self has identified.

An ego-state, for example, may be in a group of five ego-states, two of whom are from past lifetimes. All five may be afraid of a spirit that accessed the group at some point and, under some pretext, threatened to punish anyone who tried to leave. The spirit also may have left two ravens perched on posts on either side of the door. The group was told the birds would peck at anyone who tried to leave – and if the birds were triggered, the spirit would know and return. In effect, the spirit was able to *lock in place* these parts of the self/soul.

A second example: the higher self identifies a past-life ego-state as the source of a block. It's a young woman who died in childbirth and could not even hold her baby. She is with three other ego-states. They are small children. They were created in the client's present life following the accidental death of her mother. With her own unresolved grief and longing, this past life part was triggered and drawn to these young ego-states who were calling for their mother.

Now, years later, in the healing process, if the higher self identifies one of the three children as the one to communicate with first, that very contact can begin to trigger that ego-state's pain and grief. In turn, the other two ego-states become triggered as well. Their pain, too, is starting to surface. At this point, the past life mother steps in to block the therapist's communication thereby stopping the children's pain from coming forward. Unless that mother ego-state understands about the healing process, from her point of view the process is only causing the children pain. The therapist will have to deal with this past-life woman, then, before addressing the pain these children carry.

The bottom line is that the therapist in Soul-Centered Healing cannot know ahead of time what kind of web or complex of entities and devices may be keeping the problem conditions in place and actively blocking the healing process. The therapist has to be ready for anything and anyone. He or she has to be ready to follow wherever the trail leads. This is where the protocols come into play. The protocols in Part 2 deal with the most common sources of blocking. So, when dealing with a complex block that involves more than just one ego-state, the therapist can work his or her way through the configuration by switching from one protocol to another as the situation demands.

These complex blocks are all part of the story, though. More than likely, whoever or whatever is behind the blocks, is probably also part of the problem the client is presenting. Paradoxically, the block or blocker cannot stop the healing process without also revealing itself, the very thing it wants to avoid. Ultimately, healing is a process of encountering and clearing blocks so the Light can be brought to all parts of the self, and all separate entities and energies removed.

Exercise 2:

Once you've gained some facility in communicating with a person's higher self, the next step is to ask the higher self to review a problem.

This is a clinical step. You're asking the person's higher self to open up their inner world without knowing for sure what will present. It's even likely that what presents will involve something painful or traumatic. So, for Exercise 2 you have to be prepared to follow through. Because of emotional bonds and conflicts of interest that can be involved, I would suggest not doing this with a friend or family member. You don't know what you might open up and whether you will be in a position to follow up.

In Exercise 2, once the person is in trance, re-establish communication with the higher self. Ask if it is willing to review the identified problem or symptom. If so, ask that it carry out the review and signal when the review is complete. When you receive the yes signal, the goal of Exercise 2 is to identify who or what the higher self has found. If it's someone, then the goal is to identify who it is: An ego-state? A spirit? An entity? If it's something, like a device or energy, then the goal is to identify what it is.

Because it's a clinical situation, you may not be able to stop at just identifying whether it's something or someone. It may demand to be addressed, or the client may begin to experience an abreaction, or is frightened by something that is happening. In either case, the therapist may need to follow it up, either immediately or in a subsequent session.

The following is an example of mixing and matching protocols. It starts with a twelve-year-old ego-state that has tried to share memories that it carries involving abuse by her stepfather. A sixteen-year-old ego-state dressed in black has come forward and told 12yo to be quiet. She threatens her.

Mixing and Matching Protocols: Example 1

TH 12yo: if you needed to stop the sharing, first finger lifting. If not, second finger can lift.

12yo Second finger lifts.

TH 12yo, did someone or something get in the way of your sharing? If so, first finger. If, not, second finger lifting. If you're not sure, the hand can lift.

12yo First finger lifts.

TH If it was someone, first finger. If something, second finger. If you're not sure, the hand can lift.

12yo Hand lifts.

TH Higher self, I'm asking that you find the source of that block. First finger when you have found it, second finger if you do not.

HS First finger lifts.

TH Higher self, were you able to find the source of that block?

HS Yes finger lifts.

TH Higher self is that one blocking part of the self/soul?

HS	Yes finger lifts.
TH	Higher self, are you in agreement that I communicate with that one?
HS	Yes finger lifts.
TH	Higher self, I'm asking that you help that one come forward here with me, and to this one: are you willing now to communicate with me?
__	Yes finger lifts.
TH	Do you know yourself to be part of this self and soul I'm working with?
__	Yes finger lifts.
TH	Are you receiving Light for yourself there where you are?
__	No finger lifts.
TH	Are you willing to have some Light/Love energy sent to you?
__	No finger lifts.
TH	Are you afraid of the Light?
__	No finger lifts.
TH	Are you angry at the Light?
__	Yes finger lifts.
TH	Do you blame the Light for what happened?
__	Yes finger lifts.
TH	To this one: are you one first created in this present life of Jenny's?
__	Yes finger lifts.
TH	Are you younger than twelve?
__	No finger lifts.
TH	Are you younger than twenty?
__	Yes finger lifts.
TH	Are you younger than eighteen years old?
__	Yes finger lifts.
TH	Are you sixteen?
__	Yes finger lifts.
TH	16yo: do you have a name?
16yo	Yes finger lifts.
TH	Is it all right for us to know your name?
16yo	Yes finger lifts.
TH	I'm going to ask that you say it right to the conscious mind on the count of three. One, two, three… just say your name, nice and loud, right to the conscious mind, and Jenny, first finger when you've received that, second finger if not.

Je   The name I'm getting is Blaze.
TH   Sixteen year old: is this right? Is your name Blaze?
16yo Yes finger lifts.
TH   Blaze, do you know about the healing process we are working with?
Bz   No finger lifts.
TH   Are you willing to have some information sent to you about that?
Bz   Yes finger lifts.
TH   Okay. On three then: One, two, three… and higher self please send this information to Blaze about the healing process…. how she can be free of all pain, hurt and distress. Blaze, first finger when you've received that information, second finger, if you do not.
Bz   Yes finger lifts.
TH   Blaze, did you receive that information?
Bz   Yes finger lifts.
TH   Does that make sense to you?
Bz   Yes finger lifts.
TH   Would you like to have that healing and release for yourself?
Bz   Yes finger lifts.
TH   Are you willing, then, to receive some of the Light/Love energy for yourself now, knowing you can stop it if you need to?
Bz   No finger lifts.
TH   Is that still because you're angry at the Light?
Bz   No finger lifts.
TH   Is there someone or something in your way?
Bz   Yes finger lifts.
TH   If it's someone, first finger. If it's something or some energy, second finger.
Bz   No finger lifts.
TH   Blaze, if it looks more like an object or device, first finger; if more like an energy, then second finger.
Bz   First finger lifts.
TH   Blaze, do you know what that thing is?
Bz   Yes finger lifts.
TH   I'm going to ask that you share that right here to the conscious mind on three. One, two, three… and Blaze, just share what you can about that device – a thought, a word, a picture… first finger when you've shared that; second finger if not.
Bz   First finger lifts.

TH	Jenny, here with me: Jenny did you receive that?
Bz	It looks like a gold necklace. She's wearing it.
TH	Blaze: is this right. Is it a gold necklace?
Bz	Yes finger lifts.
TH	Are you wearing it?
Bz	Yes finger lifts.
TH	Is that stopping you from receiving the Light?
Bz	Yes finger lifts.
TH	Did someone give you that necklace?
Bz	Yes finger lifts.
TH	Are you willing to have it removed now?
Bz	No finger lifts.
TH	Do you think you need that to live?
Bz	Yes finger lifts.
TH	Did someone tell you that?
Bz	Yes finger lifts.
TH	Blaze, whoever gave you that necklace lied to you. You don't need that to survive. As part of this soul, you already have your own soul-source energy. It is a life sustaining energy. Whoever gave you that necklace does not want you to find out about your own connection to your soul energy. They know that once you find that out they will have no more power over you. Blaze, would you be willing for higher self to send you just a tiny piece of that Light and let you decide for yourself. You can stop it immediately if you need to, or you can keep it for yourself if you wish. It will be totally up to you. Would you be willing to do that – just a tiny piece of Light?
Bz	Yes finger lifts.
TH	Higher self, please send Blaze just that tiny piece of Light. Blaze let yourself touch that piece and decide for your self. Stop it if you need to, or you can bring it inside if you wish. First finger lifting when that's complete, either way.
Bz	First finger lifts.
TH	Blaze, did you touch that all right?
Bz	Yes finger lifts.
TH	Did you decide to keep it for yourself?
Bz	Yes finger lifts.
TH	Does that feel all right?
Bz	Yes finger lifts.

Mixing and Matching Protocols

TH Would you like to have more of that Light/Love energy for yourself?
Bz Yes finger lifts.
TH Blaze, are you willing to have that necklace removed now?
Bz Yes finger lifts.
TH Higher self, please dissipate and remove the necklace from the self/soul; and higher self, send Blaze more of the Light/Love/warmth energy. Blaze, let yourself receive that Light to whatever level is comfortable. First finger when that feels complete; second finger if there's a problem.
Bz First finger lifts.
TH Blaze would you wish to have the healing and release now for yourself?
Bz Yes finger lifts.
TH Are you willing to share what you need to so that you and others can have that full release?
Bz Yes finger lifts.
TH Do you know what you need to share for your release?
Bz Yes finger lifts.
TH I'm going to ask that you share it right here to the conscious mind. On three: one, two, three... and Blaze, just share now what you need to, what happened. Let it come right to the present. First finger when that's complete, second finger if the sharing is stopped or blocked.
Bz First finger lifts.
TH Jenny did you receive that?
Je Yes finger lifts.
TH Anything to comment on about that?
Je I think she took the necklace from this dark man thinking it would give her the power to protect the younger ones by keeping them quiet and away from the Light. Instead, she understands now she was being used.
TH Blaze, is there anything else now that needs to be shared?
Bz No finger lifts.
TH Higher self, can she have a full release now?
HS Yes finger lifts.
TH Blaze, on three then, let yourself release the pain, the fear, the hurt. Release it right through the body and out. On three now: one, two, three... and just release any pain, hurt, anger... let it release through the body and out. And as you release, you can bring in that full Light/

Love energy for yourself and with it will come any self-forgiveness needed. First finger when all has been released that's ready. Second finger, if there's a problem.
Bz Yes finger lifts.
TH Blaze, is there any distress or anger you're still feeling there?
Bz No finger lifts.
TH Are you in agreement now that 12yo share what she needs to for release?
Bz Yes finger lifts.
TH Higher self, before 12yo shares, should Blaze move to her own place of integration – that's first finger – or wait for the others here before integrating – that's second finger?
HS First finger lifts.
TH Higher self, should she have a conscious experience before integrating?
HS Yes finger lifts.
TH Higher self, help Blaze then move here to the conscious mind. Blaze, let yourself have this conscious experience here in the present. Higher self, when that's complete, help her move to her own place of Light and integration here with Jenny in the present. First finger when these moves are complete. Second finger, if there's a problem.
HS First finger lifts.

In situations like this where ego-states, a spirit(s), and devices are present, the protocols act as a set of tools. You switch from one to another depending on the problem before you. You don't want a pair of pliers when the job calls for a screwdriver. You don't want to treat a spirit the same as you do an ego-state. Trying to re-integrate something that is not part of your client in the first place is only going to lead to more problems and confusion.

Here is a second example of the mix and match of protocols. The example starts with an eight-year-old ego-state that has been identified, received the Light, and is ready to share.

Mixing and Matching Protocols: Example 2

TH 8yo, you're alone where you are there, is that correct?
8yo Yes finger lifts.
TH Are you willing to share now what you need to share for release?

Mixing and Matching Protocols

8yo   Yes finger lifts.

TH   I'm going to ask then that you share on the count of three what you need to share. Beginning, one, two, three… and just share it right here to the present, what you need to share. Yes finger when that's complete, second finger if it is stopped or blocked?

8yo   Second finger lifts.

TH   8yo, was that sharing stopped?

8yo   Yes finger lifts.

TH   If you needed to stop that, yes finger lifting. If someone or something seemed to get in the way, the no finger can lift.

8yo   No finger lifts.

TH   If someone got in the way, yes finger lifting; if something or some energy, the no finger lifting; if you don't know, the hand can lift.

8yo   Hand lifts.

TH   Are you still receiving Light there?

8yo   Yes finger lifts.

TH   Okay. I'm going to have higher self come forward to communicate about this, and I'll come back. Higher self, are you still able to communicate?

HS   Yes finger lifts.

TH   Higher self, are you aware of some block to 8yo's sharing?

HS   Yes finger lifts.

TH   If it's someone, yes finger lifting; if some thing or some energy, the no finger lifting; if it's not clear, the hand can lift.

HS   No finger lifts.

TH   Higher self, if it's something like a device or object, the yes finger can lift, if more like an energy, then the no finger can lift. If neither of those fit, the hand can lift.

HS   No finger lifts.

TH   Is that device or object part of the self/soul energy?

HS   No finger lifts.

TH   It's separate from the soul, is that correct?

HS   Yes finger lifts.

TH   Is there more than one?

HS   Yes finger lifts.

TH   More than five?

HS   No finger lifts.

TH   Is it more than three?

HS Yes finger lifts.
TH More than four?
HS No finger lifts.
TH Higher self, is it four?
HS Yes finger lifts.
TH Can you remove those devices now?
HS Yes finger lifts.
TH I'm going to ask that you dissipate and remove them on three: one, two, three… and higher self, using the Light, I'm asking that you find those devices and remove them from the self/soul. Yes finger when that's complete; no finger, if there is a problem.
HS No finger lifts.
TH Higher self, were you blocked from removing those devices?
HS Yes finger lifts.
TH If someone stopped you, the first finger lifting, if it was something or some energy, the no finger can lift. If you don't know, the hand can lift.
HS First finger lifts.
TH If that one is part of the self/soul, the first finger lifting. If it is separate, the no finger can lift.
HS First finger lifts.
TH Higher self, please identify that one, help them come forward here with me, and to this one: are you willing now to communicate with me?
___ No finger lifts.
TH To this one: did you know you are part of this self and soul I'm working with?
___ No finger lifts.
TH I want you to know first of all, that we are here to help. Whether you are part of this soul or not, we want you to know there is a way to be free of all pain and fear. To this one: as long as it is safe, are you willing to know whether you are part of this soul or not?
___ Yes finger lifts.
TH That information will come to you then, on three. Beginning, one, two, three… and higher self send to this one that information on whether they are, or are not, part of the self/soul; communicate to them also any further understandings that can be helpful, especially about the healing process. To this one: the yes finger can lift when

Mixing and Matching Protocols 247

you've received that information, the no finger lifting if you do not.
— No finger lifts.
TH To this one: if you needed to stop that communication, the yes finger lifting. If not, the no finger can lift.
— No finger lifts.
TH If someone got in the way, first finger lifting, if something, the second finger lifting, if you don't know, the hand can lift.
— First finger lifts.
TH To this one: is that one there with you?
— Yes finger lifts.
TH I'm going to ask that one to come forward here with me, and to this one: do you know yourself to be part of this self and soul?
— No finger lifts.
TH If you believe you are separate, first finger. If you just aren't sure, the no finger can lift.
— First finger lifts.
TH To this one: if you believe you are a soul, the yes finger lifting, if a created entity or from another soul, the no finger lifting, if you're not sure, the hand can lift.
— Yes finger lifts.
TH To this one: if you are a soul, then you have your own soul-source energy inside. Are you willing to look now and see if that soul-source energy is there?
— No finger lifts.
TH Is there some scare or apprehension for you about that?
— No finger lifts.
TH Are you angry at the Light?
— No finger lifts.
TH Are you being threatened by someone or something there?
— Yes finger lifts.
TH If it's someone, yes finger lifting. If something or an energy of some kind, the no finger lifting. If you're not sure, the hand can lift.
— Yes finger lifts.
TH To this one: is the one threatening right there with you?
— No finger lifts.
TH Is that one in direct communication with you right now?
— No finger lifts.
TH Are you afraid that one will come back if you look inside for your

own Light?
— Yes finger lifts.
TH To this one: you need to know that as a soul, you have the absolute freedom to choose. As a soul, you have the right to end any contact or agreement with any of those who are threatening. Would you be willing for a high-level teacher from the Light to come forward and communicate about the choices available to you?
— Yes finger lifts.
TH Just turn then towards the Light and I'm asking that high-level teacher to step forward. Yes finger when you see them, no finger if you do not.
— Yes finger lifts.
TH I'm asking the teacher then to communicate to you this understanding about yourself as a soul, and the choices you have available. Yes finger when you've received that. No finger if you do not.
— Yes finger lifts.
TH To this one: did you receive that communication all right?
— Yes finger lifts.
TH Does it seem that you are yourself a soul?
— Yes finger lifts.
TH Are you receiving Light now for yourself there?
SP Yes finger lifts.
TH Do you know now that you can return to your own place in the Spirit Realm of Light?
SP Yes finger lifts.
TH Are you willing to go now with the teacher?
SP Yes finger lifts.
TH Are there any other separate ones with you where you are?
SP No finger lifts.
TH You can go to the teacher, then, on three. One, two, three… and move now right to the teacher, right into that corridor of Light. Higher self, yes finger when that one has gone, no finger if they do not.
HS Yes finger lifts.
TH Higher self, if we should go back to the one who blocked 8yo originally, the yes finger can lift. If better to go back to 8yo, the no finger lifting. If someone or something else should be addressed first, then the hand can lift.

HS	Yes finger lifts.
TH	Please bring that one forward, then, who had blocked 8yo, and to this one: are you willing again now to communicate with me?
__	Yes finger lifts.
TH	Does that feel safer for you now?
__	Yes finger lifts.
TH	Are you receiving Light for yourself there now?
__	Yes finger lifts.
TH	Does that feel all right to you?
__	Yes finger lifts.
TH	Does it seem that you are part of this self and soul I'm working with?
__	Yes finger lifts.
TH	Are you one first created in this present life of Dave's?
__	Hand lift.
TH	Are you willing to have a safe review about that?
__	Yes finger lifts.
TH	I'm going to ask higher self then to help you with a safe review. On three: one, two, three… higher self, help this one to safely review inside what it is they carry, what's happened, what needs to be shared for release. To this one: yes finger when you have had that review, no finger if it is stopped or blocked.
__	Yes finger lifts.
TH	To this one: were you able to have that review all right?
__	Yes finger lifts.
TH	If you were first created in this present life of Dave's, the yes finger lifting, if you are from a past or different lifetime, the no finger can lift. If it's still not clear the hand can lift.
__	No finger lifts.
TH	To this one: you first came in a past or different lifetime, is that correct?
__	Yes finger lifts.
TH	Are you a male?
__	No finger lifts.
TH	Are you a female?
__	Yes finger lifts.
TH	Do you know your name?
__	Yes finger lifts.
TH	Is it all right for me to know your name?

—	Yes finger lifts.
TH	I'm going to ask then that you say it right here to the present, on three, beginning, one, two, three… and just say the name nice and loud, right here to the conscious mind.

(Pause)

TH	Dave, anything come to you?
Da	I'm getting the name Morgan.
TH	To this one: is that right? Is your name Morgan?
Mo	Yes finger lifts.
TH	Morgan, do you know about the healing process that we are working with?
Mo	Yes finger lifts.
TH	Is there anyone else with you where you are Morgan?
Mo	Yes finger lifts.
TH	Are there more than three of you?
Mo	No finger lifts.
TH	More than two?
Mo	No finger lifts.
TH	There are two of you, is that right?
Mo	Yes finger lifts.
TH	Morgan, is that other one also part of the self/soul?
Mo	Yes finger lifts. (They don't always know the answer to this question.)
TH	Morgan, I first communicated with you when you stepped forward to block 8yo. Do you still need to block him now?
Mo	No finger lifts.
TH	Do both of you there know about the healing process?
Mo	Yes finger lifts.
TH	Are you willing to share now what you need to in order to have a release?
Mo	Yes finger lifts.
TH	I'm going to ask that you share it then. On three: one, two, three… and just share what you need to right here to the conscious mind. It's safe to do that now. First finger when that's complete, second finger if there's a problem.
Mo	Second finger lifts.
TH	Morgan, if you needed to stop that, first finger lifting. If someone or something seemed to interfere, the second finger can lift. If you don't know, the hand can lift.

Mo First finger lifts.
TH You needed to stop the sharing, is that right?
Mo. Yes finger lifts.
TH If you needed to stop it because of your pain, the first finger can lift. If you being threatened in some way, the second finger lifting. If neither of those fit, the hand can lift.
Mo Second finger lifts.
TH If it's someone threatening you, the first finger. If something or some energy is threatening, then lift the second finger. If neither of those fit, the hand can lift.
Mo. First finger lifts.
TH The higher self is able, Morgan, to help you both break any sharing into very small and tolerable pieces. Are you willing for higher self to communicate information to you about this?
Mo. Yes finger lifts.
TH Higher self, please communicate to them how you can help them break any sharing into small pieces. Morgan, first finger can lift when you have received that, second finger if you do not.
Mo First finger lifts.
TH Did you receive that information all right?
Mo Yes finger lifts.
TH Are you willing for higher self to help you in this way for sharing release?
Mo. Yes finger lifts.
TH Okay. Higher self, please help them now break the sharing into pieces. Morgan, yes finger when ready to share that first piece. No finger lifting if there's a problem
Mo. Yes finger lifts.
TH Morgan, I'm asking higher self now to surround you both with that Light and support. On three just share the piece you can. One, two, three... and just share it now right to the conscious mind...
Continue with the Ego-State Protocol.

The protocols do not predict or try to explain all the phenomena that come forward in a client's healing process. The purpose of the protocols is to help the therapist classify what has come forward and then apply the proper formula to help bring it to healing and resolution.

The protocols are formulas, and different phenomena call for different formulas. At this level, what applies to one ego-state applies to them all; or what applies to one spirit applies to all spirits. Using the appropriate protocol can help guide the therapist through what can at times be a labyrinth of obstacles, fears, and confusion.

When confronted with complex blocks, the rule of thumb is to keep your eye on the ball. Whatever was happening in the session when the block presented is the place you want to get back to. It may be re-establishing communication with the higher self, or a specific ego-state, or removing a suffocating energy. This is where the block was triggered and so this is what we need to go back to and continue where we left off. If we can do that, then it is a good indication that the block has been resolved and the work can continue on its course. It may require a number of steps and procedures to get back there, especially when evil souls and networks are involved. Focusing on this aim—getting back to where the block started—the task becomes one of clearing away any obstacles that are in the way of that. This constant focus can also, I think, keep the therapist from becoming lost in what at times can seem a hall of mirrors.

Having said this, once more I need to acknowledge that there are always exceptions. Sometimes, for example, a series of blocks leads to a more significant level of the issue than where the block started. It's as though in resolving the block you have broken through a wall and who or what is on the other side is now what it is important to address. The point is, though, if we did go back and communicate to the original ego-state, we would now find it free to communicate.

16

Soul-Centered Healing: Closing Comments

The Soul Journey

The practice of Soul-Centered Healing begins with the recognition of the client as a soul, a being of Light, who incarnated from the Light and will return to the Light when the body dies. There can, of course, be exceptions where souls take indirect paths in their search for home. This is what we share in common with every client—we are all souls. We are all beings of Light. We come from the same Source, and at our deepest level, we know we are all part of the Oneness of the Light. This is what I see as the basis for the therapeutic relationship.

Soul-Centered Healing assumes that the client, as a soul, has lived other lifetimes (99% of the time), and that he or she has come into this life with a soul history. It also assumes that those past lifetimes have played some part in or have some connections to the client's present life. From a clinical point of view, soul history may or may not become an issue in the client's healing process. Usually, I find that past-life material does present. Sometimes it's a major focus; sometimes it's even the root cause of a client's problem.

It might be that events or conflicts in the client's present life have triggered past-life conflicts or traumas that begin erupting into the conscious reality. It's also possible that parts of the client's soul created in past lives have been active at unconscious levels since the client was born and right up to the present. It remains to be seen with each client whether past lives play a significant part in his or her healing process.

A second assumption about past lives is that every soul freely chooses to incarnate. A soul is not forced into a lifetime. In addition, in line with many other esoteric and metaphysical teachings, SCH assumes that a soul chooses each specific incarnation. This does not mean that the soul chooses every detail about a life. Free choice doesn't permit that. It's more as though it sets the stage for the coming human lifetime. As Gerod described it, every soul incarnates with a basic blueprint for that lifetime. This blueprint includes the soul's choice of parents, and the genetic body it will possess. It chooses the date, time, place, and circumstances of its birth. The blueprint also includes the probability of major events, relationships, and challenges occurring in a person's life that the soul has chosen for particular purposes and with certain aims to achieve.

Ego-consciousness has a natural resistance to this soul level of reality, first, because it is an unknown, and secondly, because it cannot comprehend the level of knowledge and choice in which souls exist beyond the body and physical reality. As persons, we can know or have faith that these dimensions exist. We can resonate with them. We can feel them. Some people do perceive them, at least in limited ways. Ego-consciousness, however, cannot grasp them in terms of the reality it knows through its physical senses and its body.

Ego-consciousness must step beyond those boundaries if it is to know the nonphysical and soul level realities. As chef, Emeril Lagasse, would say, the ego would have to "kick it up a notch." And the ego-consciousness cannot make that leap without surrendering the primacy of the body as the basis of identity. It's where the ego would recognize that it is not ultimately about the body, it is about consciousness and the Light.

In Soul-Centered Healing, no assumptions are made about what a client's soul purposes may be, only that the client has a soul story, and it may or may not become a focus in the healing process. Regardless, it's always in the background. Once incarnate, things may not go according to the soul's blueprint. Gerod described each person as the focus of the soul's consciousness in the present and so possesses the soul's freedom to choose. There are people who make choices that turn the blueprint upside down—may even go against the soul. From a soul point of view, even this is not a problem for the soul. Gerod said to me more than once, "There are no wrong choices, only choices." The soul learns from all experience and it has all the time it needs to plan future lifetimes to correct its course if necessary.

The idea that a soul chooses its incarnations has two major implications for clients. The first is that he or she is not a victim. It says they have not come into this world through happenstance and bad luck. It implies to the client that what has happened in their life and where they are now are at least partly, if not largely, the result of their own soul's choices made before birth. This shift of ultimate causality, and therefore responsibility, is what I see as a shift from an *egocentric* to a *soul-centered* perspective, from a three-dimensional to a multi-dimensional reality, and from physics to metaphysics.

In our Western culture, this shift can be a source of anxiety or even psychological shock to clients who have not addressed the issue of reincarnation in their own life. Reincarnation demands a radically different way of thinking than the current Judeo-Christian doctrine that holds that every soul lives only one lifetime. This shift implies a different basis for identity. From my point of view, it is an expanded identity, not an either/or. This psychological shock can also trigger the client's ego defenses against the confusion, loss of control, and fear of the unknown that is implied in this shift to a new perspective. In Transpersonal Psychology, we would call it the "death of the ego." This is a common experience when talking about conversion, and the same thing can happen in the therapeutic setting when a client begins to acknowledge other dimensions of reality and being.

Another threat to the ego when confronted with other realities is what psychologists term *ego-deflation*. This is when the ego's perception of its primacy and importance is significantly diminished relative to the higher order realities that are being revealed. The ego is losing its place. From the ego's limited point of view, however, it may even perceive the loss as impending death. From the point of view of healing, however, this is where the ego may start to move into alignment with the self, and where the self then awakens to the soul.

Once we get beyond the ego defenses, the client's recognition of soul choices implies his or her own power to choose in the present. As an incarnate soul, the person possesses the soul's absolute freedom to choose. Gerod said this is why the conscious person's choices can have far reaching effects on the soul as compared to the choices of ego-states. When a person learns that where they are in their present life is partly the result of soul choices, it opens them also to the realization of their own power to choose. It also implies the logic: "If I chose my way into it, then I can choose my way out of it." This knowledge is empowering to a client, even if he or she is not aware of it at a conscious level. In recognizing soul choices, the client is reclaiming his or her own power to choose.

In terms of Soul-Centered Healing, what I have been describing here I would consider a backdrop in the healing process. Past lives and soul choices before birth may not present directly as issues or problems in the healing process, but I assume they are part of the picture for every client. Even when not addressed directly, I assume that major issues and conflicts in a client's present life most probably resonate within the soul's history and the client's working it out in the present can resonate healing to these levels as well.

The Inner Labyrinth

A major problem in talking about the practice of Soul-Centered Healing is that each client's soul story and healing journey are absolutely unique. In this method, there is no prediction of where a client's healing process will lead or what phenomena you will encounter. I have talked about the phenomena that I have encountered most frequently. I have focused on what can be talked about generally. I've not talked about everything. Using this method, you are likely to encounter phenomena that don't fit the categories or characteristics I've presented here. For those of us who practice in these realms, we are still on the frontier of discovery and the development of a language.

When working with a client, I do not believe I know the way through the soul's labyrinthine twists and turns. I do believe, though, that the client's higher self knows, or can find, the way through and can guide the healing process. There often does appear to be a certain sequence of steps that need to be followed in the healing process, and the higher self usually knows what the sequence is.

I also believe there are spirit guides that do assist at etheric levels to the extent they are able and to the extent that it is in accord with the soul's free choice. These guides will not violate a soul's choices, as those souls in Darkness will readily do if they can. Without knowing specifically how much guides from the Light can help, my attitude is for a client to have all the help he or she can have. So, I often ask that the higher self make contact with the client's spirit guide(s) just to make sure this connection is open. Many times in my work with clients I will directly request assistance from guides for specific situations. I might be asking spirit healers to work with a client at an etheric level during a coming surgery; or that a guide come to a child ego-state that is terrified; or call for guides who can help remove dark souls whose accesses have been closed, but that are still resisting.

I believe it is our role as therapists to facilitate the client's unfolding journey of healing guided by the soul's Light.

Consulting Psychics

Soul-Centered Healing developed out of an ongoing consultation with a psychic. It would be more accurate to say it was a consultation with a spirit using the services of a psychic. Just like with mechanics or chefs, there's a combination of skill, talent, and natural ability involved in their practice. Different psychics have different kinds of information. They come in all shapes and sizes.

The question for us as therapists is whether a particular psychic has access to information that can be helpful in a client's healing or our work with clients in general. This is something that has to be determined by the therapist. It's not an easy thing to do in a profession that officially denies or ignores the existence of these realms. It would be easier if we had a directory of psychics, along with their areas of expertise and specific abilities. In the end, the benefits of consulting with a particular psychic needs to be evaluated in terms of its results. Is it helping?

I know there are other therapists who consult with psychics or possess their own psychic abilities, which they use in their work with clients. It is difficult, if not impossible, to know how many therapists fit into these categories. I believe it would be significant, at least five percent. It could be much larger. Most of this population would be comprised of therapists using their own abilities, ranging from intuition to direct communication with spirits.

This whole issue of consulting psychics is complex and controversial. In the first place, how are we going to talk about something we don't even acknowledge exists? This may be changing in our culture. We may be moving closer to a paradigm shift in our Western culture. We may be opening up as a culture to the collective awareness of other dimensions of consciousness and reality. Acknowledging the existence of spirits, for example, would be part of that paradigm.

If I were to pick out one major caution for therapists in working with psychics it would be the danger of prediction and foresight becoming part of the therapeutic process. If clients make decisions, wittingly or unwittingly, based on a psychic's information about future events, it risks becoming an interference in the client's healing process, or maybe worse, an obstruction. This is why my work with Gerod remained focused in the present. Gerod would not make predictions. The information he gave did not get far ahead of the client's healing process. It was focused on what was happening in the healing sessions with higher self, with the ego-states, with the spirits, with other beings, etc.

People do consult psychics. They seek guidance, information about a loved one, signs to look for. People consult psychics for all kinds of reasons. Clients can do this too if they wish, but in the clinical setting, I would be very careful about predictions. The ultimate responsibility for what one chooses resides with the chooser, the client. It's not that the reliance on psychic information will take that away, it can't. We can surrender our freedom, but as souls, we cannot surrender our free choice.

A central aim of Soul-Centered Healing is to help a person reclaim the knowledge of their soul freedom and power to choose. The focus of healing is most often on identifying for a client what is in the way of achieving that aim. If a psychic can offer specific information that helps in that process, then it can be of benefit for both the client and the therapist.

Summary

I view the protocols as the backbone of Soul-Centered Healing. They are constants that the therapist relies on to engage and work with a client's inner world. The protocols identify and keep communications straight between the therapist and the different entities and phenomena that are presenting. *Communication* is key. In dealing with these invisible beings and dimensions, communication is the only means we have to work directly with the inner world and be able to verify what is happening. Without this clear and valid communication, it would not take much for the process to dissolve into guesswork and confusion. The protocols enable us to carry on that communication using only ideomotor signals and yes/no questions.

I would characterize the protocols as *inclusive*. They begin with the most general of categories and work their way to specifics, as needed.

At the same time, the protocols are flexible enough to apply to a whole range of phenomena that might otherwise be dismissed as nonsensical, fabrication, or delusion. The protocols allow the therapist to remain open to whomever or whatever is presenting without prematurely labeling a phenomenon and deciding a course of treatment. This means that the truth of a client's experience will guide his or her healing process as it seeks to identify the sources of pain, distress, or disease.

The protocols are also a tool for opening the inner world to the Light by identifying and resolving any blocks that would stop it. This is the process I talked about it in my first book.

> By bringing Light to parts of the self that hold pain and bringing Light into areas of the soul that have become clouded or dark, Soul-Centered Healing helps a person to know his or her own Light. This is not merely a cognitive recognition. It's an experience. It's a knowing, and the healing itself occurs through the person's experience of the Light. This is the part that cannot be passed on through a book.

Hopefully, what I have given to you with these protocols are the tools to facilitate this experience with your clients.

Appendix A: Trance Induction

In my work with clients, trance induction begins with the suggestion of relaxation moving from the feet to the scalp as I count from 1 to 10. Once I reach 10, the induction continues:

> Now the conscious mind can go where it wishes, think what it likes. The conscious mind doesn't even need to listen to what I say.
>
> But those parts of the unconscious mind – the protective part, the higher self, those inner personalities – are all able to respond in whatever ways are most helpful to the entire self.
>
> Now as a child, you learned to nod the head up and down in order to say "yes." After a number of those times, nodding the head up and down, it became an automatic movement.
>
> You've been in a church or a classroom. You've seen people, as they listen to the teacher or the minister, you've seen them nod their heads as if to say, "yes, I agree." And they're not even aware that their heads are moving. It's an automatic movement, an unconscious communication.
>
> As a child, you also learned to shake the head back and forth to communicate no. After a number of those times, shaking the head back and forth, that too became an automatic movement.
>
> Now those parts of the unconscious can use these kinds of non-verbal movements in order to communicate.
>
> What we ask is that these parts inside create a lifting of the right index finger to communicate, "yes." A lifting of the second finger to communicate "no." And a lifting of all the fingers, or the entire hand, to communicate, "stop," or "I'm not sure."

The protective part, the higher self, those parts of the unconscious are able to create these nonverbal signals in order to communicate. Lifting the right index finger to communicate, "yes." Lifting the second finger to communicate "no." And a lifting of all the fingers, or the entire hand, to communicate, "stop," or "I'm not sure."

Now I'm asking the protective part of the mind, that part that is always aware and has always served to protect _____ from threat, hurt, and pain. To the protective part, as long as it is safe, are you willing now to communicate with me? If so, the first finger can lift to let me know. If not, the second finger can lift.

As stated in the Introduction, proficiency in hypnosis is a requirement for practitioners. The above simple approach produces first-time trance and finger responses in about 80% of my clients. Some clients require repetition, different kind of induction, and/or trance deepeners. Hypnotherapists will be familiar with such problems and will know how best to address them.

www.ingramcontent.com/pod-product-compliance
Lightning Source LLC
Chambersburg PA
CBHW060029180426
43196CB00044B/2055